Cultural Methodologies

To Lesley

Cultural Methodologies

edited by
Jim McGuigan

SAGE Publications
London • Thousand Oaks • New Delhi

Editorial arrangement and Introduction © Jim McGuigan, 1997
Chapter 1 © Douglas Kellner, 1997
Chapter 2 © Tony Bennett, 1997
Chapter 3 © Nick Stevenson, 1997
Chapter 4 © Ann Gray, 1997
Chapter 5 © Carolyn Steedman, 1997
Chapter 6 © Martyn Lee, 1997
Chapter 7 © Helen Thomas, 1997
Chapter 8 © Sabina Sharkey, 1997
Chapter 9 © Graham Murdock, 1997
Chapter 10 © Michael Green, 1997

First published 1997

SAGE Publications Ltd
6 Bonhill Street
London EC2A 4PU

SAGE Publications Inc
2455 Teller Road
Thousand Oaks, California 91320

SAGE Publications India Pvt Ltd
32, M-Block Market
Greater Kailash - I
New Delhi 110 048

British Library Cataloguing in Publication data

A catalogue record for this book is available
from the British Library.

ISBN 0 8039 7484 1
ISBN 0 8039 7485 X (pbk)

Library of Congress catalog card number 97-061940

Typeset by Photoprint, Torquay, Devon
Printed in Great Britain by The Cromwell Press Ltd,
Broughton Gifford, Melksham, Wiltshire

Contents

Notes on Contributors

Tony Bennett is Professor of Cultural Studies at Griffith University, Brisbane, where he is also Director of the Australian Key Centre for Cultural and Media Policy. His many publications include *Outside Literature* (1990), *The Birth of the Museum* (1995) and *Culture: A Reformer's Science* (forthcoming).

Ann Gray is a Senior Lecturer in Cultural Studies at the University of Birmingham and joint editor of the *European Journal of Cultural Studies*. Her publications include *Video Playtime: The Gendering of a Leisure Technology* (1992), *Studying Culture* (1993, 1997), edited with Jim McGuigan, and, with Helen Baehr, *Turning it On: A Reader in Women & Media* (1996). She is currently writing a book on research methods in cultural studies.

Michael Green is Head of the Department of Cultural Studies and Sociology at the University of Birmingham. He joined the original Centre for Contemporary Cultural Studies in the 1960s and has also taught in California, Montreal, Montpellier and Munich. He has written widely on cultural policy, educational and media issues.

Douglas Kellner is Professor of Philosophy in the University of Texas at Austin and is the author of many books, including *Camera Politica* with Michael Ryan (1988), *Critical Theory, Marxism and Modernity* (1989), *Jean Baudrillard* (1989), *Postmodern Theory* with Steve Best (1991), *Television and the Crisis of Democracy* (1990), *The Persian Gulf TV War* (1992) and *Media Culture* (1995). He has recently completed another book with Steve Best, *The Postmodern Turn* (1997).

Martyn Lee is Senior Lecturer in Communication, Culture and Media at Coventry University. He is the author of *Consumer Culture Reborn: The Cultural Politics of Consumption* (1993) and is currently working on a book on aspects of modernism. He is also editor of *The Consumer Society Reader* (forthcoming).

Jim McGuigan is Reader in Cultural Studies at Coventry University. His publications include *Cultural Populism* (1992), *Studying Culture* (1993, 1997), *Culture and the Public Sphere* (1996) and the forthcoming *Technocities*. He is currently editing a thematic issue of the *International Journal of Cultural Policy* and writing a book on modernity and postmodern culture.

Graham Murdock is Reader in the Sociology of Culture at Lough-borough University and a Professor in the Department of Mass Communication at the University of Bergen. He has published widely on the social and economic organization of culture and communications, and his work has been translated into over a dozen languages. His latest book is a two-volume collection, *The Political Economy of the Media* (1997), with Peter Golding. He is currently working on books about modernity and about global consumption.

Sabina Sharkey is Course Director of the MA programmes in cultural studies and in Irish studies at the Graduate Centre for British and Comparative Cultural Studies, University of Warwick. She has contributed to edited collections and journals including *Women: A Cultural Review, Paragraph, A Journal of Critical Theory* and *Textual Practice*, and is currently completing a monograph on identity politics in seventeenth-century Ireland.

Carolyn Steedman is Professor in the Centre for Social History at the University of Warwick. Her publications include *Landscape for a Good Woman* (1986), *The Radical Soldier's Tale* (1988), a biography of the educationalist Margaret McMillan entitled *Childhood, Culture and Class in Britain* (1990) and *Strange Dislocations: Childhood and the Idea of Human Interiority, 1780–1930* (1995). She is currently researching the role of servants, service and servitude in the making of modern identity.

Nick Stevenson lectures in Sociology at the University of Sheffield. His publications include *Understanding Media Cultures* (1995) and *Culture, Ideology and Socialism: Raymond Williams and E.P. Thompson* (1995). His recent work includes editing a collection of essays on culture and citizenship, and completing a book called *The Transformation of the Media* (forthcoming). In addition, he is researching consumption, identity and men's life-style magazines with Kate Brookes and Peter Jackson.

Helen Thomas is Head of Sociology at Goldsmiths' College, University of London. She has published widely on dance, including her *Dance, Gender and Culture* (1993), *Dance, Modernity and Culture* (1995) and *Dance in the City* (1997), and is currently working on *The Body, Dance and Cultural Theory*. She has also conducted survey research into the conditions of cultural work in theatre and the electronic media.

Acknowledgements

I must thank the contributors to this book for their endurance. It has turned out to be a much longer and more drawn out project than was originally anticipated. I also thank Chris and Robert Rojek at Sage for being such excellent editors. Their good humour, imagination and efficiency are greatly appreciated. Finally, I am grateful yet again to Lesley for her patience and Christopher and Jenny for their healthy scepticism of the 'gobbledegook' that I produce and have here incited others to produce as well.

Leamington, July 1997

Introduction

Jim McGuigan

This book comes out of a practical concern with the still rather indeterminate status of cultural studies in terms of academic legitimacy and, hence, research funding. Research students in cultural studies have typically had to conduct their work under the cover of something else, say, art history, literary criticism or sociology. It is not just that research-funding bodies have been reluctant, in the past, to recognize cultural studies but also that the self-definition of cultural studies has tended to be resistant to academic legitimation, seeing itself as part of an intellectual guerilla movement waging war on the borders of official academia. This romantic and heroic conception of cultural studies is now decidedly *passé*, not least because of the sheer success, in spite of obstructions to it, of cultural studies educationally and, indeed, in terms of research. The institutionalization of cultural studies and what David Chaney (1994) has called 'the cultural turn' in the human sciences, and perhaps even to some extent in the natural sciences as well, have changed the situation. Yet still it remains difficult to say quite what cultural studies amounts to methodologically. Few attempts have been made to spell out the methodologies of cultural studies. Pertti Alasuutari's *Researching Culture* (1995) is a rare and eccentric exception to this general rule of avoidance.

Cultural studies is eclectic in the methods it uses, drawing liberally from across the humanities and social sciences. Moreover, cultural studies itself is by no means a unitary authority for intellectual work. It is insistently plural and it has become harder, not easier, to say anything very general about cultural studies. In putting together a book on methodology, it quickly became evident that this would have to be about *methodologies* and, more slowly, it also became evident that it was impossible to do this comprehensively. I am tempted myself to list all the sins of omission that, undoubtedly, will be listed by reviewers and readers. However, as Sabina Sharkey, one of the contributors to this book, remarks, '[l]isting as an activity seems to be unavoidably reactive and defensive' (p. 163). Taking this observation to heart, I will not get my retaliation in first by listing all the sins for which I and the contributors to this volume are likely to be accused.

Let's face it, you can't please all the people all of the time. I am not sure that you can please some of the people all the time. The best one can hope for is perhaps to please most of the people some of the time, albeit at different times. The treatment of methodology in this book is pluralistic yet coherent, but not comprehensive. There should be something here to please most tastes. What all the contributors would probably agree upon, if nothing else, is that method should not be separated from theory, which is frequently the case with 'methodology' textbooks in the social sciences. Method is about procedure. Methodology is about the conceptual grounds for research. Methods can be adopted and adapted to realize methodological aims. But, as most good researchers know, it is not unusual to make up the methods as you go along. The methods should serve the aims of the research, not the research serve the aims of the method. This book, then, does not give a great deal of advice in terms of methodical procedure; instead it addresses methodological issues as they relate to theory and practical research in actual conditions.

The book is divided into three parts: Methodologies, Researches and Reflections. The first part outlines a set of methodological issues concerning critique and practicality in cultural studies. It also includes consideration of ethics and the feminist relationship to cultural studies. The second part concretizes matters with reference to actual research, presenting illustrative samplers rather than a catalogue of findings. The final part reflects upon where cultural studies has reached as an intellectual project and the institutional conditions in which it is conducted. In general, the book aims to equip new researchers with a broad understanding of what they are letting themselves in for. It should be of use not only to career researchers but also to students conducting projects that involve research from undergraduate to postgraduate levels.

We start with Douglas Kellner's reconstructive essay on the critical tasks of a multiperspectival cultural studies. He is concerned with 'the missed articulation' between the British tradition of cultural studies (see Turner 1996) and the critical theory tradition of the Frankfurt School launched in Germany during the 1920s and carried on in exile in the USA during the 1940s (see Bronner and Kellner 1989; Jay 1973). The very field of critical communications research from a 'transdisciplinary' perspective was first marked out by the Frankfurt School, most notably in the work of Adorno, Horkheimer and Marcuse, yet this whole tradition has tended to be treated with indifference or scorn in mainstream cultural studies, especially in Britain, due to its 'elitist' critique of mass culture and 'passive' consumerism. On the other hand, the British tradition became, during the 1980s, increasingly 'populist' in its perspective, and problematically so when it attended exclusively to the 'active audience' and, in effect, the 'sovereign consumer' (McGuigan 1997).

Kellner does not simply want to counterpose the critical theory of the Frankfurt School to 'British' cultural studies. There are differences but there are also important similarities in the way they both break with the standard academic division of labour and refuse to stop at the border of the text, which is particularly where the third important tradition in the development of cultural studies, that of French structuralism and post-structuralism, has been most faulted. A complementarity can be achieved by reconnecting cultural analysis with the political economy of the cultural and media industries. The 'global postmodern' cannot be understood only as a matter of signification, identity and difference; the material powers of multinational business and politics must also be taken into account. Kellner's model is quite straightforward. It involves, first, the study of the production and political economy of culture; second, textual analysis and cultural critique; and, third, study of audience reception and how cultural products are used. While not all research would deal with all three dimensions, there is no reason for the field as a whole to privilege any one dimension over the other two. Kellner illustrates the viability of a multiperspectival approach, in his chapter, with reference to the political economy of television genres and 'stardom' (see Kellner 1995 for a fuller version of the argument and illustrative case studies).

On a rather different note from Douglas Kellner, Tony Bennett also distances himself from what came to be known for a while as the mainstream position in cultural studies. For him, however, this was characterized not so much by its populism but by its oppositionalism. Against the unrealistic political pretensions of such cultural studies, Bennett argues for a pragmatism in which the cultural intellectual is better seen as a technician of governmentality rather than as an organic intellectual heroically representing subordinate social movements and political forces. Bennett's (1992) Australian agenda for 'putting policy into cultural studies' has been controversial (see McGuigan 1996), yet it clearly does attend to the actual institutional conditions of education and research in cultural studies.

Cultural studies has become institutionalized with its courses and textbooks and, I would add, 'professional training'. It has to be recognized that students want jobs and there is little funding or facility for research that is not in some sense policy-related. These are real conditions and not at all peculiar to Australia. The rule of Lyotard's (1984) performativity criterion of knowledge is, no doubt, ubiquitous. In his contribution to this volume, Bennett stresses the need for a more modest and practical politics for cultural studies than was typically so in the past whilst also retaining, however, much of what is distinctive about the field: its interdisciplinarity, inclusiveness, attention to multiple forms of power associated with the triad of class, gender and 'race', and a realistic understanding of its particular emplacement within university systems.

There are pragmatic considerations in cultural research, and it would be foolish to neglect them. However, there are also ethical and moral considerations, and it would be irresponsible to neglect them too. It is not uncommon for books on methodology to include an afterthought on ethics. Better than this, however, is to raise ethical and moral questions early on so that they may inform the research process in its various aspects, not only those questions directly germane to tactful research and respect for the subjects of research but much more generally related to how objects of study are formulated, where the priorities lie in studying the practices of meaning-making and circulation, particularly through and within the modern media. In his contribution, Nick Stevenson addresses ethical and moral considerations with specific reference to the work of Jürgen Habermas (1990), Carol Gilligan (1982), Raymond Williams (1980) and Zygmunt Bauman (1993).

Stevenson begins by reminding the reader of his own distinction (Stevenson 1995) between three ways of conceptualizing and studying the media: first, critical theory, which is concerned with the role of media in relation to social power and ideology; second, reception analysis, which is concerned with the interpretive understanding of audiences and instances of semiotic resistance; and, third, the kind of analysis that is concerned with the historical role of media in the formation of modernity and the properties of different media (Thompson 1995). Behind much study of the modern media, in whatever particular form, there is an ethical concern with purpose and democratic communication. One might go so far as to argue that such considerations are at the core of critical analysis of how the media old and new operate. Stevenson declares that his own intellectual inquiries are thus motivated.

Habermas's key notion of the public sphere is crucial to political debate regarding culture and media. His discourse ethics and distinction between system and life-world, rather more abstractly, are also relevant. The difficulty, however, is that Habermas's arguments are very much based on universalistic criteria of dialogue and value. Any kind of universalism has been called into question for suppressing difference and, in particular, has been disputed by feminist theory (see Meehan 1995). Gilligan's 'ethic of care', as Stevenson notes, has been a challenge to the gender blindness of universalistic reasoning and to the excessive rationalism of masculine thought. Habermas's discourse ethics is also in danger of dematerializing the politics of communication and culture. For this reason, Stevenson finds much in Williams's cultural materialism to qualify and complement the Habermasian view. Finally, Bauman's postmodern ethics is yet another call for modesty, placing enormous emphasis on ethical individualism in a world which no longer seems to believe in great narratives of emancipation. By discussing these various counterpoints to Habermas, Stevenson indicates just how good Habermas is to argue with, which is one clear demonstration of the efficacy of discourse ethics. The goal of achieving mutual understanding, of necessity, operates routinely in everyday life so as to bring about the accomplishment of the most practical tasks. It can occasionally be found in academia as well, though mutual misunderstanding there is probably more common.

The relationship between feminism and cultural studies has been extremely productive yet not without its problems. Ann Gray notes the earlier tensions in this relationship, specifically, in her account, regarding how they were played out at the Birmingham Centre for Contemporary Cultural Studies during the 1970s and 1980s. For the most part, however, she stresses their intellectual affinities. Feminism, it has to be said, is first and foremost a politics rather than an academic subject and, for this reason, needs to be distinguished from women's studies. Feminism in its diverse manifestations impacts upon all fields of knowledge as it engages with all aspects of life. Cultural studies might more obviously, then, be compared with women's studies since they are both inter-disciplinary fields of academic study, albeit similarly controversial and comparatively recent additions to the university curriculum. Feminism, on the other hand, is a political project which, amongst other things, influences both cultural studies and women's studies. Feminist commit-ment is clearly at the heart of women's studies, though it does not define it as an academic subject; feminism is quite close to the heart of cultural studies as well, according to Gray.

Feminism and cultural studies are most strongly affined to one another in their common concern with the existence of the marginalized, the silenced and the oppressed, which is very much the source and con-tinuing sense of their mutual embattlement within official academia. Both have aimed to represent the experiences of subaltern groups. Early cultural studies sought to articulate working-class experience and par-ticularly the spectacular subcultures of the young. Recent work in cultural studies has been increasingly concerned with 'race' and, also to an extent, with sexuality (see, for instance, Gilroy 1993a, 1993b; Mercer 1994). Sexuality, and not only the articulation of gendered subordination and resistance, has been of focal concern for the various feminisms. On the question of 'experience', Gray argues, feminists have made greater effort to clarify its epistemological status than is characteristic of cultural studies in general. This is connected to a developing debate on the politics and methodological protocols of feminist research in the work of writers like Sandra Harding (1987). There has been considerable reflec-tion upon the slipperiness of 'experience' and the researcher's role in studying and representing the experience of women. Insofar as cultural studies has paid close attention to these matters it has been required to do so by feminism and, similarly, by black researchers in the field.

In addition to exploring these general matters concerning reflexive research, Gray makes some very specific suggestions of method. She seeks to circumvent the anthropological critique (Nightingale 1993) of 'ethnography' in cultural studies and in feminist cultural studies. The term 'ethnography' has been used to refer to research which has not typically fulfilled the anthropologist's rigorous demands; rarely is there, for example, lengthy 'immersion' in fieldwork, the traditional touchstone and rite of passage of the professional anthropologist (see Murdock's discussion of these matters in this volume). There are good practical and material reasons for the deficiencies of cultural studies in this respect. Gray herself stresses the utility of a more modest approach and outlines a selection of practical methods of an 'ethnographic' yet realistic kind. She stresses the importance and complexity of the interview as a common though infrequently commented upon source of 'data', and she discusses autobiography and life story as valuable and defensible methods.

One of the originary myths of cultural studies, now virtually forgotten, but to which the present writer has a certain sentimental attachment, is that of 'the Scholarship Boy', the working-class lad who through the good offices of the welfare state and educational opportunity acquires 'culture'. As Carolyn Steedman observes, '[t]he Scholarship *Boy* (who is not so much a brother to the Scholarship Girl, as an organising paradigm) came into named literary existence in 1957, the creation of Richard Hoggart' (p. 117). Hoggart's (1957) *The Uses of Literacy*, the life and career of Raymond Williams (Inglis 1995) and the different class and racial but comparable personal trajectory of Stuart Hall (Chen and Morley 1996) all feature in this myth. 'Uprooted, anxious, and very badly dressed, inadequate in so many ways, Hoggart's Boy is simply not in the same league' (p. 118) as the success-conscious, successful and sexually confident Scholarship Girls in the literature surveyed by Steedman in her chapter.

Steedman pays close attention to the extraordinary efflorescence of the autobiographical mode in contemporary culture. It is captured in Giddens's (1991) notion of the reflexive self and bespeaks the widespread injunction to make sense of ourselves. It is not just, however, about authorial navel-gazing:

> When a literary genre becomes more than itself – when it becomes, variously, a cognitive form, a mode of academic writing, a way of being in the world – then the time has come to investigate its production at a particular point in time and in a limited setting; the time has come to submit large-scale claims about autobiography to some kind of historical scrutiny. (p. 107)

Carolyn Steedman's own writerly craft, best exemplified perhaps by her *Landscape for a Good Woman: A Story of Two Lives* (1986), draws attention to the literary origins of cultural studies and, also, the way in which literary study has become to a significant extent cultural studies. In addition to this, however, is Steedman's reflection upon the socialized version of the subjective pole of cultural studies. She is interested substantively in how this literary interrogation and construction of the self occurred in a particular historical context, post-Second World War Britain, and within a particular institutional context, that of 'progressive' English teaching.

In his chapter, Martyn Lee explores the mutually informing relationships between cultural studies and human geography. While it is clear that cultural studies has in recent years been very positively influenced by the geographical attention to space (for instance, by Harvey 1989; Massey 1994; Soja 1989), Lee argues that there is, however, a danger of missing the specificities of location and locality, especially when the principal object of analysis is 'globalization'. There is a temptation to simply replicate the universalizing, standardizing and homogenizing tendencies of modernity which have, according to Lee, been undermined by both the post-Fordist turn of capitalism and 'the postmodern turn' (Seidman 1994) in theory.

Influenced by Doreen Massey's 'power-geometry' and the way that she emphasizes the particularities and dynamic qualities of place, a perspective which holds out the prospect of 'a progressive sense of place', Lee formulates the conceptual terms for analysing empirically the 'character' of cities. He appropriates and extends the applicability of Pierre Bourdieu's (1984) concept of 'habitus' in order to specify how material conditions of existence generate habitual practices that become sedimented in cities over time. The case is made out for a strongly historical understanding of place and particularly the formation of city cultures. Lee sketches such an analysis concretely with reference to the 'open city' of Coventry in the English Midlands, a city which typifies certain processes of economic and cultural transformation yet in a very distinctive and peculiar manner.

Helen Thomas, in her contribution to this volume, discusses the complexities of a certain kind of ethnographic research in which the researcher is in reflexive dialogue with the subjects of the research. Her interest is in dance, the dancing body and its representation, and how discourses of gender, sexuality and 'race' operate in relation to dance. The Geertzian approach to ethnography adopted and celebrated here is especially attuned to the complexities of meaning in everyday life and may be used to illuminate the difficulties of negotiating identity in a multicultural society. For instance, Thomas comments particularly upon some young black male dancers' anxieties about the sexual meanings of dance, especially their heterosexual fears of being interpreted as homosexual in the Western 'feminized' culture of dance.

The research focuses upon a youth and community dance project at the Laban Centre for Movement and Dance in south-east London. Helen Thomas discusses her deployment of individual interviews and group discussions of videotaped dance in a reflexive manner. The treatment of the practicalities of such research and problems of representation both in producing the research and in dealing with the focal topics of research in this chapter illustrates in a very practical way some of the more general issues concerning ethnographic method that are discussed by Ann Gray and Graham Murdock elsewhere in this volume. And, interestingly,

Thomas raises the sensitive issue of 'thin description' which is the main topic of Murdock's later chapter.

Cultural studies, particularly in the strand developed from early work in Britain, is strong on the local. It is now persistently called upon, however, to address the global or at least the 'transnational' (Ang and Stratton 1996). Such calls are, however, always situated in particular local, national and international configurations, such as the 'Asianization of Australia', rather than in some virtual 'global' space. This book largely concentrates on recent developments in a mainly Anglo-American set of traditions yet it has to be registered that cultural studies is becoming increasingly dispersed and that it will inevitably go through dramatic transformations with such dispersal. The trends are difficult to chart and perhaps it is too early even to try, although brave efforts have been made to do so (see, for instance, Davies 1995). Two key sites of debate arise in this respect: the condition of post-colonialism and the fate of the nation-state. Post-colonial studies (see Ashcroft et al. 1995) is a comparatively new and burgeoning field and the eclipse of the nation-state in a globalizing economy has been seriously questioned (Hirst and Thompson 1996). The position of Ireland as a post-colonial nation and object of study is an interesting case in point and one which is somewhat neglected in the wider field of post-colonial studies. Yet, in recent years in the old post-imperial state of Britain, Irish studies has emerged in a companionate space to cultural studies, sharing with other 'studies', such as women's studies, a rebellious and controversial status in academia, frequently derided as trivial and marginalized as such. This is the topic of Sabina Sharkey's chapter.

Sharkey provides a close reading of the section of Joyce's *Ulysses* when Leopold Bloom encounters 'the citizen' in a Dublin pub and a dispute over nationality and identity ensues. The Jewish Irishman Bloom at one point observes hilariously, '[a] nation is the same people living in the same place . . . or also living in different places' (pp. 161–2). The impossibility of defining such a thing as a nation is thus beautifully encapsulated in this comic interlude. The instability of nationhood is, of course, a problem for the nation-state. As Sharkey herself observes, '[i]t is the work of the nation-state to incorporate ethnically different groups into an imagined unit' (p. 162). How the nation is imagined (Anderson 1991) and re-imagined is explored throughout her chapter with regard to Ireland. She sees the methodological task as the study of 'the process of formations and deconstructions of the maps of meaning in a culture' (p. 174). This is an endless task and one which nicely encapsulates one of the ongoing projects of cultural studies.

It is wise, in my opinion, towards the end of a conference or towards the end of an edited book such as this one, to bring on someone like Graham Murdock to produce a diagnosis of current ills and to outline what should be done in a practical fashion, delivered with panache and a scattering of memorably witty remarks. Murdock fixes upon the old stand-off between empiricist and interpretive modes of research. Cultural studies has almost exclusively favoured the latter of these modes, and with good reason. It is unnecessary to rehearse at length the standard criticisms of empiricist fact-grubbing and obsessive quantification. The facts are always the construction of theorizing whether consciously or unconsciously and meaning in its real complexity is unquantifiable.

Nevertheless, Murdock does question the hostility towards about quantification in interpretive social analysis and cultural studies; and he notes how it is frequently smuggled in surreptitiously to support the validity of qualitative research findings. The fact of the matter is, however, that empiricism, like much of the scientific legacy of the European Enlightenment, is now seen to have shaky foundations, and like many of the central committee members of erstwhile communist states its proponents are only too painfully aware of that fact themselves. Qualitative research has become increasingly legitimate and, in such a context, a certain reconciliation between different modes of inquiry would appear to be on the cards.

Murdock proceeds to consider the actual messiness of qualitative research, particularly in its self-consciously 'ethnographic' styles. Always the aim must be to produce 'thick descriptions' (Geertz 1973) that are properly cognizant of the interrelations of agency, structure and history. While anthropologists might complain of the thinness of much cultural studies, anthropology itself has had to rethink what it is doing. An enhanced appreciation of writing and narrative form in various media (Clifford and Marcus 1986; MacCannell 1992) is now commonplace in anthropology and should also be reflected upon as constitutive in cultural studies.

Last but by no means least, Michael Green's concluding chapter gives priceless advice on the 'nuts and bolts' of actually doing research. It is principally addressed to the doctoral student setting out on what can be a lonely and arduous yet also an exciting journey. Green's chapter should be of interest as well to undergraduate students thinking about postgraduate work in cultural studies, and also to Master's degree students. Four ways of working are identified. There is, first, the classic model of individual research in the humanities and social sciences that is conducted full-time and for which the lucky few may still obtain grants. The second model is the one pioneered by the Birmingham Centre in the 1970s, collaborative research amongst equals, which produced some classics of cultural studies. That was a luxurious situation which is little afforded now and, besides, some of the individuals involved never did complete their own PhDs. Third, there is the model derived from the natural sciences of team projects to which funds for doctoral and postdoctoral research may be attached. The fourth model is probably the closest, however, to the actualities of research in cultural studies, doing the work for a doctoral, for instance, whilst teaching either part-time or full-time. In this context, the doctoral thesis should not be seen as one's major piece of research, though it may turn out to be so for those who do not succeed in building or even wish to build an academic career for themselves.

Michael Green recognizes that his remarks on the lived experience of research in cultural studies do not apply solely to cultural studies. What he has to say, in effect, testifies to the institutionalization of cultural studies, its integration into 'normal' conditions of academic life, and the hardening circumstances of intellectual work, especially in and around the British universities. Cultural studies has passed through its 'launch phase' and entered the 'legitimation phase', for better or for worse. While some may bemoan a diminution of radical alterity in the project of cultural studies, it is hard to see quite how the situation might have turned out differently. This book aims, in any case, to help new researchers in the field come to terms with the legitimation of cultural studies and to cope with the problems of critical inquiry in the institutional conditions where we find ourselves.

References

Alasuutari, P. (1995) *Researching Culture: Qualitative Method and Cultural Studies*, London: Sage.

Anderson (1991) *Imagined Communities: Reflections on the Origin and Spread of Nationalism*, 2nd edn, London: Verso.

Ang, I. and Stratton, J. (1996) 'Asianing Australia: Notes Towards a Critical Transnationalism in Cultural Studies', *Cultural Studies*, 10(1).

Ashcroft, B., Griffiths, G. and Tiffin, H. (eds) (1995) *The Post-Colonial Studies Reader*, London: Routledge.

Bauman, Z. (1993) *Postmodern Ethics*, Oxford: Basil Blackwell.

Bennett, T. (1992) 'Putting Policy into Cultural Studies', in L. Grossberg, C. Nelson and P. Treichler (eds), *Cultural Studies*, London: Routledge.

Bourdieu, P. (1984) *Distinction: A Social Critique of the Judgement of Taste*, London: Routledge.

Bronner, S. and Kellner, D. (eds) (1989) *Critical Theory and Society*, New York: Routledge.

Chaney, D. (1994) *The Cultural Turn: Scene-Setting Essays on Contemporary Cultural History*, London: Routledge.

Chen, K.-H. and Morley, D. (eds) (1996) *Stuart Hall: Critical Dialogues in Cultural Studies*, London: Routledge.

Clifford, J. and Marcus, G. (eds) (1986) *Writing Culture: The Poetics and Politics of Ethnography*, Berkeley and Los Angeles: University of California Press.

Davies, I. (1995) *Cultural Studies and Beyond*, London: Routledge.

Geertz, C. (1973) *The Interpretation of Cultures*, New York: Basic Books.

Giddens, A. (1991) *Modernity and Self-Identity: Self and Society in the Late-Modern Age*, Cambridge: Polity Press.

Gilligan, C. (1982) *In a Different Voice*, Cambridge, Mass.: Harvard University Press.

Gilroy, P (1993a) *The Black Atlantic: Modernity and Double Consciousness*, London: Verso.

Gilroy, P. (1993b) *Small Acts: Thoughts on the Politics of Black Cultures*, London: Serpent's Tail.

Habermas, J. (1990) *Moral Consciousness and Communicative Action*, Cambridge: Polity Press.

Harding, S. (ed.) (1987) *Feminism and Methodology*, Milton Keynes: Open University Press.

Harvey, D. (1989) *The Condition of Postmodernity*, Oxford: Basil Blackwell.

Hirst, P. and Thompson, G. (1996) *Globalization in Question*, Cambridge: Polity Press.

Hoggart, R. (1957) *The Uses of Literacy*, London: Chatto & Windus.

Inglis, F. (1995) *Raymond Williams*, London: Routledge.

Jay, M. (1973) *The Dialectical Imagination: A History of the Frankfurt School and the Institute of Social Research 1923–50*, London: Heinemann.

Kellner, D. (1995) *Media Culture: Cultural Studies, Identity and Politics Between the Modern and the Postmodern*, London: Routledge.

Lyotard, J.-F. (1984) *The Postmodern Condition: A Report on Knowledge*, Manchester: Manchester University Press.

MacCannell, D. (1992) *Empty Meeting Grounds: The Tourist Papers*, London: Routledge.

McGuigan, J. (1996) *Culture and the Public Sphere*, London: Routledge.

McGuigan, J. (1997) 'Cultural Populism Revisited', in M. Ferguson and P. Golding (eds), *Cultural Studies in Question*, London: Sage.

Massey, D. (1994) *Space, Place and Gender*, Cambridge: Polity.

Meehan, J. (ed.) (1995) *Feminists Read Habermas: Gendering the Subject of Discourse*, New York: Routledge.

Mercer, K. (1994) *Welcome to the Jungle: New Positions in Black Cultural Studies*, New York: Routledge.

Nightingale, V. (1993) 'What's "Ethnographic" about Ethnographic Audience Research?', in G. Turner (ed.), *Nation, Culture, Text: Australian Cultural and Media Studies*, London: Routledge.

Seidman, S. (ed.) (1994) *The Postmodern Turn: New Perspectives on Social Theory*, New York: Cambridge University Press.

Soja, E. (1989) *Postmodern Geographies: The Reassertion of Space in Critical Social Theory*, London: Verso.

Steedman, C. (1986) *Landscape for a Good Woman: A Story of Two Lives*, London: Virago.

Stevenson, N. (1995) *Understanding Media Cultures: Social Theory and Mass Communication*, London: Sage.

Thompson, J. (1995) *The Media and Modernity: A Social Theory of the Media*, Cambridge: Polity Press.

Turner, G. (1996) *British Cultural Studies*, 2nd edn, London: Routledge.

Williams, R. (1980) *Problems in Materialism and Culture*, London: Verso.

PART I
METHODOLOGIES

1
Critical Theory and Cultural Studies: The Missed Articulation

Douglas Kellner

For some decades now, British cultural studies has tended to either disregard or caricature in a hostile manner the critique of mass culture developed by the Frankfurt School.[1] The Frankfurt School has been repeatedly stigmatized as elitist and reductionist, or simply ignored in discussion of the methods and enterprise of cultural studies. This is an unfortunate oversight as I will argue that despite some significant differences in method and approach, there are also many shared positions that make dialogue between the traditions productive. Likewise, articulation of the differences and divergences of the two traditions could be fruitful since, as I will argue, both traditions to some extent overcome the weaknesses and limitations of the other. Consequently, articulation of their positions could produce new perspectives that might contribute to developing a more robust cultural studies. Thus, I will argue that rather than being antithetical, the Frankfurt School and British cultural studies approaches complement each other and can be articulated in new configurations.

As we approach the year 2000 and enter a new cultural environment being dramatically transformed by global media and computer technologies, we need a cultural studies that analyses the political economy of the now global culture industries, the proliferation of new media technologies and artefacts, and their multifarious appropriations by audiences. In this chapter, I will discuss some of the theoretical resources needed for these tasks. My argument is that the Frankfurt School is extremely useful for analysing the current forms of culture and society because of their focus on the intersections between technology, the culture industries and the economic situation in contemporary capitalist societies. Since the present age is being dramatically shaped by new media and computer technologies, we need perspectives that articulate the intersection of technology, culture and everyday life. In my view, both the Frankfurt School and British cultural studies offer us resources to critically analyse and transform our current social situation and thus to develop a critical social theory and cultural studies with a practical intent.

The Frankfurt School, cultural studies and regimes of capital

To a large extent, the Frankfurt School inaugurated critical studies of mass communication and culture, and thus produced an early model of cultural studies (see Kellner 1982, 1989a, 1995a). During the 1930s, the Frankfurt School developed a critical and transdisciplinary approach to cultural and communications studies, combining critique of political economy of the media, analysis of texts, and audience reception studies of the social and ideological effects of mass culture and communications.[2] They coined the term 'culture industries' to signify the process of the industrialization of mass-produced culture and the commercial imperatives which drove the system. The critical theorists analysed all mass-mediated cultural artefacts within the context of industrial production, in which the commodities of the culture industries exhibited the same features as other products of mass production: commodification, standardization and massification. The culture industries had the specific function, however, of providing ideological legitimation of the existing capitalist societies and of integrating individuals into the framework of the capitalist system.

Adorno's analyses of popular music (1941, 1978 [1932], 1982, 1989), Lowenthal's studies of popular literature and magazines (1949, 1957, 1961), Herzog's studies of radio soap operas (1941), and the perspectives and critiques of mass culture developed in Horkheimer and Adorno's famous study of the culture industries (1972; Adorno 1991) provide many examples of the value of the Frankfurt School approach. Moreover, in their theories of the culture industries and critiques of mass culture, they were the first to systematically analyse and criticize mass-mediated culture and communications within critical social theory. They were the first social theorists to see the importance of what they called the 'culture industries' in the reproduction of contemporary societies, in which so-called mass culture and communications stand in the centre of leisure activity, are important agents of socialization, mediators of political reality, and should thus be seen as major institutions of contemporary societies with a variety of economic, political, cultural and social effects.[3]

Furthermore, they investigated the cultural industries in a political context as a form of the integration of the working class into capitalist societies. The Frankfurt School were one of the first neo-Marxian groups to examine the effects of mass culture and the rise of the consumer society on the working classes which were to be the instrument of revolution in the classical Marxian scenario. They also analysed the ways that the culture industries and consumer society were stabilizing contemporary capitalism and accordingly sought new strategies for political change, agencies of political transformation and models for political emancipation that could serve as norms of social critique and goals for political struggle. This project required rethinking the Marxian project and produced many important contributions – as well as some problematical positions.

The Frankfurt School focused intently on technology and culture, indicating how technology was becoming both a major force of production and a formative mode of social organization and control. In a 1941 article, 'Some Social Implications of Modern Technology', Herbert Marcuse argued that technology in the contemporary era constitutes an entire 'mode of organizing and perpetuating (or changing) social relationships, a manifestation of prevalent thought and behaviour patterns, an instrument for control and domination' (1941: 414). In the realm of culture, technology produced mass culture that habituated individuals to conform to the dominant patterns of thought and behaviour, and thus provided powerful instruments of social control and domination.

Victims of European fascism, the Frankfurt School experienced firsthand the ways that the Nazis used the instruments of mass culture to produce submission to fascist culture and society. While in exile in the United States, the members of the Frankfurt School came to believe that American 'popular culture' was also highly ideological and worked to promote the interests of American capitalism. Controlled by giant corporations, the culture industries were organized according to the strictures of mass production, churning out mass-produced products that generated a highly commercial system of culture which in turn sold the values, life-styles and institutions of American capitalism.

In retrospect, one can see the Frankfurt School work as articulating a theory of the stage of state and monopoly capitalism which became dominant during the 1930s.[4] This was an era of large organizations, theorized earlier by Hilferding as 'organized capitalism' (1981 [1910]), in which the state and giant corporations managed the economy and in which individuals submitted to state and corporate control. This period is often described as 'Fordism' to designate the system of mass production and the homogenizing regime of capital which wanted to produce mass desires, tastes and behaviour. It was thus an era of mass production and consumption characterized by uniformity and homogeneity of needs, thought and behaviour producing a 'mass society' and what the Frankfurt School described as 'the end of the individual.' No longer was individual thought and action the motor of social and cultural progress; instead giant organizations and institutions overpowered individuals. The era corresponds to the staid, ascetic, conformist and conservative world of corporate capitalism that was dominant in the 1950s with its organization men and women, its mass consumption and its mass culture.

During this period, mass culture and communication were instrumental in generating the modes of thought and behaviour appropriate to a highly organized and massified social order. Thus, the Frankfurt School theory of 'the culture industries' articulates a major historical shift to an era in which mass consumption and culture was indispensable to producing a consumer society based on homogeneous needs and desires for mass-produced products and a mass society based on social organization and homogeneity. It is culturally the era of highly controlled network radio and television, insipid top forty pop music, glossy Hollywood films, national magazines and other mass-produced cultural artefacts

Of course, media culture was never as massified and homogeneous as in the Frankfurt School model. One could argue that the model was flawed even during its time of origin and influence and that other models were preferable (such as those of Walter Benjamin, Siegfried Kracauer, Ernst Bloch and others of the Weimar generation and, later, British cultural studies, as I argue below). Yet the original Frankfurt School model of the culture industry did articulate the important social roles of media culture during a specific regime of capital and provided a model, still of use, of a highly commercial and technologically advanced culture that serves the needs of dominant corporate interests, plays a major role in ideological reproduction, and in enculturating individuals into the dominant system of needs, thought and behaviour.

British cultural studies, then, seen from historical perspective, emerges in a later era of capital, on the cusp of what became known as 'post-Fordism' and a more variegated and conflicted cultural formation. The forms of culture described by the earliest phase of British cultural studies in the 1950s and early 1960s articulated conditions in an era when there were still significant tensions in England and much of Europe between an older working class-based culture and the newer mass-produced culture whose models and exemplars were the products of American culture industries. The initial project of cultural studies developed by Richard Hoggart, Raymond Williams and E.P. Thompson attempted to preserve working-class culture against onslaughts of mass culture produced by the culture industries. Thompson's historical inquiries into the history of British working-class institutions and struggles, the defences of working-class culture by Hoggart and Williams, and their attacks on mass culture were part of a socialist and working-class-oriented project that assumed that the industrial working class was a force of progressive social change and that it could be mobilized and organized to struggle against the inequalities of the existing capitalist societies and for a more egalitarian socialist one. Williams and Hoggart were deeply involved in projects of working-class education and oriented towards socialist working-class politics, seeing their form of cultural studies as an instrument of progressive social change.

The early critiques in the first wave of British cultural studies of Americanism and mass culture, in Hoggart, Williams and others, thus paralleled to some extent the earlier critique of the Frankfurt School, yet valorized a working class that the Frankfurt School saw as defeated in Germany and much of Europe during the era of fascism and which they never saw as a strong resource for emancipatory social change. The early work of the Birmingham School, as I will now argue, was continuous with the radicalism of the first wave of British cultural studies (the Hoggart–Thompson–Williams 'culture and society' tradition) as well as, in important ways, with the Frankfurt School. Yet the Birmingham project also paved the way, as I suggest below, for a postmodern populist turn in cultural studies, which responds to a later stage of capitalism.

The trajectories of cultural studies

It has not yet been recognized (as far as I know) that the second stage of the development of British cultural studies – starting with the founding of the University of Birmingham Centre for Contemporary Cultural Studies in 1963/4 by Hoggart and Stuart Hall – shared many key perspectives with the Frankfurt School. During this period, the Centre developed a variety of critical approaches for the analysis, interpretation and criticism of cultural artefacts.[5] Through a set of internal debates, and responding to social struggles and movements of the 1960s and the 1970s, the Birmingham group came to focus on the interplay of representations and ideologies of class, gender, race, ethnicity and nationality in cultural texts, including media culture. They were among the first to study the effects of newspapers, radio, television, film and other popular cultural forms on audiences. They also focused on how various audiences interpreted and used media culture in varied and different ways and contexts, analysing the factors that made audiences respond in contrasting ways to media texts.

The now classical period of British cultural studies from the early 1960s to the early 1980s continued to adopt a Marxian approach to the study of culture, one especially influenced by Althusser and Gramsci (see, especially, Hall 1980a). Yet, although Hall usually omits the Frankfurt School from his narrative, some of the work done by the Birmingham group replicated certain classical positions of the Frankfurt School, in their social theory and methodological models for doing cultural studies, as well as in their political perspectives and strategies. Like the Frankfurt School, British cultural studies observed the integration of the working class and its decline of revolutionary consciousness, and studied the conditions of this catastrophe for the Marxian project of revolution. Like the Frankfurt School, British cultural studies concluded that mass culture was playing an important role in integrating the working class into existing capitalist societies and that a new consumer and media culture was forming a new mode of capitalist hegemony.

Both traditions focused on the intersections of culture and ideology and saw ideology critique as central to a critical cultural studies (CCCS 1980a, 1980b). Both saw culture as a mode of ideological reproduction and hegemony, in which cultural forms help to shape the modes of thought and behaviour that induce individuals to adapt to the social conditions of capitalist societies. Both also saw culture as a form of resistance to capitalist society and, moreover, both the earlier fore-runners of British cultural studies, especially Raymond Williams, and the theorists of the Frankfurt School saw high culture as forces of resistance to capitalist modernity. Later, British cultural studies would valorize resistant moments in media culture and audience interpretations and use of media artefacts, while the Frankfurt School tended, with some exceptions, to see mass culture as a homogeneous and potent form of ideological domination – a difference that would seriously divide the two traditions.

From the beginning, British cultural studies was highly political in nature and focused on the potentials for resistance in oppositional subcultures, first, valorizing the potential of working-class cultures, then, youth subcultures to resist the hegemonic forms of capitalist domination. Unlike the classical Frankfurt School (but similar to Herbert Marcuse), British cultural studies turned to youth cultures as providing potentially new forms of opposition and social change. Through studies of youth subcultures, British cultural studies demonstrated how culture came to constitute distinct forms of identity and group membership and appraised the oppositional potential of various youth subcultures (see Hebdige 1979; Jefferson 1976). Cultural studies came to focus on how subcultural groups resist dominant forms of culture and identity, creating their own styles and identities. Individuals who conform to dominant dress and fashion codes, behaviour and political ideologies thus produce their identities within mainstream groups, as members of specific social groupings (such as white, middle-class conservative Americans). Individuals who identify with subcultures, like punk culture, or black nationalist subcultures, look and act differently from those in the mainstream, and thus create oppositional identities, defining themselves against standard models.

But British cultural studies, unlike the Frankfurt School, has not adequately engaged modernist and avant-garde aesthetic movements, limiting its focus by and large to products of media culture and 'the popular', which has become an immense focus of its efforts. However, the Frankfurt School engagement with modernism and avant-garde art in many of its protean forms strikes me as more productive than the ignoring of modernism and to some extent high culture as a whole, especially during the last decade or so, by British cultural studies. It appears that in its anxiety to legitimate study of the popular and to engage the artefacts of media culture, British cultural studies has turned away from so-called 'high' culture in favour of the popular. But such a turn sacrifices the possible insights into all forms of culture and replicates the bifurcation of the field of culture into a 'popular' and 'elite' (which merely inverts the positive/negative valorizations of the older high/low distinction). More important, it disconnects cultural studies from attempts to develop oppositional forms of culture of the sort associated with the 'historical avant-garde' (Bürger 1984). Avant-garde movements like Expressionism, Surrealism and Dada wanted to develop art that would revolutionize society, that would provide alternatives to hegemonic forms of culture.

The oppositional and emancipatory potential of avant-garde art movements was a primary focus of the Frankfurt School, especially Adorno, and it is unfortunate that British and North American cultural studies have largely neglected engaging avant-garde art forms and movements. Indeed, it is interesting that such a focus was central to the project of *Screen*, which was in some ways the hegemonic avant-garde of cultural theory in Britain in the 1970s, with powerful influence throughout the world. In the early 1970s, *Screen* developed a founding distinction between 'realism' and 'modernism' and carried out a series of critiques of both bourgeois realist art and the sorts of media culture that reproduced the ideological codes of realism. In addition, it positively valorized avant-garde modernist aesthetic practices, which were championed for their political and emancipatory effects. This project put *Screen* theory in profound kinship with the Frankfurt School, especially Adorno, though there were also serious differences.

British cultural studies developed systematic critiques of the theoretical positions developed by *Screen* in the 1970s and early 1980s which, as far as I know, were never really answered.[6] Indeed, what became known as '*Screen* theory' itself fragmented and dissolved as a coherent theoretical discourse and practical programme by the 1980s. While many of the critiques of *Screen* theory developed by British cultural studies were convincing, I would argue that the emphasis on avant-garde practices championed by *Screen* and the Frankfurt School constitutes a productive alternative to the neglect of such practices by current British and North American cultural studies.

British cultural studies – like the Frankfurt School – insists that culture must be studied within the social relations and system through which culture is produced and consumed, and that thus study of culture is intimately bound up with the study of society, politics and economics. The key Gramscian concept of hegemony led British cultural studies to investigate how media culture articulates a set of dominant values, political ideologies and cultural forms into a hegemonic project that incorporates individuals into a shared consensus, as individuals became integrated into the consumer society and political projects like

Reaganism or Thatcherism. This project is similar in many ways to that of the Frankfurt School, as are their metatheoretical perspectives that combine political economy, textual analysis and study of audience reception within the framework of critical social theory.

British cultural studies and the Frankfurt School were both founded as fundamentally transdisciplinary enterprises which resisted established academic divisions of labour. Indeed, their boundary-crossing and critiques of the detrimental effects of abstracting culture from its socio-political context elicited hostility among those who are more disciplinary-oriented and who, for example, believe in the autonomy of culture and renounce sociological or political readings. Against such academic formalism and separatism, cultural studies insists that culture must be investigated within the social relations and system through which culture is produced and consumed, and that thus analysis of culture is intimately bound up with the study of society, politics and economics. Employing Gramsci's model of hegemony and counter-hegemony, it sought to analyse 'hegemonic,' or ruling, social and cultural forces of domination and to seek 'counter-hegemonic' forces of resistance and struggle. The project was aimed at social transformation and attempted to specify forces of domination and resistance in order to aid the process of political struggle and emancipation from oppression and domination.

Some earlier authoritative presentations of British cultural studies stressed the importance of a transdisciplinary approach to the study of culture that analysed its political economy, process of production and distribution, textual products and reception by the audience – positions remarkably similar to the Frankfurt School. For instance, in his classic programmatic article, 'Encoding/Decoding', Stuart Hall began his analysis by using Marx's *Grundrisse* as a model to trace the articulations of 'a continuous circuit', encompassing 'production–distribution–consumption–production' (1980b: 128ff.). Hall concretizes this model by focusing upon how media institutions produce meanings, how they circulate, and how audiences use or decode the texts to produce meaning. Moreover, in a 1983 lecture published in 1986/7, Richard Johnson provided a model of cultural studies, similar to Hall's earlier model, based on a diagram of the circuits of production, textuality and reception, parallel to the circuits of capital stressed by Marx, illustrated by a diagram that stressed the importance of production and distribution. Although Johnson emphasized the importance of analysis of production in cultural studies and criticized *Screen* for abandoning this perspective in favour of more idealist and textualist approaches (1986/7: 63ff.), much work in British and North American cultural studies has replicated this neglect.

In more recent cultural studies, however, there has been a turn – throughout the English-speaking world – to what might be called a postmodern problematic which emphasizes pleasure, consumption and the individual construction of identities in terms of what McGuigan (1992) has called a 'cultural populism'. Media culture from this perspective produces material for identities, pleasures and empowerment, and thus audiences constitute the 'popular' through their consumption of cultural products. During this phase – roughly from the mid-1980s to the present – cultural studies in Britain and North America turned from the socialist and revolutionary politics of the previous stages to postmodern forms of identity politics and less critical perspectives on media and consumer culture. Emphasis was placed more and more on the audience, consumption and reception, and displaced attention from production and distribution of texts and how texts were produced in media industries.

A postmodern cultural studies?

In this section, I wish to argue that the forms of cultural studies developed from the late 1970s to the present, in contrast to the earlier stages, theorize a shift from the stage of state monopoly capitalism, or Fordism, rooted in mass production and consumption to a new regime of capital and social order, sometimes described as 'post-Fordism' (Harvey 1989), or 'postmodernism' (Jameson 1991), and characterizing a transnational and global capital that valorizes difference, multiplicity, eclecticism, populism and intensified consumerism in a new information/entertainment society. From this perspective, the proliferating media culture, postmodern architecture, shopping malls and the culture of the postmodern spectacle became the promoters and palaces of a new stage of technocapitalism, the latest stage of capital, encompassing a postmodern image and consumer culture.[7]

Consequently, I would argue that the turn to a postmodern cultural studies is a response to a new era of global capitalism. What is described as the 'new revisionism' (McGuigan 1992: 61ff.) resolutely severs cultural studies from political economy and critical social theory. During the current stage of cultural studies there is a widespread tendency to decentre, or even ignore completely, economics, history and politics in favour of emphasis on local pleasures, consumption and the construction of hybrid identities from the material of the popular. This cultural populism replicates the turn in postmodern theory away from Marxism and its alleged reductionism, master narratives of liberation and domination, and historical teleology.[8]

In fact, as McGuigan (1992: 45ff.) has documented, British cultural studies has had an unstable relationship with political economy from the beginning. Although Stuart Hall and Richard Johnson grounded cultural studies in a Marxian model of the circuits of capital (production–distribution–consumption–production), Hall and other key figures in British cultural studies have not consistently pursued economic analysis and most practitioners of British and North American cultural studies from the 1980s to the present have pulled away from political economy altogether. Hall's swervings towards and away from political economy are somewhat curious. Whereas in the article cited above Hall begins cultural studies with production and recommends traversing through the circuits of capital (1980b), and while in 'Two Paradigms' (1980c), Hall proposes synthesizing 'culturalism' and 'structuralism' on a higher level *à la* the Frankfurt School, he has been rather inconsistent in articulating the relationship between political economy and cultural studies, and rarely deployed political economy in his work.

In the 'Two Paradigms' article, for example, Hall dismisses the political economy of culture paradigm because it falls prey to economic reductionism. Hall might be right in rejecting some forms of the political economy of culture then circulating in England and elsewhere, but, as I will argue below, it is possible to do a political economy of culture *à la* the Frankfurt School without falling prey to reductionism yet using the same sort of model of reciprocal interaction of culture and economy. In particular, the Frankfurt model posits a relative autonomy to culture that is often defended by Hall, and does not entail economic reductionism or determinism.

Generally speaking, however, Hall and other practioners of British cultural studies (Bennett, Fiske, McRobbie, et al.) either simply dismiss the Frankfurt School as a form of economic reductionism or simply ignore it.[9] The blanket charge of economic reductionism is in part a way of avoiding political economy altogether. Yet while many practitioners of British cultural studies ignore political economy totally, Hall, to be sure, has occasionally made remarks that might suggest the need to articulate cultural studies with political economy. In a 1983 article, Hall suggests that it is preferable to conceive of the economic as determinate in 'the first instance' rather than in 'the last instance', but this play with Althusser's argument for the primacy of the economic is rarely pursued in actual concrete studies (see the critiques in McGuigan 1992: 34; Murdock 1989).

Hall's analysis of Thatcherism as 'authoritarian populism' (1988) related the move towards the hegemony of the right to shifts in global capitalism from Fordism to post-Fordism, but for his critics (Jessop et al. 1984) he did not adequately take account of the role of the economy and economic factors in the shift towards Thatcherism. Hall responded that with Gramsci he would never deny 'the decisive nucleus of economic activity' (1988: 156), but it is not certain that Hall himself adequately incorporates economic analysis into his work in cultural studies and political critique. For example, Hall's writing on the 'global postmodern' suggests the need for more critical conceptualizations of contemporary global capitalism and theorizing of relations between the economic and the cultural of the sort associated with the Frankfurt School. Hall (1991) states:

> [T]he global postmodern signifies an ambiguous opening to difference and to the margins and makes a certain kind of decentring of the Western narrative a likely possibility; it is matched, from the very heartland of cultural politics, by the backlash: the aggressive resistance to difference; the attempt to restore the canon of Western civilization; the assault, direct and indirect, on multiculturalism; the return to grand narratives of history, language and literature (the three great supporting pillars of national identity and national culture); the defence of ethnic absolutism, of a cultural racism that has marked the Thatcher and the Reagan eras; and the new xenophobias that are about to overwhelm fortress Europe.

For Hall, therefore, the global postmodern involves a pluralizing of culture, openings to the margins, to difference, to voices excluded from the narratives of Western culture. But one could argue in opposition to this interpretation in the spirit of the Frankfurt School that the global postmodern simply represents an expansion of global capitalism on the terrain of new media and technologies, and that the explosion of information and entertainment in media culture represents powerful new sources of capital realization and social control. To be sure, the new world order of technology, culture and politics in contemporary global capitalism is marked by more multiplicity, pluralism and openness to difference and voices from the margins, but it is controlled and limited by transnational corporations which are becoming powerful new cultural arbitrators who threaten to constrict the range of cultural expression rather than to expand it.

The dramatic developments in the culture industries in recent years towards merger and consolidation represent the possibilities of increased control of information and entertainment by ever fewer superconglomerates. One could argue already that the globalization of media culture is an imposition of the lowest denominator homogeneity of global culture on a national and local culture, in which CNN, NBC and the Murdoch channels, for instance, impose the most banal uniformity and homogeneity on media culture throughout the world. To be sure, the European cable and satellite television systems have state television from Germany, France, Italy, Spain, Sweden and Russia, and so on, but these state television systems are not really open to that much otherness, difference or marginality. Indeed, the more open channels, like public access television in the United States and Europe, or the SBS service which provides multicultural television in Australia, are not really part of the global postmodern, and are funded or mandated for the most part by the largess of state and are usually limited and local in scope and reach.

Certainly, there are some openings in Hall's global postmodern, but they are rather circumscribed and counteracted by increasing homogenization. Indeed, the defining characteristics of global media culture is the contradictory forces of identity and difference, homogeneity and heterogeneity, the global and the local, impinging on each other, clashing, simply peacefully co-existing, or producing new symbioses, as in the motto of MTV Latino which combines English and Spanish: *'Chequenos!'* – meaning 'Check us out!' Globalization by and large means the hegemony of transnational cultural industries, largely American. In Canada, for instance, about 95 per cent of films in movie theatres are American; US television dominates Canadian television; seven American firms control distribution of sound recordings in Canada; and 80 per cent of the magazines on newsstands are non-Canadian (*Washington Post Weekly,* September 11–17, 1995: 18). In Latin America and Europe the situation is similar with American media culture, commodities, fast-food and malls creating a new global culture that is remarkably similar on all continents.[10] Evocations of the global postmodern diversity and difference should thus take into account countervailing tendencies towards global homogenization and sameness – themes constantly stressed by the Frankfurt School.

For Hall (1991), the interesting question is what happens when a progressive politics of representation imposes itself on the global postmodern field, as if the global field was really open to marginality and otherness. But in fact the global field itself is structured and controlled by dominant corporate and state powers and it remains a struggle to get oppositional voices in play and is probably impossible where there is not something like public access channels or state-financed open channels as in Holland. Of course, things look different when one goes outside of the dominant media culture – there *is* more pluralism, multiplicity, openness to new voices, on the margins, but such alternative cultures are hardly part of the global postmodern that Hall elicits. Hall's global postmodern is thus too positive and his optimism should be tempered by the sort of critical perspectives on global capitalism developed by the Frankfurt School and the earlier stages of cultural studies.

The emphasis in postmodernist cultural studies, in my view, articulates experiences and phenomena within a new mode of social organization. The emphasis on active audiences, resistant readings, oppositional texts, utopian moments, and the like, describes an era in which individuals are trained to be more active media consumers, and in which they are given a much wider choice of cultural materials, corresponding to a new global and transnational capitalism with a much broader array of consumer choices, products and services. In this regime, difference sells, and the differences, multiplicities and heterogeneity valorized in postmodern theory describes the proliferation of differences and multiplicity in a new social order predicated on proliferation of consumer desires and needs.

The forms of hybrid culture and identities described by postmodern cultural studies correspond to a globalized capitalism with an intense flow of products, culture, people and identities with new configurations of the global and local and new forms of struggles and resistance (see Appadurai 1990; Cvetkovich and Kellner 1997). Corresponding to the structure of a globalized and hybridized global culture are new forms of cultural studies which combine traditions from throughout the world. Cultural studies has indeed become globalized during the past decade with proliferation of articles, books, conferences and Internet sites and discussions throughout the world.

The question arises as to the continued use-value of the older traditions of Frankfurt School theory and British cultural studies in this new and original condition. To begin, these traditions continue to be relevant because there are continuities between our present stage and the earlier ones. Indeed, I would argue that we are in an interregnum period, between the modern and the postmodern, and that the current regime of capital has strong continuities with the mode of production and social organization of the earlier stages described by the Frankfurt School and British cultural studies. Contemporary culture is more commodified and commercialized than ever and so the Frankfurt School perspectives on commodification are obviously still of fundamental importance in theorizing our current situation. The hegemony of capital continues to be the dominant force of social organization, perhaps even more so than before. Likewise, class differences are intensifying, media culture continues to be highly ideological and to legitimate existing inequalities of class, gender and race, so that the earlier critical perspectives on these aspects of contemporary culture and society continue to be of importance.

My argument will be that the new global constellation of techno-capitalism is based on configurations of capital and technology, producing new forms of culture, society and everyday life. I have been arguing that the Frankfurt School furnishes resources to analyse this conjuncture because its model of the culture industries focuses on the articulations of capital, technology, culture and everyday life that constitute the current socio-cultural environment. Although there is a tendency of Frankfurt School thinkers to occasionally offer an overly one-sided and negative vision of technology as an instrument of domination – building on Weber's theory of instrumental rationality – there are also aspects that make possible a critical theory of technology that articulates both its emancipatory and oppressive aspects (see Kellner 1984, 1989a; Marcuse 1941). The Frankfurt School thus complements British cultural studies in providing a more intense focus on the articulations of capital and technology, and thus theorizing contemporary culture and society in the context of the current constellation of global capitalism.

In the next section, accordingly, I will examine what theoretical resources the Frankfurt School and the tradition of British cultural studies contain to critically analyse and transform contemporary societies and culture. I will be concerned to articulate some overlapping similarities in perspective between the two traditions, but also differences in which the traditions complement each other and force us to produce yet new perspectives in order to do cultural studies in the present conjuncture. My argument is that cultural studies today should return to the earlier models of British cultural studies and put in question the current rejection of political economy, class, ideology and question the postmodern turn in cultural studies. I believe that the turn away from the problematic shared to some extent with the Frankfurt School has vitiated contemporary British and North American cultural studies and that a return to critical social theory and political economy is a necessary move for a revitalized cultural studies. This project requires a new cultural studies that articulates the sort of analysis of political economy developed by the Frankfurt School with the emphasis on subversive moments of media culture, oppositional subcultures and an active audience developed by British cultural studies. I believe that the neglect of political economy truncates cultural studies and would argue for its importance not only for generally understanding media culture, but also for analysing texts and audience use of texts which are deeply influenced by the system of production and distribution within which media products circulate and are received (see Kellner 1995a).[11]

Border-crossing, transdisciplinarity and cultural studies

I have been arguing that there are many important anticipations of key positions of British cultural studies in the Frankfurt School, that they share many positions and dilemmas, and that a dialogue between these traditions is long overdue. I would also propose seeing the project of cultural studies as broader than that taught in the contemporary curricula and as encompassing a wide range of figures from various social locations and traditions. There are indeed many traditions and models of cultural studies, ranging from neo-Marxist models developed by Lukács, Gramsci, Bloch and the Frankfurt School in the 1930s to feminist and psychoanalytic cultural studies to semiotic and post-structuralist perspectives. In Britain and the United States, there is a long tradition of cultural studies that preceded the Birmingham School.[12] And France, Germany and other European countries have also produced rich traditions that provide resources for cultural studies throughout the world.

The major traditions of cultural studies combine – at their best – social theory, cultural critique, history, philosophical analysis and specific political interventions, thus overcoming the standard academic division of labour by surmounting arbitrary disciplinary specialization. Cultural studies thus operates with a transdisciplinary conception that draws on social theory, economics, politics, history, communication studies, literary and cultural theory, philosophy and other theoretical discourses – an approach shared by the Frankfurt School, British cultural studies and French postmodern theory. Transdisciplinary approaches to culture and society transgress borders between various academic disciplines.[13] In regard to cultural studies, such approaches suggest that one should not stop at the border of a text, but should see how it fits into systems of textual production, and how various texts are thus part of systems of genres or types of production, and have an intertextual construction – as well as articulating discourses in a given socio-historical conjuncture.

The 'Rambo' films, for instance, fit into the genre of war films and a specific cycle of return to Vietnam films, but also articulates anti-communist political discourses dominant in the Reagan era (see Kellner 1995a). It replicates the right-wing discourses concerning PoWs left in Vietnam and the need to overcome the Vietnam syndrome (that is, shame concerning the loss of the war and overcoming the reluctance to again use US military power). But it also fits into a cycle of masculinist hero films, anti-statist right-wing discourses and the use of violence to resolve conflicts. The figure of Rambo itself became a 'global popular' which had a wide range of effects throughout the world. Interpreting the cinematic text of 'Rambo' films thus involves the use of film theory, textual analysis, social history, political analysis and ideology critique, effects analysis and other modes of cultural criticism.

One should not, therefore, stop at the borders of the text or even its intertexuality, but should move from text to context, to the culture and society that constitutes the text and in which it should be read and interpreted. Transdisciplinary approaches thus involve border-crossings, across disciplines from text to context, and thus from texts to culture and society. Raymond Williams was especially important for cultural studies because of his stress on borders and border-crossings (1961, 1962, 1974). Like the Frankfurt School, he always saw the interconnection between culture and communication, and their connections with the society in which they are produced, distributed and consumed. Williams also saw how texts embodied the political conflicts and discourses within which they were embedded and reproduced.

Crossing borders inevitably pushes one to the boundaries and borders of class, gender, race, sexuality and the other constituents that differentiate individuals from each other and through which people construct their identities. Thus, most forms of cultural studies, and most critical social theories, have engaged feminism and the various multicultural theories which focus on representations of gender, race, ethnicity and sexuality, enriching their projects with theoretical and political substance derived from the new critical discourses that have emerged since the 1960s. Transdisciplinary cultural studies thus draw on a disparate range of discourses and fields to theorize the complexity and contradictions of the multiple effects of a vast range of cultural forms in our lives and, differentially, demonstrate how these forces serve as instruments of domination, but also offer resources for resistance and change. The Frankfurt School, I would argue, inaugurated such transdisciplinary approaches to cultural studies, combining analysis of the production and political economy of culture with textual analysis that contextualizes cultural artefacts in their socio-historical milieu, and with studies of audience reception and use of cultural texts.[14]

Yet there are serious flaws in the original programme of critical theory which require a radical reconstruction of the classical model of the culture industries (Kellner 1989a, 1995a). Overcoming the limitations of the classical model would include: more concrete and empirical analysis of the political economy of the media and the processes of the production of culture; more empirical and historical research into the construction of media industries and their interaction with other social institutions; more empirical studies of audience reception and media effects; more emphasis on the use of media culture as providing forces of resistance; and the incorporation of new cultural theories and methods into a reconstructed critical theory of culture and society. Cumulatively, such a reconstruction of the classical Frankfurt School project would update the critical theory of society and its activity of cultural criticism by incorporating contemporary developments in social and cultural theory into the enterprise of critical theory.

In addition, the Frankfurt School dichotomy between high culture and low culture is problematical and should be superseded by a more unified model that takes culture as a spectrum and applies similar critical methods to all cultural artefacts ranging from opera to popular music, from modernist literature to soap operas. In particular, the Frankfurt School model of a monolithic mass culture contrasted with an ideal of 'authentic art', which limits critical, subversive and emancipatory moments to certain privileged artefacts of high culture, is highly problematic. The Frankfurt School position that all mass culture is ideological and homogenizing, having the effects of duping a passive mass of consumers, is also objectionable. Instead, one should see critical and ideological moments in the full range of culture, and not limit critical moments to high culture and identify all of low culture as ideological. One should also allow for the possibility that critical and subversive moments could be found in the artefacts of the cultural industries, as well as the canonized classics of high modernist culture that the Frankfurt School seemed to privilege as the site of artistic opposition and emancipation.[15] One should also distinguish between the encoding and decoding of media artefacts, and recognize that an active audience often produces its own meanings and use for products of the cultural industries.

British cultural studies overcomes some of these limitations of the Frankfurt School by systematically rejecting high/low culture distinctions and taking seriously the artefacts of media culture. Likewise, they overcome the limitations of the Frankfurt School notion of a passive audience in their conceptions of an active audience that creates meanings and the popular. Yet it should be pointed out that Walter Benjamin – loosely affiliated with the Frankfurt School but not part of their inner circle – also took media culture seriously, saw its emancipatory potential, and posited the possibility of an active audience. For Benjamin (1969), the spectators of sports events were discriminating judges of athletic activity, able to criticize and analyse sports events. Benjamin postulated that the film audience can also become experts of criticism and dissect the meanings and ideologies of film. Yet I believe that we need to synthesize the concepts of the active and manipulated audience to grasp the full range of media effects, thus avoiding both cultural elitism and populism.

Indeed, it is precisely the critical focus on media culture from the perspectives of commodification, reification, technification, ideology and domination developed by the Frankfurt School that provides a perspective useful as a corrective to more populist and uncritical approaches to media culture which surrender critical perspectives – as is evident in some current forms of British and North American cultural studies. In fact, as described by Lazarsfeld (1941) in an issue of *Studies in Philosophy and Social Science* edited by the Frankfurt School on mass communications, the field of communications study was initially divided between the critical school associated with the Institute for Social Research and, in contrast, administrative research, which Lazarsfeld defined as research carried out within the parameters of established media and social institutions and that would provide material that was of use to these institutions – research with which Lazarsfeld himself would be identified. Hence, it was the Frankfurt School that inaugurated critical communications research, and I am suggesting that a return to a reconstructed version of the original model would be useful for media and cultural studies today.

Although the Frankfurt School approach itself is partial and one-sided, it does provide tools with which to criticize the ideological forms of media culture and the ways that it provides ideologies which legitimate forms of oppression. Ideology critique is a fundamental constituent of cultural studies, and the Frankfurt School is valuable for inaugurating systematic and sustained critiques of ideology within the cultural industries. The Frankfurt School is especially useful in providing contextualizations of their cultural criticism. Members of the group carried out their analyses within the framework of critical social theory, thus integrating cultural studies within the study of capitalist society and the ways that communications and culture were produced within this order and the roles and functions that they assumed. Thus, the study of communication and culture became an important part of a theory of contemporary society, in which culture and communication were playing ever more significant roles.[16]

In the next section, I will argue that the neglect in current versions of British cultural studies of the sort of political economy and critical social theory found in the Frankfurt School work has vitiated contemporary cultural studies. I develop this argument with engagement of some key texts within British cultural studies, and criticize some current versions which are shown to be problematical precisely through their abandoning of the more Marxist-oriented perspectives that defined earlier versions of British cultural studies and the work of the Frankfurt School.

Political economy and cultural studies

Thus, against the turn away from political economy in cultural studies, I believe it is important to situate analysis of cultural texts within their system of production and distribution, often referred to as the 'political economy' of culture.[17] But this requires some reflection on what sort of political economy might be useful for cultural studies. The references to the terms 'political' and 'economy' call attention to the fact that the production and distribution of culture takes place within a specific economic system, constituted by relations between the state, the economy, the media, social institutions and practices, culture and everyday life. Political economy thus encompasses economics and politics and the relations between them and the other central dimensions of society and culture.

In regard to media institutions, for instance, in Western democracies, a capitalist economy dictates that cultural production is governed by laws of the market, but the democratic imperatives mean that there is some regulation of culture by the state. There are often tensions within a given society concerning which activities should be governed by the imperatives of the market alone and how much state regulation or intervention is desirable, to assure a wider diversity of broadcast programming, or the prohibition of phenomena agreed to be harmful, such as cigarette advertising or pornography (see Kellner 1990).

Political economy highlights that capitalist societies are organized according to a dominant mode of production that structures institutions and practices according to the logic of commodification and capital accumulation so that cultural production is profit- and market-oriented. Forces of production (such as media technologies and creative practice) are deployed according to dominant relations of production that are important in determining what sort of cultural artefacts are produced and how they are consumed. However, 'political economy' does not merely refer solely to economics, but to the relations between the economic, political and other dimensions of social reality. The term thus links culture to its political and economic context and opens up cultural studies to history and politics. It refers to a field of struggle and antagonism and not an inert structure, as caricatured by some of its opponents.

Political economy also calls attention to the fact that culture is produced within relationships of domination and subordination and thus reproduces or resists existing structures of power. Such a perspective also provides a normative standard for cultural studies whereby the critic can attack aspects of cultural texts that reproduce class, gender, racial and other hierarchal forms of domination and positively valorize aspects that resist or subvert existing domination, or depict forms of resistance and struggle against them. In addition, inserting texts into the system of culture within which they are produced and distributed can help elucidate features and effects of the texts that textual analysis alone might miss or downplay. Rather than being antithetical approaches to culture, political economy can actually contribute to textual analysis and critique, as well as audience reception and uses of media texts – as I attempt to demonstrate below. The system of production often determines what sort of artefacts will be produced, what structural limits there will be as to what can and cannot be said and shown, and what sort of audience expectations and usage the text may generate.

Consideration of Stuart Hall's famous distinction between encoding and decoding (1980b), I believe, suggests some of the ways that political economy structures both the encoding and decoding of media artefacts. As the Frankfurt School pointed out, media culture is produced within an industrial organization of production in which products are generated according to codes and models within culture industries that are organized according to industrial models of production (Horkheimer and Adorno 1972). What codes are operative and how they are encoded into artefacts is thus a function of the system of production. In a commercial system of media culture, production is organized according to well-defined genres with their own codes and modes of production.

Film, television, popular music and other genres of media culture are highly codified into systems of commercial enterprise, organized in accordance with highly conventional codes and formulas. In the system of commercial broadcasting in the United States, for instance, network television is organized into a few dominant genres such as talk shows, soap operas, action/adventure series and situation comedies. Each genre has its own codes and format, with situation comedies invariably using a structure of conflict and resolution, with the solving of the problem suggesting a moral message or upholding dominant values or institutions. Within the genre, each series has its own codes and formats which are followed according to the dictates of the production company; each series, for instance, uses a manual (or 'story bible') that tells writers and production teams what to do and not to do, defines characters and plot lines, and the conventions of the series; continuity experts enforce the following of these codes rigorously (as do network censors that do not allow content that transgresses dominant moral codes).

Sometimes, of course, the codes of media culture change, often dramatically and usually in accordance with social changes that lead media producers to conclude that audiences will be receptive to new forms more relevant to their social experience. So for some years during the 1950s and 1960s happy, middle-class nuclear families ruled the US situation comedy during an era of unparalleled post-Second World War affluence that came to an end in the early 1970s. Precisely then new working-class comedies appeared, such as Norman Lear's *All in the Family*, which focused on social conflict, economic problems, and which did not offer easy solutions to all of the standard conflicts. Lear's subsequent series on the working class, *Mary Hartman*, combined situation comedy codes with soap opera codes which endlessly multiplied problems rather than providing solutions. During the protracted economic recession of the 1980s and 1990s, triggered by a global restructuring of capitalism, new 'loser television' situation comedy series appeared featuring the victims of the economic downswing and restructuring (that is, *Roseanne, Married with Children* and *The Simpsons*). *Beavis and Butt-Head* takes loser television even further, combining situation comedy formats with music video clips and the commentary of two mid-teenage animated cartoon characters without apparent families, education or job prospects (see the discussion in Kellner 1995a).

Other popular 1990s sitcoms feature singles, reflecting the decline of the family and proliferation of alternative life-styles in the present moment (for example, *Murphy Brown, Seinfeld, Friends*, and so on). The most popular US sitcoms of the 1990s thus break the codes of happy affluent families easily solving all problems within the nuclear family ('It's all in the family'). The codes of the texts are produced by changes in production codes with media corporations deciding that audiences want a new sort of programme that better reflects their own situation and in turn creates new audience codes and expectations. The concept of 'code' therefore intersects articulations of media industries and production, texts and audience reception in a circuit of production–consumption–production in which political economy is crucial.

Increased competition from ever-proliferating cable channels and new technologies led network television in the 1980s and 1990s to break many of the conventions rigorously followed in series TV in order to attract declining audiences. Programmes like *Hill Street Blues, L.A. Law, Law and Order* and *N.Y.P.D. Blue*, for instance, broke previous conventions and taboos of the television crime drama. *Hill Street Blues* employed hand-held cameras to create a new look and feel, multiplied its plot lines with some stories lasting for weeks, and did not always provide a positive resolution to the conflicts and problems depicted. Previous TV police dramas rigorously followed a conflict/resolution model with a crime, its detection and an inevitable happy ending, projecting the message that crime did not pay and providing idealizations of the police and the criminal justice system. But the later police shows mentioned above depicted corrupt members within the law enforcement and judicial system, police committing crimes, and criminals getting away with their misdeeds.

Yet even the code-breaking series have their own codes and formulas which cultural analysis should delineate. The relatively young and liberal production team of *Hill Street Blues*, for instance, conveyed socially critical attitudes towards dominant institutions and sympathy for the oppressed marked by the experiences of sixties radicalism (see Gitlin's 1983 study of the Bochco–Kozoll production team). The team's later series *L.A. Law* negotiated the emphasis on professionalism and rising mobility of the Reaganite eighties with concern for social problems and the oppressed. Their 1990s series *N.Y.P.D. Blue* reflects growing cynicism towards police, law enforcement and the society as a whole. The success of these series obviously points to an audience which shares these attitudes and which is tiring of idealized depictions of police, lawyers and the criminal justice system.

Thus, situating the artefacts of media culture within the system of production and the society that generate them can help illuminate their structures and meanings. The encoding of media artefacts is deeply influenced by systems of production so that study of the texts of television, film or popular music, for instance, is enhanced by studying the ways that media artefacts are actually produced within the structure and organization of the culture industries. Since the forms of media culture are structured by well-defined rules and conventions, the study of the production of culture can help elucidate the codes actually in play and thus illuminate what sorts of texts are produced. Because of the demands of the format of radio or music television, for instance, most popular songs are three to four minutes, fitting into the format of the distribution system. Because of its control by giant corporations oriented primarily towards profit, film production in the United States is domin-ated by specific genres, and since the 1970s by the search for blockbuster hits, thus leading to proliferation of the most popular sorts of comedies, action/adventure films, fantasies, and seemingly never-ending sequels and cycles of the most popular films. This economic factor explains why Hollywood film is dominated by major genres and subgenres, explains sequelmania in the film industry, crossovers of popular films into television series,[18] and a certain homogeneity in products constituted within systems of production with rigid generic codes, formulaic con-ventions and well-defined ideological boundaries.

Likewise, study of political economy can help determine the limits and range of political and ideological discourses and effects, and can help indicate which discourses are dominant at a specific conjuncture. The rigid production code (the Hays code) implemented for Hollywood films in 1934, for instance, strictly forbade scenes showing explicit sexuality, use of drugs, critical references to religion, or stories in which crime did indeed pay. By the 1960s, the production code was thoroughly subverted and eventually abandoned during an era of falling audiences where the film industries broke previous taboos in order to attract audiences to the movie theatres. In addition, the wave of youth and counterculture films of the 1960s responded to what film studios saw as a new film generation which made up a significant chunk of the audience (Kellner and Ryan 1988). Low-budget films like *Easy Rider* made high profits and Holly-wood spun off genre cycles of such films. Likewise, when low-budget blaxploitation films made high profits a cycle of films featuring black heroes, often outlaws, against the white power structure proliferated. After consolidation of the film industry in the 1970s, however, and megablockbuster hits like *Jaws* and *Star Wars*, Hollywood aimed at more mainstream genre blockbuster films, driving more subcultural fare to the margins.

Thus, economic trends in the film industry help explain what sorts of films were made over the past decades. Television news and entertainment and its biases and limitations can also be illuminated by study of political economy. My study of television in the United States, for instance, disclosed that the takeover of the television networks by major transnational corporations and communications conglomerates was part of a 'right turn' within US society in the 1980s whereby powerful corporate groups won control of the state and the mainstream media (Kellner 1990). For example, during the 1980s all three US networks were taken over by major corporate conglomerates: ABC was taken over in 1985 by Capital Cities, NBC was taken over by GE, and CBS was taken over by the Tisch Financial Group. Both ABC and NBC sought corporate mergers and this motivation, along with other benefits derived from Reaganism, might well have influenced them to downplay criticisms of Reagan and to generally support his conservative programmes, military adventures and simulated presidency – and then to support George Bush in the 1988 election (see the documentation in Kellner 1990).

Reaganism and Thatcherism constituted a new political hegemony, a new form of political common sense, and the trend in the 1990s has been for deregulation and the allowing of 'market forces' to determine the direction of cultural and communications industries. Hence, in 1995–6 megamergers between Disney and ABC, Time Warner and Turner Communications, CBS and Westinghouse, and NBC and Microsoft, and mergers among other major media conglomerates were negotiated. Merger mania was both a function of the general atmosphere of deregulation and a Federal Communications Commission (FCC) ruling under the Clinton administration which allowed television networks to own and produce their own programming (whereas previously independent Hollywood production companies created programmes and the networks distributed them). Relaxing of these rules and visions of 'synergy' between production and distribution units has led to even greater concentration of media conglomerates and will thus probably lead to a narrower range of programming and voices in the future.

Thus, analysis of political economy allows illumination of the major trends in the information and entertainment industries. Furthermore, one cannot really discuss the role of the media in specific events like the Gulf War without analysing the production and political economy of news and information, as well as the actual text of the war against Iraq and its reception by its audience (see Kellner 1992a, 1995a). Likewise, in appraising the full social impact of pornography, one needs to be aware of the sex industry and the production process of, say, pornographic films, and not just limit analysis to the texts themselves and their effects on audiences. Nor can one fully grasp the success of Michael Jackson or Madonna without analysing their marketing strategies, their use of the technologies of music video, advertising, publicity and image management.

Towards a multiperspectival cultural studies

To conclude: I am proposing that cultural studies develop a multi-perspectival approach which includes investigation of a wide range of artefacts interrogating relationships within the three dimensions of: (1) the production and political economy of culture; (2) textual analysis and critique of its artefacts; and (3) study of audience reception and the uses of media/cultural products.[19] This proposal involves suggesting, first, that cultural studies itself be multiperspectival, getting at culture from the perspectives of political economy and production, text analysis and audience reception.[20] I would also propose that textual analysis and audience reception studies utilize a multiplicity of perspectives, or critical methods, when engaging in textual analysis, and in delineating the multiplicity of subject positions, or perspectives, through which audiences appropriate culture. Moreover, I would argue that the results of such studies need to be interpreted and contexualized within critical social theory to adequately delineate their meanings and effects.

Which perspectives will be deployed in specific studies depends on the subject matter under investigation, the goals of the study, and its range. Obviously, one cannot deploy all the perspectives I have proposed in every single study, but I would argue if one is doing a study of a complex phenomena like the Gulf War, Madonna, Rambo, rap music or the O.J. Simpson trial, one needs to deploy the perspectives of political economy, textual analysis and audience reception studies to illuminate the full dimensions of these spectacles of media culture. In this chapter, I have limited myself to some arguments concerning how Frankfurt School perspectives on the cultural industries can enrich cultural studies, and for a final example of the fruitfulness of this approach let us reflect on the Madonna and Michael Jackson phenomena. There have been a large number of readings of their texts and a vast literature on Madonna's effects on her audiences, but less study of how their mode of production and marketing strategies have helped create their popularity.

My argument would be that Madonna and Michael Jackson have deployed some of the most proficient production and marketing teams in the history of media culture, and this dimension should therefore be considered in analyses of their meanings, effects and uses by their audiences. Just as Madonna's popularity was in large part a function of her marketing strategies and her production of music videos and images that appealed to diverse audiences (see Kellner 1995a), so too has Michael Jackson's media machine employed topflight production, marketing and public relations personnel. Both Madonna and Michael Jackson reached superstardom during the era when MTV and music videos became central in determining fame within the field of popular music and arguably became popular because of their look and spectacular presentations in expensive music videos with exceptionally high production values. In both cases, it is arguably the marketing of their image and the spectacle of their music videos or concerts – rather than, say, their voices or any specific musical talent – that account for their popularity. Both deployed top musical arrangers, choreographers and cinematographers in the production of music videos and performed in highly spectacular and well-publicized concerts that were as much spectacle as performance. Both employed powerhouse publicity machines and constantly kept themselves in the public eye. In particular, both were celebrated constantly by MTV, which had entire weekends, and even weeks, devoted to publicizing their work and fame.

Both, therefore, succeeded because of their understanding and use of the machinery of musical production and promotion by the culture industries. Interestingly, Michael Jackson targeted mainstream audiences from the beginning, attempting to appeal equally to black and white, preteen and teenage, audiences. Indeed, his look erased racial markers as he became whiter and whiter after recurrent plastic surgery; likewise, he cultivated an androgynous look and image that collapsed distinctions between male and female, child and adult, appearing both childlike and sexy, as a naive innocent and canny businessperson, thus appealing to multiple audiences. Madonna, by contrast, targeted first teenage girl audiences, then various ethnic audiences, with performers of colour and distinct ethnic markers appearing in her music videos and concerts.

Both also appealed to gay audiences, with Madonna in particular pushing the boundaries of the acceptable in music videos, leading MTV to ban a 1990 video, 'Justify My Love', with what was deemed excessively extreme sexuality. Both became highly controversial, Madonna because of her exploitation of sexuality and Michael Jackson because of accusations of child molestation. Indeed, the latter created a serious public relations problem for Jackson, who had presented himself as a lover of children. When this image became too literal he needed to refurbish his public persona. After settling financially with the family of the boy who had claimed that Jackson had sexually abused him, Jackson undertook a series of desperate attempts to refurbish his image in the mid-1990s. He married Lisa Marie Presley, Elvis's daughter, in 1994, thus positioning him as a husband, a father (of Lisa Marie's children by a previous marriage), and as in the lineage of the King of Rock, the successor to the throne. With the 1995 release of *HisStory*, a multi-record collection of his greatest hits and current work, Jackson undertook a massive publicity campaign with Sony records supported with a $30 million budget. The record did not match his earlier sales, but at least brought Jackson back into the limelight as it was accompanied by an unparalleled media blitz in summer 1995 with ABC Television dedicating entire special programmes to Jackson and his wife, and to Jackson on-line with his fans in a live Internet interaction. Not to be outdone, MTV devoted an entire week's prime time programming to Jackson.

Yet Jackson and Lisa Marie Presley split up in 1996 and once again rumours circulated that he was continuing to engage in paedophilia. These rumours and the break-up of his marriage created bad press and retarnished his image. In the midst of this crisis, Jackson declared that a long-time friend was pregnant with his child and he married her in the fall of 1996, once again, trying to produce a positive image as husband and father. But, again, negative media reports circulated and Jackson's image is again in crisis. He who lives by the media can also die by the media, though, like old soldiers, media celebrities sometimes just fade away.

In any case, analysing the marketing and production of stardom and popularity can help to demystify the arguably false idols of media culture and to produce more critical audience perception. Analysing the business dimension of media culture can help produce critical conscious-ness as well as better understanding of its production and distribution. Such a dimension, I have been arguing, enhances cultural studies and contributes to developing a critical media pedagogy that supplements analysis of how to read media texts and how to study audience use of them.

Consequently, a cultural studies that is critical and multiperspectival provides comprehensive approaches to culture that can be applied to a wide variety of artefacts from pornography to Michael Jackson and Madonna, from the Gulf War to *Beavis and Butt-Head*, from modernist painting to postmodern architecture. Its comprehensive perspectives encompass political economy, textual analysis and audience research and provide critical and political perspectives that enable individuals to dissect the meanings, messages and effects of dominant cultural forms. Cultural studies is thus part of a critical media pedagogy that enables individuals to resist media manipulation and to increase their freedom and individuality. It can empower people to gain sovereignty over their culture and to be able to struggle for alternative cultures and political change. Cultural studies is thus not just another academic fad, but can be part of a struggle for a better society and a better life.

Notes

1. As I argue in this text, the classical texts of British cultural studies ignore or denigrate the Frankfurt School and most succeeding texts on cultural studies continue to either superficially caricature or hostilely attack the tradition of critical theory. For my own earlier

appreciations and criticisms of the Frankfurt School tradition that I draw upon here, see Kellner (1989a, 1995a).

2. On the Frankfurt School theory of the cultural industries, see Horkheimer and Adorno (1972; Adorno 1991); the anthology edited by Rosenberg and White (1957); the readers edited by Arato and Gebhardt (1982) and Bronner and Kellner (1989); the discussions of the history of the Frankfurt School in Jay (1973) and Wiggershaus (1994); and the discussion of the Frankfurt School combination of social theory and cultural criticism in Kellner (1989a).

3. I've analysed some of these effects from a reconstructed critical theory perspective in analyses of Hollywood film with Michael Ryan (1988), two books on American television (Kellner 1990, 1992a) and a series of media cultural studies (in Best and Kellner, forthcoming; Kellner 1995a).

4. See Kellner (1989a) and the texts in Bronner and Kellner (1989).

5. For standard accounts of this phase of British cultural studies, see Agger (1992); Fiske (1986); Grossberg (1989); Hall (1980b); Johnson (1986/7); McGuigan (1992); O'Connor (1989); Turner (1996). For readers which document the positions of British cultural studies, see the articles collected in During (1993) and Grossberg et al. (1992).

6. See the critique of 'Screen theory' in Hall et al. (1980).

7. For detailed description of this new form of culture and society, see Best and Kellner (1997, forthcoming); for critical analysis of the postmodern theories that emerged during the 1970s and 1980s, see Best and Kellner (1991).

8. The most extreme version of 'the end of political economy' is found in Baudrillard (1993) and French postmodern theory, but is present in some versions of British and North American cultural studies. See Kellner (1989b, 1995a).

9. Among the few engagements with the Frankfurt School in the vast literature explaining the origins and trajectory of British cultural studies, or on the positions the Birmingham School critically engaged, are an article by Tony Bennett (1982: 30ff.), in an anthology containing Open University texts used for cultural studies. Bennett tended to read the Frankfurt School as a left variant of the mass society model which cultural studies was rejecting. Earlier, there was a highly dismissive article by Phil Slater (1974) in the Birmingham Centre journal on 'The Aesthetic Theory of the Frankfurt School', and 'A Bibliography of the Frankfurt School' by Chris Pawling (1974) in the journal published by the Centre for Contemporary Cultural Studies. In one of his genealogies of the Centre, Hall (1980a: 16) notes how the British New Left encountered major works of European Marxism – including 'the Frankfurt School, then of Benjamin, and then of Gramsci' – through the translations of *New Left Review,* but Hall never describes his wrestling with the devilish angels of the Frankfurt School – as he frequently does vis-à-vis Althusser and Gramsci. Thus, there has been no real critical engagement with the Frankfurt School that I could find and certainly no recognition of the shared positions.

10. In Europe, American films constitute between 75 and 80 per cent of the market (*Time,* February 27, 1995: 36). It is predicted that new digital technologies will create even greater penetration of world markets by American media products.

11. Here I agree with McGuigan, who writes that

the separation of contemporary cultural studies from the political economy of culture has been one of the most disabling features of the field of study. The core problematic was virtually premised on a terror of economic reductionism. In consequence, the economic aspects of media institutions and the broader economic dynamics of consumer culture were rarely investigated, simply bracketed off, thereby severely undermining the explanatory and, in effect, critical capacities of cultural studies. (1992: 40–1)

12. On earlier traditions of cultural studies in the United States, see Aronowitz (1993), and for Britain, see Davies (1995).

13. Articles in the 1983 *Journal of Communications* issue on 'Ferment in the Field' (33[3], [Summer 1983]) noted a bifurcation of the field between a culturalist approach and more empirical approaches in the study of mass-mediated communications. The culturalist

approach was largely textual, centred on the analysis and criticism of texts as cultural artefacts, using methods primarily derived from the humanities. The methods of communications research, by contrast, employed more empirical methodologies, ranging from straight quantitative research, empirical studies of specific cases or domains, or historical research. Topics in this area included analysis of the political economy of the media, audience reception and study of media effects, media history, the interaction of media institutions with other domains of society, and the like. See Kellner (1995b) for analyses of how the Frankfurt School, British cultural studies and French postmodern theory all overcome the bifurcation of the field of culture and communications into text- and humanities-based approaches opposed to empirical and social science-based enterprises. As I am arguing here, a transdisciplinary approach overcomes such bifurcation and delineates a richer and broader perspective for the study of culture and communications.

14. The contributions of the Frankfurt School to audience reception theory are often overlooked completely, but Walter Benjamin constantly undertook studies of how audiences use the materials of popular media and thus inaugurated a form of reception studies (see Benjamin 1969: 217ff.). Leo Lowenthal also carried out reception studies of literature, popular magazines, political demagogues and other phenomena (1949, 1957, 1961). On Frankfurt experiments with studies of media effects, see Wiggershaus (1994: 441ff.).

15. There were, to be sure, some exceptions and qualifications to this 'classical' model: Adorno would occasionally note a critical or utopian moment within mass culture and the possibility of audience reception against the grain (see the examples in Kellner 1989a). But although one can find moments that put in question the more bifurcated division between high and low culture and the model of mass culture as consisting of nothing except ideology and modes of manipulation which incorporate individuals into the existing society and culture, generally the Frankfurt School model is overly reductive and monolithic, and thus needs radical reconstruction – which I have attempted to do in work over the past two decades.

16. In the 1930s model of critical theory, theory was supposed to be an instrument of political practice. Yet the formulation of the theory of the culture industries by Horkheimer and Adorno (1972 [1947]) in the 1940s was part of their turn towards a more pessimistic phase in which they eschewed concrete politics and generally located resistance within critical individuals, like themselves, rather than within social groups, movements or oppositional practices. Thus, the Frankfurt School ultimately is weak on the formulation of oppositional practices and counter-hegemonic cultural strategies, with the exception, as noted, of Walter Benjamin.

17. For a survey of recent literature on the political economy of the media and efforts at 'rethinking and renewal', see Mosco (1996).

18. Curiously, whereas, during the 1970s and the 1980s, there were frequent spin-offs of television series from popular movies, in more recent years the trend has reversed with popular classic television series spun off into films like *The Fugitive*, *The Beverly Hillbillies*, *The Flintstones*, *The Addams Family* series, *The Brady Bunch*, and many others. Yet the synergy continues with a 1995 TV-series based on a film derived from John Grisham's *The Client* and 1996 series based on the films *Dangerous Minds* and *Clueless*.

19. I set out this multiperspectival approach in an earlier article and book on the Gulf War as a cultural and media event (Kellner 1992a, 1992b), and illustrate the approach in studies of the Vietnam War and its cultural texts; Hollywood film in the age of Reagan; MTV; TV entertainment like *Miami Vice*; advertising; Madonna; cyberpunk fiction; and other topics in Kellner (1995a). Thus, I am here merely signalling the metatheory that I have worked out and illustrated elsewhere.

20. Curiously, in his textbook on the sociology of culture, Raymond Williams (1981) equates precisely this multiperspectival approach to a mainstream 'observational sociology' perspective, though I am suggesting more critical approaches to production, textual analysis and audience reception. Yet, interestingly, Williams privileges an institution and production approach in his sociology of culture, whereas British and North American

cultural studies have neglected these dimensions for increasing focus on audiences and reception.

References

Adorno, T.W. (1941) 'On Popular Music', (with G. Simpson), *Studies in Philosophy and Social Science*, 9(1): 17–48.

Adorno, T.W. (1978) 'On the Social Situation of Music', *Telos*, 35 (Spring): 128–64.

Adorno, T.W. (1982) 'On the Fetish Character of Music and the Regression of Hearing', in A. Arato and E. Gebhardt (eds), *The Essential Frankfurt School Reader*, New York: Continuum.

Adorno, T.W. (1989) 'On Jazz', in S. Bronner and D. Kellner (eds), *Critical Theory and Society: A Reader*, New York: Routledge.

Adorno, T.W. (1991) *The Culture Industry*, London: Routledge.

Agger, B. (1992) *Cultural Studies as Critical Theory*, London: Falmer Press.

Appadurai, A. (1990) 'Disjuncture and Difference in the Global Cultural Economy', in M. Featherstone (ed.), *Global Culture: Nationalization, Globalization and Modernity*, London: Sage.

Arato, A. and Gebhardt, E. (eds) (1982) *The Essential Frankfurt School Reader*, New York: Continuum.

Aronowitz, S. (1993) *Roll Over Beethoven*, Hanover, New Hampshire: University Press of New England.

Baudrillard, J. (1993) *Symbolic Exchange and Death*, London: Sage.

Benjamin, W. (1969) *Illuminations*, New York: Shocken.

Bennett, T. (1982) 'Theories of the Media, Theories of Society', in M. Gurevitch, T. Bennett, J, Curran and J. Woolacott (eds), *Culture, Society, and the Media*, London: Macmillan.

Best, S. and Kellner, D. (1991) *Postmodern Theory: Critical Interrogations*, London and New York: Macmillan and Guilford Press.

Best, S. and Kellner, D. (1997) *The Postmodern Turn*, New York: Guilford Press.

Best, S. and Kellner, D. (forthcoming) *The Postmodern Adventure*, New York: Guilford Press.

Bronner, S. and Kellner, D. (eds) (1989) *Critical Theory and Society: A Reader*, New York: Routledge.

Bürger, P. (1984 [1974]) *Theory of the Avant-Garde*, Minneapolis: University of Minnesota Press.

Centre for Contemporary Cultural Studies (CCCS) (1980a) *On Ideology*, London: Hutchinson.

Centre for Contemporary Cultural Studies (CCCS) (1980b) *Culture, Media, Language*, London: Hutchinson.

Cvetkovich, A. and Kellner, D. (1997) *Articulating the Global and the Local: Globalization and Cultural Studies*, Boulder, Colo.: Westview Press.

Davies, I. (1995) *Cultural Studies and Beyond*, London and New York: Routledge.

During, S. (ed.) (1993) *The Cultural Studies Reader*, London and New York: Routledge.

Fiske, J. (1986) 'British Cultural Studies and Television', in R. Allen (ed.), *Channels of Discourse*, Chapel Hill: University of North Carolina Press

Gitlin, T. (1983) *Inside Prime Time*, New York: Pantheon.

Grossberg, L. (1989) 'The Formations of Cultural Studies: An American in Birmingham', *Strategies*, 22: 114–149.

Grossberg, L., Nelson, C. and Treichler, P. (eds) (1992) *Cultural Studies*, New York: Routledge.

Hall, S. (1980a) 'Cultural Studies and the Centre: Some Problematics and Problems', in S. Hall, D. Hobson, A. Lowe and P. Willis (eds), *Culture, Media, Language*, London: Hutchinson.

Hall, S. (1980b) 'Encoding/Decoding', in S. Hall, D. Hobson, A. Lowe and P. Willis (eds), *Culture, Media, Language*, London: Hutchinson.

Hall, S. (1980c) 'Cultural Studies: Two Paradigms', *Media, Culture, & Society*, 2: 57–72.

Hall, S. (1983) 'The Problem of Ideology: Marxism Without Guarantees', in B. Matthews (ed.), *Marx 100 Years On*, London: Lawrence & Wishart.

Hall, S. (1988) *The Hard Road to Renewal*, London: Verso.

Hall, S. (1991) Lecture on 'Globalization and Ethnicity', University of Minnesota, videotape.

Hall, S., Hobson, D., Lowe, A. and Willis, P. (eds) (1980) *Culture, Media, Language*, London: Hutchinson.

Harvey, D. (1989) *The Condition of Postmodernity*, Oxford: Basil Blackwell.

Hebdige, D. (1979) *Subculture: The Meaning of Style*, London: Methuen.

Herzog, H. (1941) 'On Borrowed Experience: An Analysis of Listening to Daytime Sketches', *Studies in Philosophy and Social Science*, IX(1): 65–95.

Hilferding, R. (1981 [1910]) *Finance Capital*, London: Routledge & Kegan Paul.

Horkheimer, M. and Adorno, T.W. (1972) *Dialectic of Enlightenment*, New York: Herder & Herder.

Jameson, F. (1991) *Postmodernism, or the Cultural Logic of Late Capitalism*, Durham, North Carolina: Duke University Press.

Jay, M. (1973) *The Dialectical Imagination*, Boston: Little, Brown & Company.

Jefferson, T. (ed.) (1976) *Resistance through Rituals*, London: Hutchinson.

Jessop, B., Bennett, K. and Bromley, S. (1984) 'Authoritarian Populism, Two Nations, and Thatcherism', *New Left Review*, 147: 32–60.

Johnson, R. (1986/7) 'What is Cultural Studies Anyway?' *Social Text*, 16: 38–80.

Kellner, D. (1982) 'Kulturindustrie und Massenkommunikation. Die Kritische Theorie und ihre Folgen', in W. Bonss and A. Honneth (eds), Frankfurt: Suhrkamp, 482–514.

Kellner, D. (1984) *Herbert Marcuse and the Crisis of Marxism*, London and Berkeley: Macmillan and University of California Press.

Kellner, D. (1989a) *Critical Theory, Marxism, and Modernity*, Cambridge and Baltimore: Polity Press and Johns Hopkins University Press.

Kellner, D. (1989b) *Jean Baudrillard: From Marxism to Postmodernism and Beyond*, Cambridge and Palo Alto, Calif.: Polity Press and Stanford University Press.

Kellner, D. (1990) *Television and the Crisis of Democracy*, Boulder, Colo.: Westview Press.

Kellner, D. (1992a) *The Persian Gulf TV War*, Boulder, Colo.: Westview Press.

Kellner, D. (1992b) 'Toward a Multiperspectival Cultural Studies', *Centennial Review*, XXVI(1) (Winter): 5–42.

Kellner, D. (1995a) *Media Culture: Cultural Studies, Identity, and Politics Between the Modern and the Postmodern*, London and New York: Routledge.

Kellner, D. (1995b) 'Media Communications vs. Cultural Studies: Overcoming the Divide', *Communication Theory*, 5(2) (May): 162–77.

Kellner, D. and Ryan, M. (1988) *Camera Politica: The Politics and Ideology of Contemporary Hollywood Film*, Bloomington, Ind.: Indiana University Press.

Lazarsfeld, P. (1941) 'Administrative and Critical Communications Research', *Studies in Philosophy and Social Science*, IX(1): 2–16.

Lowenthal, L. (1949) (with Norbert Guttermann) *Prophets of Deceit*, New York: Harper.

Lowenthal, L. (1957) *Literature and the Image of Man*, Boston: Beacon Press.

Lowenthal, L. (1961) *Literature, Popular Culture and Society*, Englewood Cliffs, New Jersey: Prentice-Hall.

McGuigan, J. (1992) *Cultural Populism*, London and New York: Routledge.

Marcuse, H. (1941) 'Some Social Implications of Modern Technology', *Studies in Philosophy and Social Science*, IX(1): 414–439.

Mosco, V. (1996) *The Political Economy of Communication: Rethinking and Renewal*, London: Sage.

Murdock, G. (1989) 'Cultural Studies at the Crossroads', *Australian Journal of Communication*, 16.

O'Connor, A. (1989) 'The Problem of American Cultural Studies', *Critical Studies in Mass Communication*, December: 405–413.

Pawling, C. (1974) 'A Bibliography of the Frankfurt School', *Cultural Studies*, 6: 212–215.

Rosenberg, B. and White, D. (eds) (1957) *Mass Culture*, Glencoe, Ill: The Free Press.

Slater, P. (1974) 'The Aesthetic Theory of the Frankfurt School', *Cultural Studies*, 6: 172–211.

Turner, G. (1996) *British Cultural Studies: An Introduction*, 2nd edn, New York: Unwin Hyman.

Wiggershaus, R. (1994) *The Frankfurt School*, Cambridge: Polity Press.

Williams, R. (1961) *The Long Revolution*, London: Chatto & Windus.

Williams, R. (1962) *Communications*, London: Penguin.

Williams, R. (1974) *Television, Technology, and Cultural Form*, London: Fontana.

Williams, R. (1981) *Communications*, London: Penguin.

2

Towards a Pragmatics for Cultural Studies

Tony Bennett

Perhaps my title begs a question or two. For, putting aside what a pragmatics for cultural studies might look like, it is not altogether clear that cultural studies either is, or will come to be, greatly troubled with or by the need for one. After all, from the perspective of a certain style of radicalism, the concept of a pragmatics might seem inherently compromised, conceding from the outset the oppositional stance which, in some accounts, has defined the cultural studies project. To be pragmatic means, according to my dictionary, to be concerned 'with practical consequences or values' or with matters 'pertaining to the affairs of a state or community'. Few of the traditions within cultural studies with which I am familiar have been notably pragmatic in the first of these senses. There has, it is true, always been a clear insistence on the practical, in the sense of political, relevance of the concerns of cultural studies. However, this theoretical interest in practice has seldom resulted in any developed interest in the conditions – institutional, discursive, political – which define the limits and forms of the practicable. As to the second definition – the affairs of a state or community – these, in their actually existing forms, are often precisely what cultural studies has defined itself against.

To suggest that cultural studies might aspire to, and stand in need of, a pragmatics, then, is to propose a revisionary programme for cultural studies. This is partly a matter of arguing the need for cultural studies to be developed in a closer association with the policy concerns of government and industry as a means of developing a more prosaic concept of practice, one that will sustain actual and productive connections with the field of the practicable. This is not a new argument. Indeed, it is one which, although often using a different vocabulary, has been made a number of times in earlier phases in the development of cultural studies in critique of the reluctance to tether questions of culture and policy too closely together that stems, in part, from the history of the concept of culture itself. It will therefore be useful to bring an historical perspective to bear on this question in order to rediscover an earlier pragmatic strain within cultural studies that now needs to be retrieved 'against the grain' of, and as a corrective to, what have since proved to be more influential libertarian and oppositional formulations of the practical stances that should be adopted by cultural studies. In doing so, however, I shall also seek to locate questions concerning the relations between cultural studies and policy as part of a broader pragmatics rooted in a recognition of the real institutional conditions of cultural studies' existence within the education system.

It is, indeed, from considerations of this kind that I want to take my initial bearings as a way of signalling the need to root debates about the theoretical and political agendas of cultural studies more closely in the circumstances affecting the forms in which it is, and is most likely to be, produced and disseminated. Two such factors might usefully be mentioned at this point. The first consists in the growing body of writing that is concerned to describe and assess the limitations of cultural studies from the perspective of rival critical paradigms. This is not to say that cultural studies has previously lacked critics. To the contrary, its claims to intellectual seriousness have had to be advanced in the face of those familiar kinds of elitist disdain which typically greet any intellectual project concerned with the power relations of the cultural field rather than simply training a new generation of cultic consumers. Then also, politically, there have been sharp disputes within cultural studies, as well as between it and closely related intellectual traditions, regarding its understandings of the relations between culture, race, gender and class. On the whole, however, throughout most of the 1980s, cultural studies registered what seemed to be a more-or-less irresistible advance. Its currency as a term became widespread internationally as its spiralling ascent – registered in terms of publications, conferences and the growth of cultural studies curricula – encountered little serious criticism or opposition.

The early 1990s, by contrast, witnessed the publication of a number of critical studies which – mostly from the disciplinary paradigm of sociology – sought to call cultural studies into question on both theoretical and political grounds. Jim McGuigan's (1992) criticism of the populist aspects of cultural studies is a case in point, whilst David Harris, in his *From Class Struggle to the Politics of Pleasure* (1992), casts a broader critical net in chastising cultural studies for what he characterizes as the narrowing and doctrinaire qualities of its most influential intellectual styles and paradigms. As it happens, I think both books fall short of their targets. This is not to deny that many of their criticisms of cultural studies are valid; far from it. But both tend to attack positions which had already been substantially criticized within cultural studies while failing to register the new positions that have been taken up in their place. Both also limit their attention more or less exclusively to Britain, and consequently take inadequate account of the extent to which much of the impetus for new initiatives and directions in cultural studies has come from 'other' places (see Blundell et al. 1993). For all that, the tendency which such studies represent is, I believe, to be welcomed – and welcomed precisely because it places much needed limits on the kind of intellectual project cultural studies might aspire to be. While a claim to embody new kinds of interdisciplinary understandings of cultural forms and practices by placing these in the context of relations of power has always been an important aspect of the self-definition of cultural studies, this view has also often been tangled up with the more polemical argument that cultural studies has the potential both to displace and to surpass those specialist disciplines which also have a stake in the analysis of culture.

While the first of these arguments is, in my view, valid and in need of further development, the second is not. Cultural studies may, of course, influence the concerns of sociology, history, art history, literary studies, and so on. Indeed, there are ample signs that it already has. However, to expect that it might displace or transcend these disciplines, or that it is in some way inherently superior to them because of its interdisciplinary characteristics, is a fantasy that is neither to be wished nor desired. To the contrary, the value and specificity of distinctive intellectual skills and trainings within the social sciences and humanities need to be both defended and promoted instead of being 'white-anted' by misplaced and overgeneralizing assessments of the value of interdisciplinariness. In place, then, of imagining a future for cultural studies in which it provides for a kind of intellectual wholeness in overcoming disciplinary specialisms, the need, now, is to fashion a clearer sense of the specific and therefore limited frameworks of analysis and inquiry that cultural studies might claim as its own in relation to and alongside the concerns of more established humanities and social science disciplines. This will involve thinking clearly about its place in the education system. For the success of cultural studies, the rate at which it has become a regular feature of the curriculum landscape of higher education is not unrelated to its value as a device for organizing broadly based undergraduate degrees for an expanded student population most of whose members have little need for specialist disciplinary trainings so far as their likely career trajectories are concerned.

This brings me to my second point: that if cultural studies now has its critics, it also has its textbooks and primers. If publishers' catalogues are anything to go by, this looks set to become a burgeoning industry. This development has, predictably, been vehemently opposed by many work-ing within cultural studies as embodying a form of institutional cooption which represents the beginning of the end so far as its radical credentials are concerned. Where cultural studies is seen as an inherently opposi-tional and resistive intellectual practice, the very concept of a cultural studies textbook is something of an oxymoron since, in place of seeing cultural studies as a constantly mobile tactics of intellectual opposition, it reduces it to a body of knowledge which has been codified to allow for its transmission to be institutionalized. For Stuart Hall (1992: 285), for example, the prospect of institutionalization represents 'a moment of profound danger' for cultural studies. In contrast to such views, then, I want to argue that the cultural studies textbook is very much to be welcomed (the issue is not whether cultural studies should or can have its textbooks, but whether it gets good ones), and welcomed precisely because it calls attention to the fact that, among other things, cultural studies has always been, and is always likely to be, an institutionalized form of pedagogy.

Yet this is a contentious proposition. In many of the more influential versions of cultural studies that we have, its relations to educational institutions and practices have been portrayed as less important than its relations to social movements of various kinds. Indeed, in some versions, cultural studies itself figures as a kind of phantom social movement, a substitute for the working class or for the counter-hegemonic alliances of social forces which, in the days of 'rainbow coalitions', were to take the proletariat's place. This view of cultural studies as, in essence, 'politics by other means' has resulted in a regrettable neglect of the respects in which, to the degree that its primary institutional location is within tertiary educational institutions, cultural studies is inescapably shaped by the agendas of such institutions and so must consciously seek to shape its own future in ways which take account of those agendas.

The general direction of my arguments, then, will be in favour of more limited and circumscribed – but, by the same token, more specific and clearly formulated – understandings of the ambit, concerns and procedures of cultural studies. If, hitherto, its ambitions have often seemed vaunting and ill defined, my purpose in proposing a pragmatics for cultural studies is to map out more definite and practicable paths for its future development. As this will involve a critical assessment of more conventional views of cultural studies, it will be useful, first, to distinguish the kinds of criticism to which cultural studies can validly and usefully be subjected from less helpful forms of critique and commentary.

Cultural studies in the plural

In a number of essays written in the late 1980s and early 1990s, Ian Hunter – who has been more astringent than most in his criticisms of cultural studies – has argued that, far from having transcended traditional aesthetic conceptions of culture, cultural studies has remained powerfully subject to the influence of such conceptions in ways which, although largely unacknowledged, have had a significant bearing on the direction and tenor of its intellectual projects and on the manner in which such projects have been conducted. Having argued that the 'cultural studies movement conceives of itself as a critique of aesthetics', here is how Hunter summarizes its central ambitions in this regard:

In short, the limits that cultural studies establishes for aesthetics are those of a knowledge or practice of cultivation segregated from the driving forces of human development – labor and politics – and retarding further development by diverting culture into the ideal realm of ethics and taste. Given this specification, the way to transcend these limits is clear. The narrowly ethical practice of culture associated with aesthetics must be subsumed within culture as the whole way of life. Then it will be possible to actualise the promise of self-realisation by harnessing aesthetics to the processes of economic and political development. (1992: 348)

It is precisely in this ambition to restore a lose form of wholeness, Hunter argues, that cultural studies most readily bears witness to the continuing influence of Romantic aesthetics as inflected, via the work of Raymond Williams, through the prism of Marxist thought. Romantic aesthetics, Hunter suggests, was essentially a practice of the self through which the aesthetic personality sought to overcome incompleteness and aspire to full humanity by using techniques of self-cultivation which aimed to harmonize and reconcile – to bring to interactive fullness – the different and, in themselves, fractured and divisive aspects of personhood. One part of the argument, then, is that the intellectual agendas of cultural studies translate this dialectical technique of person-formation into a dialectical-historical method through which the antinomies which have racked the sphere of culture are to be both traced and, through a political project aimed at the production of a common culture – of a shared way of life as a whole – overcome. Second, and as a corollary, cultural studies places its political bets on those social and cultural tendencies within the present which, in being interpreted as attempts to pierce through alienating cultural divisions, seem to prefigure new and emerging forms of cultural wholeness. This is the role accorded the concept of emergent culture within Williams's conception of the relations between dominant, residual and emergent forms of culture (see Williams 1977). In a third aspect of the argument, however, Hunter relates the legacy of Romantic aesthetics more directly to the style and persona that cultural studies intellectuals seek to construct for themselves. Speaking of the tendency within cultural studies to eschew any determinate and definite knowledge claims in favour of grand and general claims to an interdisciplinarity that is beyond existing divisions of intellectual labour, Hunter relates this to that current of thought within cultural studies which expresses disdain for making use of available and existing instruments of political action in favour of practices of critique that will make the intellectual ready to act only once more auspicious political circumstances have been produced, and sees in both of these an adaptation of the styling of the self derived from Romantic aesthetics. 'Both ideas', as he puts it, 'are symptomatic of a practice of the self that displaces the objectives of existing knowledge and politics with the objective of the permanent preparation of a self worthy to know and to act' (Hunter 1992: 355).

These are powerful arguments which, in the main, hit their targets although it can fairly be said that the bow Hunter draws is sometimes a long one, with the mechanisms of connection between historical discourses and present practices remaining somewhat obscure and conjectural. There are times also when the targets Hunter has in view seem too generalized and diffuse. For it is doubtful how far the positions he takes issue with can be attributed to cultural studies as a whole, as distinct from particular traditions and branches of inquiry within cultural studies. And if this is so, it is because it is also doubtful how true it is to say either that cultural studies can be defined as a critique of aesthetics or that, where this is so, its criticisms of aesthetics necessarily take the form Hunter attributes to them. It is true, of course, that work within cultural studies both depends on and contributes to criticisms of aesthetic conceptions of culture to the degree that it holds all forms of culture to be worthy of analysis irrespective of the places they occupy within the rankings of conventional aesthetics hierarchies. It is also true that, throughout the history of cultural studies, Williams's concept of culture as a whole way of life has been more-or-less routinely invoked to legitimate such a concern – but often as no more than a convenient shorthand which carries few of the specific and complex meanings associated with the concept in Williams's own work. When the editors of *Resistance through Rituals* wish to define what they understand by the term 'culture' in ways that will justify its extension to deal with the everyday cultural practices of young people, for example, they draw on Williams's notion of culture as a way of life. Here is the definition they offer:

> The 'culture' of a group or class is the peculiar and distinctive 'way of life' of the group or class, the meanings, values and ideas embodied in institutions, in social relations, in systems of beliefs, in mores and customs, in the uses of objects and material life. Culture is the distinctive shape in which this material and social organisation of life expresses itself. A culture includes the 'maps of meaning' which make things intelligible to its members. These 'maps of meaning' are not simply carried around in the head: they are objectivated in the patterns of social organisation and relationship through which the individual becomes a 'social individual'. Culture is the way the social relations of a group are structured and shaped: but it is also the way those shapes are experienced, understood and interpreted. (Hall and Jefferson 1976: 10–11)

This definition is not without its difficulties, not the least of which are the respects in which culture doubles as both itself (a distinctive organization of social life) and its own representation (maps of meaning). However, these difficulties have nothing to do with those aspects of Williams's usage of the concept in which culture as a whole way of life anticipates the restoration of a lost cultural wholeness in which hierarchizing and divisive forms of cultural difference will have been overcome. To the contrary, the analytical agenda of *Resistance through Rituals* is one in which relations of cultural division and subordination – between different class cultures and, within the same class, between youth subcultures and their parental class cultures – proliferate with a view to understanding how particular ways of life (youth subcultures) are structured by relations of multiple social contradiction. Something similar is involved when John Frow and Meaghan Morris refer to Williams to define culture as 'the "whole way of life" of a social group as it is structured by representation and by power . . . a network of representations – texts, images, talk, codes of behaviour, and the narrative structures organising these – which shapes every aspect of social life' (1993: x). In both cases, the reference to Williams is a more or less ritual incantation; and, in both cases, the object of analysis that is established is significantly detached from the semantic horizons in which the concept of culture as a whole way of life is embedded in Williams's own writing. The usage proposed by Frow and Morris, for example, is perhaps closer to Bourdieu's concept of habitus than it is to Williams's own usage, while, in *Resistance through Rituals*, the interpretation of culture as a way of life draws far more on sociological subcultural theory than on Williams.

My point, then, is that Hunter offers too generalized a critique of cultural studies and does so mainly because he places too much stress on the originating context of some of its key terms in Williams's work and vocabulary and, consequently, is not always fully alert to the wider range of uses and meanings that have come to be associated with those terms when deployed in contexts which have little to do with the specific kind of critique of aesthetics offered by Williams. Such concerns are simply not visible in *Policing the Crisis* (Hall et al. 1978). Yet, in view of its ambitious orchestration of relations between media practices, the shifting ground of class cultures and the changing field of political discourses in post-war Britain, this study is deservedly regarded by many as an exemplary text of and for cultural studies. Moreover, even where a concern with the critique of aesthetics has predominated, such work has not always been conducted under the aegis of Williams. Indeed, a good case could be made for seeing Bourdieu's work as having been more influential in this respect.

The more general issue to which these considerations point – and my reason for raising them here – is that cultural studies is now, and always has been, too diverse and polyglot for it to be susceptible to any general form of critique. It lacks, and always has lacked, the kind of unity of a developed discipline, say, or, indeed, of a movement, which might render it liable to successful prosecution on the grounds of the general effects of any single set of foundational concepts. Yet, for all that, although it is important to set some limits to the potential purchase of Hunter's criticisms, these remain of compelling relevance to contemporary concerns and debates within the field in view of the light they throw on the question of the institutional location of cultural studies. Hunter's remarks thus most clearly hit home where they are directed against those tendencies within cultural studies which have been developed in a close association with the field of literary studies. For it has been here – where cultural studies has been thought of as both heir and successor to English while also furnishing a critique of its winnowing specialisms – that those formulations of Williams most clearly derived from Romanticism have been most influential. And it this aspect of cultural studies which, in Hunter's view, is likely to be responsible for its most significant long-term institutional legacy. For, to the degree that the critique of aesthetic culture derived from Williams's work is one that is still dependent on Romantic aesthetics, and to the degree, therefore, that such a critique signals a renewal rather than an end of aesthetic forms of social and cultural criticism, Hunter suggests, in a more recent assessment, that this 'helps to explain why the most lasting contribution of the cultural studies movement looks like being its refurbishment of literature departments in Australia and the USA' (1993: 172).

Of course, there are literature departments and literature departments and, within these, many approaches to the study of literature that remain unaffected by these developments. It is not the choice of literary texts as an object of study that is at issue here, but rather the question as to how such texts should be studied and with what purpose. The downside of Hunter's prognosis consists in the suggestion that cultural studies may well prove to be merely the catalyst through which aesthetic and moralizing forms of critique and pedagogy regroup themselves and, in being applied to an extended array of objects (culture as a 'whole way of life'), extend their influence. And, again, it is not critique that is at issue but the form of critique and the purposes for which it is conducted. Where cultural forms are examined from the point of view of understanding the role which they play within specific fields of power relations, of criticizing their political consequences in this regard and debating the forms of practical action through which their existing political articulations might be modified, all well and good. There are ample signs, however, that where cultural studies is being fashioned as an heir to English, so the forms of critique it lays claim to are concerned more with cultivating a certain ethical style and demeanour than with the pursuit of any practicable courses of action with specific political or policy goals in view. One sign of this has been the enduring concern with 'speaking positions', which, in its focus on where the intellectual speaks from (as opposed to what he or she speaks to, and with what competence), has embodied precisely that interest in the endless preening of the intellectual's persona that is the hallmark of aesthetico-moral styles of criticism.

However, institutions connected to the literary field (which, let me stress again, I do not wish to falsely unify) have not supplied the only contexts from which cultural studies has emerged and in which it is presently practised. During its formative years in Britain it was closely connected to developments in the fields of media and communication studies, sociology, history and art history, and often with important institutional bases in these different fields. It has also, but in plural and diverse ways, and from the beginning, been shaped by its connections with socialist, feminist and anti-racist political movements. When viewed in relation to this dispersed set of institutional and political contexts, it is not difficult to locate areas of cultural studies debate where the influence of the Romantic legacy traced by Hunter has been either, to say the least, marginal or, on some issues, actively opposed. Paul Gilroy, for example, was quick to identify the respects in which notions of the organic community lay behind Williams's argument that Britain's black migrants could be regarded as only legally, but not wholly – that is culturally – British. He was also quick to argue the importance of formal, legal definitions of citizenship, and of the role of the state in securing these, against Williams's Romantic fantasy that such matters are super- ficialities, reflecting 'the limited functional terms of the ruling class' (1983: 195) compared with the deeper and more authentic cultural aspects of national identity (see Gilroy 1987). Stuart Hall, in tactfully disentangling himself from this aspect of Williams's work – and doing so in a way which shows his clear awareness of the extent to which Williams's assessments on this matter derive from the elements of Romanticism that linger on in his commitment to the view of culture as a whole way of life and the criteria of cultural belongingness that this generates – is emphatic in his insistence that, for black migrants, ' "formal legal definitions of citizenship" matter profoundly' and 'cannot be made conditional on cultural assimilation' (1993: 360). If, then, we are going to speak of origins for cultural studies, we need to recognize that these have always been plural and diverse just as have been the traditions to which these 'origins' have given rise. This is even more so when we consider cultural studies in its international formation. This is, indeed, where the problematic of origins most evidently breaks down. However much the early developments in British cultural studies may have influenced the early formation of cultural studies in Australia or Canada, for example, it is equally clear that this influence was inflected via, and interpreted through, nationally specific intellectual traditions and concerns to which the agendas of aesthetic critique derived from Williams were of only passing interest. The relationship of cultural studies to the traditions of radical nationalism were of more pressing relevance in Australia, whereas, in Canada, the concern with the role of communications technologies in organizing socio-spatial relation- ships derived from the work of Harold Innes has proved of enduring relevance, accounting for what is often most distinctive in Canadian cultural studies.

Given such an understanding of cultural studies, two questions arise. First, what do these dispersed traditions of work have in common that merits their being called cultural studies and makes such a common designation useful? And, second, which tendencies in this body of work are most worthy of support and further development, and which now need to be jettisoned or revised? Although each begets a whole series of further questions, these are, in the main, the questions that have to be faced in developing an intellectual programme for cultural studies. Let me, then, offer some brief indications as to how I should like to answer them.

Cultural studies: elements of a definition

The first question is perhaps the most difficult to deal with. For the rate of growth of cultural studies has been such that some, including Michael Green, have doubted whether it is any longer possible, or desirable, to meet the 'urgently needed sense of what the whole area is about' (Green 1993: 519). My own view is that the enterprise is both possible and worth undertaking, but only provided that not too much weight is invested in such definitions and that what is aimed for via them is relatively limited in scope and practical in orientation. Certainly, any attempt to impose a highly unified definition on the field, to describe it in terms of such and such a set of theoretical and political positions, will meet with failure. Instead, then, let me propose a number of propositions which might, if they are relatively loosely formulated, recruit broad assent.

First, work in cultural studies is characterized by an interdisciplinary concern with the functioning of cultural practices and institutions in the contexts of relations of power of different kinds. Its interdisciplinariness, however, does not take the form of an alternative to or transcendence of those disciplines (history, sociology, literary studies, linguistics) which may lay a claim to similar interests. To be sure, it may challenge the effects of particular specialist focuses within these disciplines, but it does not offer, or aspire to offer, a wholesale critique of them as disciplines any more than it dispenses with the need to draw on the specialist techniques, skills, knowledges and trainings associated with these disciplines where these are appropriate to the topic under investigation. Rather, cultural studies supplies an intellectual field in which perspectives from different disciplines might be (selectively) drawn on in examining particular relations of culture and power. In this respect, cultural studies performs a clearing-house function in coordinating the methods and findings of different disciplines insofar as they bear on the role played by cultural practices, institutions and forms of cultural classification in the organization and transmission, or contestation, of particular relations of power. It does not embody a putative intellectual synthesis in which existing disciplinary specialisms would be overcome or rendered redundant (although it will promote, and clearly has promoted, new forms of alliance within and between existing disciplines).

Second, if relations of culture and power supply cultural studies with its object, the understanding of culture that animates its concerns is a broadly inclusive one. For reasons that have already been alluded to, and that will become clearer, the formulation that cultural studies is concerned with culture in the sense of whole ways of life as well as the officially valorized forms of high culture creates more problems than it solves. A more open-ended formulation might be to say that cultural studies is concerned with all those practices, institutions and systems of classification through which there are inculcated in a population particular values, beliefs, competencies, routines of life and habitual forms of conduct. To say this is not to assume that all the practices, institutions and systems of classification that are thus brought under the heading of 'culture' are constituted in the same way or function in a common manner. The likelihood is that they don't and that, therefore, the search for a common set of principles underlying the terrain of the cultural will prove abortive. Establishing such a set of principles, however, is not a necessary condition for securing cultural studies as a coherent enterprise.

Third, the forms of power in relation to which culture (as defined above) is to be examined are diverse, including relations of gender, class and race as well as those relations of colonialism and imperialism which exist between the whole populations of different territories. The forms and manner in which these relations of culture and power might be interconnected is also a matter for concern within cultural studies. This concern with the nature, make-up and interactions between the different ways in which culture operates in the context of different power relations, however, is not scholastic in motivation. The ambition of cultural studies is to develop ways of theorizing relations of culture and power that will prove capable of being utilized by relevant social agents to bring about changes within the operation of those relations of culture and power. This inescapably involves competing political estimations of who the relevant social agents are, how they/we are to be involved in the process of changing the functioning of such power relations, and who the beneficiaries of those changes will be.

Fourth, the primary institutional site for cultural studies has been, and will continue to be, within tertiary educational institutions. It is, in this sense, like any other academic discipline, and like them, too, in that it faces the problem of how most effectively to arrange for the dissemination of its arguments, ideas and perspectives in ways calculated to maximize their influence with and upon those social agents capable of utilizing its intellectual resources in specific regions of practical social action. In some formulations, this is posed as a problem regarding the relations between cultural studies and the various social movements (the women's movement, post-colonial struggles, black liberation movements) which, from time to time, it has claimed as its constituencies. In other formulations, the issue is posed as one of establishing appropriate relations with those who work in specific cultural institutions or fields of cultural management. In others, again, the polarity between these two options is viewed as a meaningless one, with cultural studies needing to establish both kinds of relations depending on the point at issue. Whichever the case, the political agendas of cultural studies pose problems of mediation or connection that need to be resolved if cultural studies is not to be *merely* academic.

I am aware that, already, in some of these formulations, I have introduced elements that some will find contentious. To suggest that some relations of culture and power might be regarded positively, for example, rather than regarding any twinning of culture and power as inherently repressive, is to introduce a perspective, derived from Foucault, that would not recruit the assent of everyone working in the field. For the most part, however, the positions sketched out above are susceptible to different interpretations that are capable of accommodating a broad spectrum of the opinion that defines current controversies within cultural studies. In answering my second question – which tendencies in this body of work should be supported, and which jettisoned? – I shall obviously need to be less ecumenical.

That said, it's not a question of opting for this or that theory, for this could only result in a doctrinaire definition, so much as one of defining an orientation for theory. I would define that orientation as materialist in the sense proposed by Brian Moon when he suggests that the term 'materialist' should now be 'deployed in a limited sense to designate a mode of analysis that grounds explanations of social phenomena in historical conditions without constructing those conditions as the expression or general effect of a more fundamental cause' (1993: 7). Contrary to the associations of historical materialism, then, the stress here is on contingency, on the forms of social life and conduct that result from the interaction of multiple historical conditions and forces, without the form of their interaction being subject to any general form of determination, and therefore explanation, arising from the effects of an underlying causal mechanism – be it that of a mode of production, the principles of structural causality, patriarchy or, for that matter, the putative unity of culture as a whole way of life. To argue for a cultural studies that would be materialist in this sense, then, is to argue for a cultural studies that will be differentiating and particularizing in its focus, that will be densely historical in its attention to the specific make-up and functioning of particular relations of culture and power, understanding these as the outcomes of complexly interacting conditions and giving rise to equally dispersed and complexly organized effects.

Such, then, is the nature of the intellectual programme I would propose for cultural studies. However, it will not have escaped the reader's attention that revisions of the kind I am suggesting affect the political orientations of cultural studies just as much as they do its theoretical concerns. It is to these questions that I now turn.

A prosaic politics

In an earlier essay, I suggested that cultural studies might usefully 'envisage its role as consisting in the training of cultural technicians: that is, of intellectual workers less committed to cultural critique as an instrument for changing consciousness than to modifying the functioning of culture by means of technical adjustments to its governmental deployment' (Bennett 1992: 406). The basis for this suggestion consisted in the argument that modern forms of cultural politics have to be seen as closely related to, and partly generated by, the ways in which the sphere of culture has been, in Foucault's sense, so deeply governmentalized that it now makes no sense – if it ever did – to think of culture as a ground situated outside the domain of government and providing the resources through which that domain might be resisted. The suggestion has provoked some disagreement, some of which has been of great value and highly productive (see, especially, O'Regan 1992). None the less, I should like to stick by it and, indeed, explore its implications further as a way of developing a more prosaic conception of the intellectual politics of cultural studies. Pierre Bourdieu has recorded, in connection with the Frankfurt School, that he felt 'a certain irritation when faced with the aristocratic demeanour of the totalising critique which retained all the features of grand theory, doubtless so as not to get its hands dirty in the kitchens of empirical research' (1990: 19). As a way of countering this traditional style of intellectual work in the cultural field, Bourdieu advises that he has sought constantly to develop a pragmatic, even barbaric, relation to culture and to work hard at 'considering the job of being an intellectual as a job like any other, eliminating everything that most aspiring intellectuals feel it necessary to do in order to feel intellectual' (1990: 29–30). In a similar way, then, my conception of the cultural studies intellectual as a technician who needs to think of her or his work as being related, and needing to be related, to the sphere of government is informed by a similar ambition to establish more mundane protocols for both the form and substance of intellectual work that addresses and situates itself in the cultural field.

It might help, in elaborating the implications of this view, to consider the contrasting formulations which tend to predominate when intellectuals are trying to puzzle out what cultural studies is, or ought to be, about. Frederic Jameson's essay 'On "Cultural Studies" ' – a review of the collection of essays derived from the cultural studies conference held at the University of Illinois in 1990 – provides a convenient counterpoint. 'The desire called Cultural Studies', Jameson begins his essay, 'is perhaps best approached politically and socially, as the project to constitute a "historic bloc", rather than theoretically, as the floor plan for a new discipline' (1993: 17). If this is so, Jameson continues, then its aspirations were most clearly expressed by Stuart Hall when he argued that the formation of cultural studies in Britain had been shaped on the model of the Gramscian notion of the organic intellectual. It was a project shaped by the will or hope that intellectual work might be aligned with an emerging historical movement and was therefore predicated, as Hall put it, on 'living with the possibility that there could be, sometime, a movement which would be larger than the movement of petit-bourgeois intellectuals' (1992: 288). Jameson argues that formulation entails cultural studies being thought of as a project committed 'to the forging of a heterogeneous set of "interest groups" into some larger political and social movement', although he is quick to note that the practice is often different, at least in the American context, where isolationist conceptions of identity politics often prevail over such synthesizing political aspirations. None the less, while clearly acknowledging its utopian aspects, the view of cultural studies as 'the expression of a projected alliance between various social groups' (Jameson 1993: 17) is the one Jameson prefers. As a consequence, he suggests, 'its rigorous formulation as an intellectual or pedagogical enterprise may not be quite so important as some of its adherents feel' – a position that renders as relatively unimportant those questions relating to the form that it might take as an academic programme and the position it might occupy in educational institutions.

This is, I think, a fair rendering of what has been, and remains, an important tendency within cultural studies. But I think it is a seriously mistaken one in at least two respects. First, insofar as cultural studies comprises (among other things) a set of teaching and research programmes located within or otherwise dependent on and related to academic institutions, it underestimates the significance of attending closely and in detail to the consequences of this, its primary institutional locale. From this perspective, questions concerning the forms of knowledge, instruction and training that are to be offered in cultural studies programmes, and the kinds of future destinies for which these are envisaged to equip students, are crucial to the kinds of long-term practical effects that it will prove capable of exerting.

However, perhaps the more important question – and this brings me to my second point – concerns the kinds of practical effects cultural studies might intelligibly aspire to. The prospect that it might furnish a stratum of intellectuals who will prepare the way for an emerging historical movement to which that stratum will then attach itself in a moment of organicity seems increasingly unlikely, and for a number of reasons. First, the political imaginary sustaining such expectations is now too seriously damaged and the attempts to suture it back into place, as in the writings of Ernesto Laclau and Chantal Mouffe, for example, have too evidently failed for this to be thought of as a realistic or even desirable prospect in any of the western societies in which cultural studies has developed. Second, and perhaps ultimately more telling, the prospect of organicity that it offers is an incoherent one. Of course, individual figures may well, and importantly, function as organic intellectuals so far as the positions they take up in relation to the agendas of specific social movements or groups are concerned. It is quite another matter, however, to think of cultural studies as providing a stratum of organic intellectuals for an emerging alliance of progressive social forces. For, even supposing that such an alliance were a realistic or, indeed, an intelligible political prospect, cultural studies simply is not the kind of thing that could undertake such a task. Its institutional placement does not allow it to do that kind of work, and those who work within the field – for we are all, by virtue of the social position established by our work, petit-bourgeois intellectuals, no matter what our biographical back-grounds and credentials might be – do not have the qualifications or capacities for it.

This is not to argue that, in an appropriately more limited usage, the notion of the 'organic intellectual' is without its value. McKenzie Wark has argued that Marcia Langton is 'very much the image of an "organic intellectual" – someone whose knowledge grows directly out of the particular struggles and forms of organisation of the community she identifies herself with – the Aboriginal people', and notes that her work in this regard has encompassed the roles of 'administrator, advocate, actor and anthropologist' (1994: 23). John Frow and Meaghan Morris, generalizing this perspective, suggest that, if the notion of the organic intellectual is detached from 'those phantom "emergent" subjects of history', it can help clarify 'the actual practices developed by real intellectuals in Australia' (1993: xxv) in patterns of work that are partly institutionally and partly constituency-based in a country whose political traditions and limited resources allow for a good deal of cross-over and exchange between intellectuals working in different institutional fields: the academy, cultural institutions, government.

In such a context, the question of the relationship between cultural studies and organic intellectuals – which is also a question concerning the relations that might most usefully be developed between the forms of teaching and research conducted within academic institutions and the political agendas and constituencies that have been formed in relation to different fields of social conflict in society at large – can be reformulated. For, viewed in this light, it is no longer an issue of trying to coordinate different movements into a historic bloc under the banner of cultural studies, or one of each and every cultural studies intellectual trying to become organic. Rather, it would concern the development of forms of work – of cultural analysis and pedagogy – that could contribute to the development of the political and policy agendas associated with the work of organic intellectuals so defined. Of course, work produced in accordance with such an understanding would point in many directions. One of the directions in which it would point, however, would be towards the politics of the bureau. For it is often within or in relation to the bureau – that is, the machineries of government in its broadest sense – that the work of organic intellectuals is conducted.

It was considerations of this kind that I had in mind when, in my contribution to the collection of essays Jameson reviewed, I suggested that intellectuals working in cultural studies needed to begin to 'talk to the ISAs'. My purpose in doing so was to argue that, if it aspired to any practical forms of social application, then it was imperative that cultural studies engage with the actually existing practical horizons, agendas and constituencies evident within different fields of cultural policy debate and formation comprised by the relevant sections of government and by the practices of cultural and media institutions. Jameson took issue with this suggestion, arguing that while it might 'have some relevance in a small country with socialist traditions', it could have no applicability in the United States, where most readers on 'the left' (wherever that now is) would find the suggestion 'obscene' (1993: 43). He was similarly perturbed by Ian Hunter's suggestion that, to the degree that it is still caught up in the slipstream of aesthetic critique, cultural studies might have relatively little to offer once it goes beyond the comforting illusions of the typical arts faculty to concern itself with other cultural regions. He thus found the following passage 'truly chilling and comical' (1993: 43):

> To travel to these other regions though – to law offices, media institutions, government bureaus, corporations, advertising agencies – is to make a sobering discovery: They are already replete with their own intellectuals. And they just look up and say, 'Well, what exactly is it that you can do for us?' (Hunter 1992: 372)

The division of opinion here, then, is real and substantial. On the one hand, cultural studies is invited to subscribe to an understanding of the connections between intellectual work and practice through which intellectuals bypass existing forms of social administration and management in order to connect more directly with social movements of different kinds. On the other, cultural studies is urged to find a way of answering the bureaucrat's question – 'What can you do for us?' – as a precondition for connecting the work of intellectuals to the fields of social administration and management in which the social and political demands of different constituencies are translated into practicable administrative options. This is, admittedly, a somewhat polarized way of posing the matter. However, these options do, I believe, clearly summarize the key issues at stake in present debates about the future directions cultural studies should take.

I shall not, however, pursue Jameson's remarks further here except to situate them. For it is clear that what speaks through them is precisely that disjunction of the aesthetic and the worldly, of culture and the mundane concerns of the practical affairs of government, that is the legacy of Romantic aesthetics – in this case, in perhaps its most influential contemporary Marxist version. How else are we to account for a Marxist who regards work developed in 'a small country with socialist traditions' as a negative model, and who regards as repugnant the prospect of 'talking to the ISAs' even though he works in one, and who can see no possible areas of interaction between the work that might be conducted in the academy and that of intellectuals in other cultural regions outside the academy? Views of this kind are, perhaps, understandable when viewed in the American context, where both the sheer size of the higher education sector and the significant role of private institutions within that sector provide the kind of institutional conditions which allow critical debate to circulate in a semi-autonomous realm which might seem removed from those of government and administration. There are, however, few places outside the United States where similar conditions apply and where, therefore, indigenous intellectual traditions are likely to prove of more service than the radical versions of American liberalism that now blight much of the debate in this area. In his review, Jameson rightly notes that Raymond Williams's work is now frequently 'appealed to for moral support for any number of sins (or virtues)' (1993: 22). As I have already indicated, there are many aspects of Williams's theorization of culture in which the legacy of the Romantic tradition is clearly visible. However, his work was more complex and many-sided than such an evaluation, starkly stated, would suggest, and it is from the ambivalences of Williams that I should like to take my final bearings in relation to the question of policy.

For when, in *Culture and Society*, Williams began the process – never really finished – of his reckoning with the Romantic tradition, he criticized it not merely for the elitism of its selective definition of culture. He was just as alert to the powerfully anti-practical and anti-reformist tendencies which might arise from the totalizing forms of critique to which Romanticism was prone. He was also at pains to dissociate himself from those forms of intellectual analysis and engagement which suggest it is possible to bypass the need for a real entanglement with those agendas of social, political and cultural reform which define the effective horizon of presently existing policy processes and concerns. He was thus terse in his disparagement of the view that the lofty heights of culture might provide a vantage point from which the mundanities of social and political life might be transcended. This was, indeed, the constitutive tension of Romanticism which Williams was concerned to argue against:

> The attachment to culture which disparages science; the attachment which writes off politics as a narrow and squalid misdirection of energy; the attachment which appears to criticise manners by the priggish intonation of a word: all these, of which Arnold and his successors have at times been guilty, serve to nourish and extend an opposition which is already formidable enough. The idea of culture is too important to be surrendered to this kind of failing. (1963: 135)

It was, Williams continues, the tension between Arnold's view of culture as a process of growth and development and his failure to find adequate evidence for that process in the social conditions of his day that led to the transformation of culture into an increasingly abstract and transcendental standard of judgement. The result, Williams argues, was a wholly disabling contradiction. 'Culture', as he put it, 'became the final critic of institutions, and the process of replacement and betterment, yet it was also, at root, beyond institutions' (1963: 136).

It is clear, moreover, that this was not merely a theoretical matter for Williams, not just something he said. It also affected a good deal of what he did, and in particular his engagement, over a number of decades, with the practical agendas and institutions of cultural policy in post-war Britain – and without ever surrendering his intellectual independence or critical voice. In this regard, Williams didn't just speak to 'the ISAs'; so far as his relationship to the Arts Council was concerned, he was a fully functioning member of one of the most important instruments of cultural policy formation in post-war Britain. What he had to say about this in an essay he wrote in 1981 is revealing. Reviewing four different conceptions of the objectives of cultural policy – 'state patronage of fine arts; pump-priming; an intervention in the market; and expanding and changing popular culture' (1989: 142) – that might guide the policies of a body like the Arts Council (or, we might add, the Australia Council, the Canada Council or the Endowment for the Humanities – and the whole host of related bodies which now proliferate in the cultural-governmental spheres of advanced Western societies), Williams, unsurprisingly, states his preference for the last of these conceptions as providing the only valid grounds on which 'we can, in good conscience, raise money for the arts from the general revenue' (1989: 148). While recognizing that this is not the prevailing view in the Arts Council, Williams is clear that 'because it [the Council] – is there it is where the argument has to start':

> Thus instead of apologising for the principles of public funding of the arts, or nervously excluding or reducing those aspects of policy which either the pillared and patented or the political and commercial hangers-on disapprove of, we should get together, in such numbers as we can, and fight the real battles. (1989: 149)

Williams concluded his essay by looking to Keynes – the architect of the Arts Council – acknowledging his important contribution in 'an open and recognising spirit' (1989: 149). It is, then, this Williams that I suggest we should now look to in a similar spirit while acknowledging that there are other aspects of his work, and in particular some of this more general theoretical formulations, from which we now need to register our distance. In his essay 'The Uses of Cultural Theory', Williams, in a phrase that has been made much of, asks, in a chastizing tone, whether there is 'never to be an end to petit-bourgeois theorists making long-term adjustments to short-term situations' (1989: 175). Andrew Milner (1993: 88) entertains the prospect, only to dismiss it as unlikely (and quite rightly), that Williams might have had myself in mind when making this remark, only to conclude, although improbably in my view, that his target was more likely to have been Stuart Hall.

In fact, Williams is perfectly clear about whom he has in mind: namely, the advocates of those forms of intellectual and cultural avant-gardism 'which are based practically only on their negations and forms of enclosure, against an undifferentiated culture and society beyond them' (1989: 175). The first part of this phrase reveals tellingly enough Williams's impatience with those who would take their stand on the purely negatively and transcendentally constituted ground of critique. It is, however, in the second part – in the notion that practical engagements within actually existing political agendas should be directed towards the creation of an 'undifferentiated culture and society' shaped by 'the acceptance and the possibility of broader common relationships' (1989: 175–6) – that the limitations of Williams's own position are evident. In the political and cultural situations which now obtain in the societies where cultural studies has made some headway and where, albeit in different ways and as a result of different histories, the recognition and promotion of cultural diversity is a more pressing priority, the long-term vision that Williams proposes here loses its coherence and purchase. For this particular petit-bourgeois theorist, then, the issue is not one of making long-term adjustments to short-term situations, but of making long-term adjustments because the long-term situation itself now has to be thought in new ways.

Equally important, there are a multitude of day-to-day issues pertaining to the administration of culture and, indeed, to the use of cultural resources in a wide range of government and governmental programmes whose resolution bears consequentially on all our ways of life. Only by recognizing that culture is ordinary in this sense will it be possible for both theory and practice to take account of the fact that, like any other area of activity, its actual futures will be determined, in significant measure, by the ways in which such practical questions of cultural policy are routinely posed and resolved.

References

Bennett, T. (1990) *Outside Literature*, London: Routledge.
Bennett, T. (1992) 'Useful Culture', *Cultural Studies*, 6(3).
Blundell, V., Shepherd, J. and Taylor, I. (eds) (1993) *Relocating Cultural Studies: Developments in Theory and Research*, London and New York: Routledge.
Bourdieu, P. (1990) *In Other Words: Essays Towards a Reflexive Sociology*, Cambridge: Polity Press.
Frow, J. and Morris, M. (eds) (1993) *Australian Cultural Studies: A Reader*, St Leonards: Allen & Unwin.
Gilroy, P. (1987) *There Ain't No Black in the Union Jack*, London: Hutchinson.
Green, M. (1993) 'Vox Populi', *Cultural Studies*, 7(3).
Hall, S. (1992) 'Cultural Studies and its Theoretical Legacies', in L. Grossberg, C. Nelson and P. Treichler (eds) (1992) *Cultural Studies*, London and New York: Routledge.
Hall, S. (1993) 'Culture, Community, Nation', *Cultural Studies*, 7(3).
Hall, S. and Jefferson, T. (eds) (1976) *Resistance through Rituals: Youth Subcultures in Post-war Britain*, London: Hutchinson.
Hall, S., Critcher, C., Jefferson, T., Clarke, J. and Roberts, B. (1978) *Policing the Crisis: Mugging, the State, and Law and Order*, London: Macmillan.
Harris, D. (1992) *From Class Struggle to the Politics of Pleasure: The Effects of Gramscianism on Cultural Studies*, London and New York: Routledge.

Hunter, I. (1992) 'Aesthetics and Cultural Studies', in L. Grossberg, C. Nelson and
  P. Treichler (eds), *Cultural Studies*, London and New York: Routledge.
Hunter, I. (1993) 'Mind games and body techniques', *Southern Review*, 26 (2).
Jameson, F. (1993) 'On "Cultural Studies" ', *Social Text*, 34.
McGuigan, J. (1992) *Cultural Populism*, London and New York: Routledge.
Milner, A. (1993) *Cultural Materialism*, Melbourne: Melbourne University Press.
Moon, B. (1993) 'Reading and Gender: From Discourse and Subject to Regime and Practice',
  D.Phil thesis, Curtin University.
O'Regan, T. (1992) '(Mis)taking Policy: Notes on the Cultural Policy Debate', *Cultural
  Studies*, 6(3).
Wark, M. (1994) 'Distorted View of Black Culture', *The Australian*, 12 January.
Williams, R. (1963) *Culture and Society, 1780–1950*, Harmondsworth: Penguin.
Williams, R. (1977) *Marxism and Literature*, Oxford: Oxford University Press.
Williams, R. (1983) *Towards 2000*, London: Chatto & Windus.
Williams, R. (1989) *The Politics of Modernism: Against the New Conformists*, London: Verso.

3

Media, Ethics and Morality

Nick Stevenson

The community stagnates without the impulse of the individual, the impulse dies away without the sympathy of the community.

William James

In thinking about mass communications, Raymond Williams once wrote, 'it matters greatly where you start' (1962a: 1). Indeed in thinking about the mass media, social theorists of various kinds have started from a multitude of positions. If we step back a moment it is evident that there are basically three places to start discussing the media. These include the responses of critical theory, reception analysis and those mostly concerned with the functioning of different media of communication. My concern here is that they very rarely give direct answers to the question: 'What are the media for?' Arguably such a question presupposes issues that are of a moral and ethical nature. The reason that many continue to argue that the mass media should represent a plurality of viewpoints is that they take the view that democracy has a certain normative relevance: that is, that most definitions of democracy are connected with the idea that power is invested in the people, rather than a social elite or a bureaucratic apparatus. Overall democratic societies would wish to uphold that the practices of collective decision making are better than authoritarian rule. This might be justified through a variety of arguments proposing that democracies potentially allow for the acceptance of difference, the fostering of relations of solidarity, and the acceptance of the principles of liberty and equality. More likely such arguments would turn on the necessity of the channels of communication being kept open in order to enable processes of consensual democratic will formation. Obviously in actually existing democracies these values can come into conflict, be passed over in favour of efficiency criteria, or fall into disuse through neglect. Despite all of these obstacles, substantive human values can be called upon to press the case for democracy. But, for the most part, media theory has either presupposed such values, relegating them to the background of the analysis, or has ignored arguments related to the normative relevance of instituted communication networks. These considerations lead unavoidably to a consideration of the current status of media theory in respect of ethical questions.

The first approach suggested by media theory offers a critical theory of mass communication, where the organizational structures, content and reception of media cultures are examined as a source of social power and ideology. Here the media are often linked to accumulation strategies on the part of capital, hegemonic attempts by powerful social groups aiming to legitimate certain 'world views' over others, or the ways in which state power silences dissenting voices that are potentially embarrassing for the status quo. Yet, as many theorists have been aware, such arguments contain within them normative claims that pose critical questions for the dominant means of image production. For instance, there is little sense in protesting against the overwhelmingly biased nature of much media production unless we are also informed as to how such relations might be reformulated. To argue that the media currently give a distorted impression of AIDS sufferers implicitly suggests that we have some idea as to how they might be more fairly or impartially represented. In short, if we are to enter into a critique of relations of dominance, we can only do so if we make certain normative claims we feel will find a wide acceptance in the community as a whole.

The second strand of media research is provided by a more interpretive approach. Audience research of various kinds has argued that media interactions normally take place within private as opposed to public settings, and involve complex symbolic work on the part of viewers, listeners and readers. Much of this work has uncovered the ways in which media messages are variously negotiated and resisted by audiences located within public and private networks of power and authority. Again, most of this writing has been motivated by the concealed normative desire to uncover the voices and perspectives of ordinary people. These excluded perspectives, it is argued, are rarely heard in the everyday outpourings of centralized media messages. The semiotic struggle from below offers an ethics of resistance against the incorporation of 'the people' into dominant ideological strategies. Such an approach is not merely descriptive but opens out a plurality of voices where it was previously assumed there was only one. Difference is discovered in the place of a previously prevailing sameness. The introduction of audience analysis thereby unsettled previously held assumptions that the subjectivity of the audience mirrored that of media content. Again, the desire to reveal difference affirms that human individuality is worthy of our respect.

Finally, the other main strand of thinking about the media has built the development of media of communication into the history of modernity. Such views have argued that the mechanisms by which modern societies communicate with themselves are primary rather than secondary phenomena. The historical passage of human societies through oral, written and electric cultures has significantly restructured modernity. In assuming this standpoint, the shifting of time and space achievable through technical media became significant mechanisms by which

human experience could be both unified and fragmented. Each time we
turn on the television we are caught up with expert cultures and the life-
worlds of others which are all distant from the places in which we live.
Media forms both compress the world while rapidly expanding the
amount of information regularly made available, thereby emphasizing
the significance of individual choice. Again, we could argue, despite the
fact that many who have worked within this paradigm remain indif-
ferent or even hostile to ethical considerations, that such dimensions
have a normative relevance. That human beings are continuing to
develop ever new and more sophisticated means of communicating with
one another alters the moral boundaries of our world. That we are
informed as to democratic movements in Burma, genocide in Rwanda
and war in Bosnia presumably opens new moral and ethical dilemmas
for modern subjects. Further, we could also ask how the development of
new communication media could become subject to ethical rather than
instrumental criteria. Yet, while I have dealt more fully with the complexity of these different traditions elsewhere, what is obvious, to me at
least, is the subordinate nature of moral and ethical problems when it
comes to discussing the media of mass communication.[1] We should not
forgo more concerted attempts to link the domains of media practice and
ethics. It is obvious, then, that what is really at issue in considering the
kinds of mass communications environments we wish to foster are
questions which are of an ethical and moral nature. This is, if you like,
where I start.

While I have perhaps painted an overly pessimistic picture of the
current state of media theory, there remain considerable resources to call
upon in addressing questions of media and ethics. First, I shall consider
the contributions of Jürgen Habermas, who attempts to link a moral and
ethical theory of communication to a substantive model of the public
sphere. While many of the arguments presented here are well known, I
want to concentrate more generally on the idea of discourse ethics. In
this respect, I will show how such a position is linked to certain
universalistic assumptions concerning the moral development of the
subject. The problem with most contemporary discussions of Habermas
and the media, and here I include my own, is that they fail to link such
concerns to his more recent writing. In this the argument will propose
that the figures of both Kohlberg and Mead have been central for the
development of communicative ethics, while demonstrating how such
concerns continue to impinge upon modern media cultures. Second, and
more briefly, I will look to Raymond Williams's attempt to formulate a
cultural materialist basis to ethical questions related to mass communication structures. Again I am aware that most discussions of Williams's
work on communications fail to make this vital link. In respect of both
Habermas and Williams, I shall also relate their concerns to feminist
arguments related to an ethic of care and the deconstruction of the
masculine subject. Finally, it could be argued that both Habermas's and

Williams's universalistic concerns are misplaced in current postmodern conditions. The argument here will question the relevance of the forms of universalistic thinking that were developed by modernity in favour of a more ambivalent linkage between the subject and structures of communication.

The public sphere: from refeudalization to colonization and juridification

The idea of discourse ethics is based upon the notion that the rightness or the justness of the norms we uphold can only be secured by our ability to give good reasons. In turn, these norms are considered valid if they gain the consent of others within a shared community. The moral principles that we uphold must be more than the prejudices of the particular group to which we happen to belong. Such collectively held norms can only be considered valid if they are judged impartially. In this sense, our ethical claims can be said to be deontological in that their rightness cannot be secured by social conventions or appeals to tradition (Habermas 1990a). The achievement of a universal ethical stance, therefore, requires that participants in practical discourse transcend their own egoistic position in order to negotiate with the horizons of other cultures and perspectives. A norm can only be considered valid if it would be freely accepted by all those it would potentially affect. These remarks, as should be clear, represent a radical reworking of the universalistic thinking of Kant, and a forcible rejection of relativistic standpoints.

In making these claims, however, Habermas is clear that we need to separate moral questions from ethical reflections that are related to the good life. This is especially necessary in modern multicultural societies that juxtapose and mix different cultural traditions and orientations. For example, we are unlikely to be able to reach universal agreement on questions such as to which particular communities we owe loyalty. We might have obligations to a particular region, football team, nation-state, religious group or family members. These networks of identity-sustaining connection are likely to inform collective and individual forms of self-understanding. Habermas argues that such questions are best described as ethical rather than moral, and are largely driven by the issue as to 'what is right for me'. On the other hand, moral concerns are more properly associated with whether or not particular maxims are appropriate for the whole community. Thus whereas participants in processes of self-clarification inevitably remain tied to their communities and identities, moral questions require that we break and distance ourselves from our immediate ties to consider questions of universal rightness and justice (Habermas 1993a). The distinction between morality and ethics could be said to apply to television. The programmes that I decide to watch obviously have a bearing on my social identity given the implications they might have for my communally negotiated view of the good life. However, such questions are radically distinct from finding agreement with others on the moral principles that should regulate television content and production. For instance, my favourite television soap opera is *East Enders*, and I am sure some of the reasons I watch regularly are connected with the feelings of community and the participation in 'ordinary' national life that it generates. These sentiments, however, are radically distinct from the principles of quality and difference which should arguably govern the institutional organization of television.

These reflections bring us onto one of Habermas's central ideas, namely communicative action. For Habermas there are basically two types of action: they are instrumental forms of action, which depend upon egocentric forms of calculation and strategy, and communicative action, where actors are prepared to commit themselves to norms which are the outcome of rational agreement. Communicative action holds out the possibility of coming to agreement over: (1) the objective world; (2) the social world of institutions, traditions and values; and (3) our own subjective worlds. We are able to reach an understanding of these three interrelated worlds due to the fact that human beings are part of an intersubjective linguistic community. For Habermas (1981), the very fact that we are language users means that we are communicatively able to reach an understanding of one another. Habermas argues that in every act of speech we are capable of immanently raising three validity claims in connection with what is said. These three validity claims, he adds, constitute a background consensus of normal everyday language use in Western society. The three claims – which are used by agents to test the validity of speech – could be characterized as: propositional truth claims, normative claims related to appropriateness, as well as claims connected to sincerity. These claims notably map onto the objective, social and subjective worlds mentioned above, which allows us to intersubjectively investigate questions of truth, justice and taste.

Given Habermas's stance on questions of morality, it is not surprising that he pays particular attention to the mechanisms of mass communication. In an early study of the public sphere, Habermas (1989a) argues that the development of a bourgeois public between 1680 and 1730 in coffee houses and salons opened out the principle of public reflection. These early exclusive conversations, Habermas explains, began to accept the principles of open and wide-ranging public debate on the domains of state and civil society. However, with the development of media conglomerates and statist concerns to manipulate public opinion, the communicative concerns of the public sphere were increasingly bracketed off by the dual mechanisms of money and power. Habermas argues at this juncture that the public sphere had become refeudalized. By this he means that systemic social forces had successfully trivialized, depoliticized and stage-managed matters that would properly warrant public reflection. The public sphere which had previously fostered rational debate amongst a male propertied elite had been replaced by new mechanisms of communication that depended upon privatized forms of reception and the promotion of politicians as media stars. In his more recent work on these themes, Habermas has rarely sought to extend his analysis of the media to take account of more contemporary transformations. This said, for Habermas, such concerns can never be far from the surface. Indeed he seems to have replaced questions of refeudalization with those that address the colonization of the life-world and processes of juridification. Such notions are intended to supplement and update his earlier reflections.

Habermas explains the internal colonization of the life-world through what he perceives as the 'indissoluble' tension that exists between capitalism and democracy. Democracy holds out the principle that institutions should be subordinable to discursive forms of argument and consensus seeking, whereas capitalism presumes a system of profit maximization irrespective of normative concerns. These two basic principles mean that the formation of public opinion through mediated public debate is articulated differently by these dual perspectives. The key area of antagonism between these two principles, however, is not the media of mass communication but the welfare state. Following Offe (1984), Habermas argues that the material separation between the economy and the state displaces the centrality of class conflict in modern societies. The contradictory development of the welfare state has meant that it has been asked to perform paradoxical social functions. The welfare state is dependent on the successful workings of the economy for revenue, while being asked to compensate for the disruptive and disorganizing consequences of capital.

Habermas is clear that the compromise between capital and labour is bought at the price of a de-politicized political sphere and the enhancement of consumerism. Democratic, or what Habermas calls 'life-world', initiatives become predefined around the systemic importance of the reproduction of consumptive life-styles and the role of the welfare client. Through these processes the life-world (the realm of intersubjectively shared knowledge) becomes robbed of its capacity to form coherent political ideologies, giving way to cynicism and fragmented forms of consciousness. The media of mass communication, if this argument is followed, become increasingly oriented around large-scale conglomerates and the structural requirement of the state to impose mass loyalty. Media therefore must obey the structural necessity of securing a profit or of legitimating the political order of modern society. Further, a point Habermas mostly ignores, publicly instituted media are subject to similar pressures to those most evident in welfare services. As Habermas (1989b) is aware, the New Right have sought to solve the crisis of legitimation currently being experienced by welfare regimes by privatization measures, tax reductions and supply-side economics. This has meant that public as opposed to commercial systems of communication have been progressively deregulated during the eighties and nineties. Thus, the relations between the system and the 'life-world' have not only had impacts upon social welfare, but have also greatly impoverished the economic and political base of public forms of communication.

At this point it is important to introduce the concept of juridification. Generally speaking, by this, Habermas means the increasing tendency of diverse areas of social life to fall under the guise of the law. The historical development of 'individual' civil, political and social rights formally guarantees certain freedoms while increasing the involvement of the state in social life more generally. Citizenship rights that have been won through civil, political and social struggles serve to bureaucratize every-day life while providing certain individual entitlements protected by the law. Viewed in terms of the public sphere, rights to free speech can be said to have a regulative rather than a constitutive power. This, perhaps, allows Habermas to develop a more fully dialectical view of the public sphere than was previously evident. The public sphere can be said to be subject to countervailing pressures and demands that are not adequately captured by notions of refeudalization. The idea of a collectively shared democratic public space is built at the point between system and life-world. It is systemically regulated by certain formal rights and the pressures of money and power while maintaining its dependence upon the more communicative social matrix of the life-world. Habermas (1981: 389–91), in this sense, articulates a more complex and ambivalent view of media cultures.

To briefly unpack some of these features. First, mass communication is important for communicative ethics as it detaches viewpoints and per-spectives from 'provincial' perspectives and makes them widely avail-able in space and time. In this respect, the media have the capacity to simultaneously hierarchize (by only including certain voices) and democratize (making views widely available) political views and per-spectives. Second, media of mass communication, at present, are largely centralized structures which are based on one-way forms of communica-tion, flowing from centre to periphery. This enhances forms of social control by reproducing a division of labour between the producers of media messages and their consumers. On the other hand, the capacity to transport images in time and space, making them publicly visible and widespread, also potentially opens them to validity claims in a variety of social contexts. Finally, Habermas (1989b) is aware that the public sphere is being reshaped through the emergence of 'life-world' movements such as ecological and feminist groups. These groups both have a more reciprocal relationship with the 'life-world' and have helped carve out more autonomous public spaces so as to openly resist ideological forms of incorporation in a way that is not reflected in mainstream political parties. Hence, these developments in Habermas's thinking position the media of mass communication as caught between systemic imperatives and the democratic considerations of communicative action. This leaves the media of mass communications torn between democracy and colonization, discussion and profit, and freedom and silence. These spheres, Habermas contends, can only be reformulated by socially containing the expression of money and power through the application of discourse ethics. This would make the restructuring of social life the responsibility of the whole community rather than groups of self-selected experts. In complex mediated societies like our own, therefore, discourse ethics would have to be applied not only to media structures but also to styles of media presentation and reporting. Only then would the whole community be in a position to be able to discursively rethink its currently perceived interests in respect of relations between culture and society.

The public sphere and moral progress

It is impossible to read Habermas without a clear notion that the democratic foundations of everyday life remain underdeveloped in modernity. Habermas's preoccupation with discourse ethics is nothing if it is not an argument for a more emancipated and less reified social order. While Habermas resolutely argues that the application of the moral principles agreed upon in dialogic negotiations are not properly the concern of the philosopher, we are left in little doubt that certain material preconditions would have to be satisfied if the democratic possibilities of modern culture are ever to be reawakened. These would include the attainment of certain levels of education, an egalitarian distribution of wealth, and of course the maintenance of a democratic, electronically mediated public space. Of the other preconditions, Habermas has spent a considerable amount of effort in outlining how discourse ethics is dependent upon a particular view of the subject. To put matters differently, there would be little point in Habermas championing the cause of communicative action unless social subjects are endowed with the cognitive capacity to construct universally binding norms. This leads Habermas away from the macro dimensions of money and power into an investigation, primarily through Kohlberg and Mead, into the moral development of the self.

In seeking to develop these arguments, I shall show how Habermas's view of a rational, plural and inclusive public sphere presupposes certain conceptions of subjective development. Habermas (1979) argues that a fully emancipated society is dependent upon the ego development achievable by its citizens. Our ability to form an understanding of our unconscious desires and our cognitive capacity to embrace a universal morality contributes significantly to the cultural development of a mature citizenship. The growth in our common capacity to become fully cognitive human beings therefore is dependent upon the moral evolution of the ego. In this, Habermas follows Kohlberg, by highlighting six developmental stages which are necessary for the emergence of the universal principles that become attached to rights, reciprocity and justice. Habermas and Kohlberg, by outlining the stages of moral-cognitive development, are seeking to understand how an initially biologically and socially dependent human being becomes capable of a post-conventional morality. The argument, common to much ego psychology, charts the separation of the mature ego from the initial bonds of the early socialization process, eventually becoming a fully independent member of the community. In order for this stage to be reached the role identity formed within the family has to be weakened to allow for an ego identity to be based upon city, state and more global forms of identification. Both Kohlberg and Habermas posit an idea of the mature individual who is able to evaluate moral norms from the standpoint of the community rather than the particular concerns of his or her family or social group. To illustrate this case, Habermas draws a homology between the moral and ethical development of human society and individual self-identity. Just as human societies have sought to question the binding power of tradition, so a post-conventional morality would hold that moral maxims and particular orientations should seek justification through universal ethics. As the social world loses its capacity, once and for all, to fix moral hierarchies through tradition, this opens the cosmos to differing value ideas related to personal fulfilment. The fully developed ego therefore should in principle be capable of questioning the authority of previously held identities within the private sphere as well as communally transmitted norms and values. Habermas invites us in our most intimate personal relations and public affiliations to subject ourselves to the reasoned discourse of others. We would, if these reflections are accurate, have to learn to live without the ontological or metaphysical guarantees that we are currently living within truth. Such a view of human beings most obviously has implications for the maintenance of an open, pluralistic and noisy public sphere that is able to reveal to us the fragility of our current practices and beliefs.

Nowhere is the notion that the formation of our identities is dependent upon intersubjective forms of recognition and moral notions of community better developed than within Mead. Habermas (1981, 1992) himself clearly realizes the historical importance of Mead in developing notions of intersubjectivity and an ethical understanding of the subject. For Mead (1934), the self emerges through a three-way conversation between the I, me and generalized other. Mead produces a theory of self-development similar to Kohlberg in that we can only understand the self by radically decentring monadic notions of consciousness. In this, Mead clearly states that 'the individual is not a self in the reflexive sense unless he is an object to himself' (1934: 142). Human selfhood can be said to develop out of our capacity to view ourselves from the particular and general attitudes of other people. Until the individual is capable of viewing him- or herself from the concrete and generalized standpoint of others, he or she cannot be said to have developed a personality. It is in 'taking the attitude of the other' that the 'me' learns to control actions, attitudes and social expressions. A subject only gains consciousness of itself to the extent to which it is able to perceive its own actions through the lens of the other. Mead distinguishes in this regard the 'I' – the spontaneous, creative response of personhood to others – from the 'me' – the organized set of attitudes of the other which we take as our own. The 'I', then, is the acting ego and the 'me' is the attitude of others which have been assumed as our own. If we take this ongoing conversation together it constitutes our personality. These features, according to Mead, allow us to talk to ourselves, and grant human beings with a shared capacity for inner dialogue and reflection. The self is caught in the constant ebb and flow of conversation between ourselves and others. For Mead these features crucially form the basis for self-understanding as well as self-regard and self-respect. We are able to develop a feeling of trust in our own capacities the extent to which we are able to reciprocally negotiate mutual reciprocity and obligations through an intersubjective dimension (Honneth 1995).

The final part in the dialogic puzzle of self-formation is provided by the 'generalized other'. For Mead, mature selfhood can only arise once we learn to take the 'attitude of the other' in a wider communal sense. This is not a description of moral conformity, but a recognition, by Mead, that the 'self-regarding self' can only handle community disapproval by setting up higher moral standards which 'out-vote' presently held societal norms (Mead 1934: 168). When there is a conflict between the individual and the community, the self is thrown back into a reflective attitude examining whether the values and norms that are currently held are in need of revision. The necessity of the individual bringing her values to bear upon the community opens out a universalistic morality and lifts us out of our more concrete ties. The individual can be required to come into conflict with their community over the defence of a universalistic morality. Moral and ethical universality is only possible, according to Mead, because individuals have the capacity to take the role of the other. To live in a democratic order has as many implications for identity formations as it does for societal structures. Hence in Habermasian terms the shared moral worth of ourselves as human beings is dependent upon the constant conversational revision of our identities, and by an institutional openness to change through procedures of rational communication (Jonas 1985). Habermas himself best sums up this point when he says Mead consistently represents, 'individualism as the flipside of universalism' (1992: 186).[2]

Habermas (1981) remains sympathetic to the overall direction of Mead's project, but offers a number of detailed criticisms. There is not the space to replay all of these arguments, so here is a brief outline of three of them. First, in Mead's terms, collective identities would have to be the direct outcome of the negotiation between the 'I' and the 'me'.

This seemingly ignores the prehistory of collective symbols and their ability to reinforce relations of authority prior to questions related to their normative validity. For instance, Habermas might, although it is not clear, have in mind national forms of consciousness that have been historically imposed by the nation-state. Here symbolic mechanisms are employed in order to sanction national hierarchies, relations between generations and feelings of in-group loyalty that are not merely the result of dialogic processes. Next, as we have outlined above, Mead fails to make a clear distinction between specifically moral and ethical questions. As Habermas makes clear, the cultural uniformity necessary for agreement on ethical questions is no longer evident in the modern world. These changes, as we saw, necessitate the division between properly ethical and moral questions. Finally, the functional material reproduction of the social order is almost entirely neglected by Mead. Mead's analysis of modern society seemingly neglects wider questions of power and ideology. Habermas consistently makes the case, in respect of this criticism, that communicative action, and societies' moral development generally, would have to operate within empirical limits imposed by certain functional requirements. The social order, for Habermas, is not subordinable to the complex interplay of self and other. To argue that this is the case would merge questions of system (dependent upon material reproduction) and social integration (dependent upon cultural traditions and socialization processes). Indeed in modernity the functioning of the systems of economy and state have become increasingly detached from questions of social integration. The regulation of society by money and power brings us back to Habermas's main political point that such domains need to become remoralized rather than collectively owned. A radical politics can no longer be characterized through particular demands, but would focus on a redistribution of power and an opening up of communicative social processes. The struggle to remoralize social conflicts in an age which has seen the increasing polarization of social groups could only appear if the public sphere were communicatively redrawn (Habermas 1990b).

This is not the place to assess the validity of Habermas's criticisms of Mead – especially as this has already been done elsewhere (Crossley 1996). What is more pertinent for our concerns is that Habermas, through the work of Mead and Kohlberg, upholds a normative conception of the mature citizen. This is an extremely bold move given certain tendencies within social theory that would either take the Foucauldian position and warn against the deep dangers of setting up normative hierarchies or move with the Baudrillardian current by arguing that the moral self is a mere fiction of Enlightenment nostalgia. My own sense is, however, that, while we might be able to explore the limitations of Habermas's attempts to rejoin subjective processes to universal concerns through a number of perspectives, contemporary feminism asks the most difficult questions. Rather than dismissing Habermas's concerns with morality and ethics as being part of an outmoded rationalist culture, many currents within contemporary feminism have sought to engage with Habermas precisely because he takes these domains seriously. Habermas, then, is important because he recognizes that the development of the self is not merely a matter of power or discourse but has ethical and moral implications. If a more democratic public sphere is to be envisaged in a future society it will be because we think of ourselves as having something to offer beyond the recidivism of cynical reason. The reinvigoration of the public sphere will only be possible if we are able to link the concerns of dialogue to those of morality and ethics as Habermas has sought to do.

Feminism, the subject and an ethic of care

Some feminist theorists have begun to argue that child-rearing arrangements are central elements in the construction of gender identity and help maintain male dominance. Further, the consequences of these cultural practices extend widely into almost every domain of social life, deeply shaping the nature of power, knowledge and ethics (Flax 1990). In terms of moral reasoning, it has been the work of Carol Gilligan that has posed the most difficulties for universalists such as Habermas. Gilligan's (1982) 'big idea' is that the moral development that leads to a consideration of universal rights and justice takes masculinity as the norm. According to Gilligan, such thinking presupposes a universal dis-embodied subject who has no concrete ties and obligations towards others. Women, therefore, are less likely to satisfy the requirements of the fully mature subject due to different patterns of socialization. Further, universalistic models of development actually repress the 'difference' of women. Much of the work done within feminist psychoanalysis, for example, has heightened our understanding that for men to imagine themselves as rational autonomous egos in search of universal principles they must first repress powerful unconscious feelings of dependency. They are able to do this as men's primary role continues to be sought within the public rather than the private sphere. It is more commonly men's experience to become progressively detached from early feelings of relatedness and care than it is women's. In Habermas's notion of the mature public 'man' who has a well-developed capacity to reason universally it is not clear what status the capacity to feel empathy, benevolence and care actually has. To put the point in more overtly psychoanalytic terms: the development of the kind of moral reasoning Habermas describes not only more fully encompasses masculine development but is, of itself, born of psychic repression. Men are only able to conceive of themselves as universal subjects to the extent to which they are able to deny the infantile experience of dependency, and the concrete ties that bind.[3]

These are powerful charges. Habermas (1990c) has, however, sought to reply to these and similar arguments made in accordance with Gilligan's views. The claims of Gilligan, charges Habermas, are more properly concerned with the application of norms than with questions of universal justification. The rightness of moral questions can only be decided through a wide-ranging communal conversation, not it seems from the particularity of our ethical attachments. Notions of care and sensitivity only come into play when we are seeking to relate universal norms in a context-sensitive manner. Similar to the critique he makes of communitarians – and indeed Mead – Habermas claims that feminists who raise questions connected with an ethic of care are confusing ethical and moral questions.

This reply seems unsatisfactory for a number of reasons. The first is that Habermas is not properly attentive to the feminist argument that to become a mature self we should have the capacity to experience autonomy as well as dependency. Jessica Benjamin (1996) has argued that a critical feminist politics should attempt to deconstruct masculine and feminine identities and the principles of public autonomy and private care that have been historically associated with them. To problematize the realms of masculine and feminine, as well as public and private, would introduce nurturance into the public realm and questions of autonomy into the private sphere. This would seemingly threaten a masculine identity whose presumed autonomy is based upon the exclusion of affective feelings from an instrumentally defined public. Such a bold move could also inform the argument that universalism and an ethic of care might be reconcilable. As Benhabib (1992) has argued, it is not clear what purposes are being served to counterpose the personal and the moral. This view might be able to remoralize public conflicts but leaves questions of sexual morality, personal integrity, child care and domestic responsibility outside of the moral domain. Again, we are brought back to the argument that the mature human subject should be capable of formulating problems in terms of universal rights and justice, as well as having the capacity to feel sympathy and empathy. Indeed Habermas himself, more recently, has begun to be persuaded by the logic of this view. This is evident when he writes that moral reasoning must reconcile two aspects:

> The first postulates equal respect and equal rights for the individual, whereas the second postulates empathy and concern for the well-being of one's neighbour. Justice in the modern sense of the term refers to the subjective realm of inalienable individuality. Solidarity refers to the well-being of associated members of a community who intersubjectively share the same life-world. (1990a: 200)

This brings me on to a second related argument: communitarian writers have consistently argued, with some justification, that Habermas's moral minimalism presupposes more than he realizes. For wide forms of discussion to take place we must have equal respect, free speech and the redistribution of social resources. Habermas presupposes a particular political community, which is exactly what he says he wants to avoid (Walzer 1994). The argument here, put more robustly, is that while Habermas claims to be upholding a politics of process over specific aims, he actually presupposes a radicalized version of social democracy. For communitarians, like Walzer, Habermas's discourse ethics is more properly understood as the radicalization of principles that are already held within the political community. What is missing in his universalism, therefore, is not only his lack of concern for the gendered nature of moral questions, but how they, in complex global societies, are likely to be worked through differently by diverse cultural communities. Habermas, therefore, is not only masculinist but ethnocentric as well. However, even communitarians like Walzer, reversing previously held perspectives, now believe in the need for a globally shared moral minimalism. Otherwise how are we to criticize other cultures very different from our own who refuse to respect very basic human rights? If we only have a contextual morality, then how are we to object to cultures which attempt to ethnically cleanse shared public spaces? As with the feminist argument regarding care, what is required, in my view, is a more reciprocal relation to be drawn between social context and morality. This would point to the interconnections between how our needs, specific identities and normative concerns can be said to interconnect. The problem with Habermas's extreme formalism is that questions of ethics and morality are very neatly separated. Both feminist and communitarian critics would argue that the kinds of moral claims we make would be informed by our current identities, affective ties and communal obligations. However, the critical point that Habermas makes in reply is that our immediate commitments should not be allowed to override more universalistic criteria. As Said argues, 'never solidarity before criticism' (1994: 24). My argument is that instead of rigidly separating the moral and the universal from the ethical and particular we should seek to appreciate how these domains intercut one another. What implications, if any, could these arguments have for a mediated public sphere? Arguably they are two-fold: (1) that the regulation of global media cultures should indeed be subject to universal moral principles; and (2) we must make sure that the importance of achieving a more participatory public culture is not allowed to overshadow the ways in which moral self development is underwritten by private domains.

The first point is to accept the critical argument opened by Habermas that we can indeed make a connection between the moral development of society and the subject. This allows us to make the case for a plural public space where opinions and identities can be revealed, tested and scrutinised. Globally, however, the actual shape of this communicative sphere will depend upon the cultural traditions and political practices that are already present. For instance, in Western Europe it is likely that the principles of public service broadcasting will remain important whereas in many African societies any future public sphere is likely to be developed around radio rather than television. The relationship between different political and cultural traditions and a universal morality is better represented dialectically rather than riven apart abstractly. The principles of process rather than outcome should be regarded as informing universal human rights to which all have access. Such a demand is built upon the recognition that when plural public cultures are deformed by money and power they do great violence to the fragile domain of mutual recognition.

The second point concerns questions of moral development in relation to both public and private spheres. The feminist argument that moral development is only partially dependent upon our ability to act in the public is an important insight. Our shared capacity to write letters to newspapers, participate in radio talk shows and make our own minds up about mediated public events is related to questions of communicative ethics. These interventions into the public should enlarge our horizons and build relations of mutual respect while being guided by perspectives we hold until defeated by a better argument. But, as feminist critics well realize, our ability to be able to empathize with the problems of our neighbour also depend upon shared emotional resources which are not matters of rational discourse alone. Further, moral development cannot be measured by our capacity to break free of our primary bonds while misrecognizing ourselves to be autonomous from related others. This points to a doubly differentiated understanding of moral development which crosses both public and private. Such a view also underlines Arendt's view that 'a life spent entirely in public, in the presence of others, becomes, as we would say, shallow' (1958: 71).

Raymond Williams, communications and materialist ethics

There is a strong temptation to stress the value of Raymond Williams because of the obvious parallels that can be drawn between himself and Habermas – the most obvious being their shared stance as public intellectuals and their involvement in the post-war New Left. If we wanted to continue this comparison we could also point to their shared orientations in the field of media and communications. Williams, more willing to offer detailed prescriptions than Habermas, argued that the media should be taken out of the control of commercial and paternal institutions, underwritten by capital and the state, and be both democratized and decentralized. Once institutionally separate from the government and the market this would provide cultural contributors with the social context for free expression. Williams creatively imagines a mediated utopia of free speech which is built around the rights of contributors to authentic expression. Open democratic forms of 'talk' would have no necessary end-point, given that all of those who contribute must remain open 'to challenge and review' (Williams 1962b: 134). The intention here is to promote what Williams called a 'culture in common' rather than a

common culture, and strengthen communal bonds by including previously excluded perspectives. Williams's idea of a democratic community is complex and built upon difference rather than homogeneity.
These differences, however, also have to be reconciled, as we shall see,
with what human beings have in common. And yet, for Williams, this
was not a conversation that could begin unless democratic and civil
spaces were opened up free from the pressures of the capitalist economy
and the state. Again, similarly to Habermas, Williams explains that the
capitalist economy and nation-state serve to hegemonically shape social
needs in the interests of power rather than the community as a whole.[4]

However, if the theory of communicative action takes the linguistic
turn in philosophical thinking, Williams's later work on media and
culture takes a more overtly material twist. Through the development of
cultural materialism, Williams sought to counter the evident strains
within and between Marxism and post-structuralism. First, Marxism in
its many guises had failed to represent cultural practices as being
properly material. For Williams the activity of listening to the Beatles is
no less material than working in a car plant. He suggests that in making
a cultural practice superstructural Marxists were claiming that 'intellectual' activities were either a reflection of the economic base, or were
somehow less real. Such a view mistakenly disallows the ontology of
culture and the relative autonomy of political and cultural spheres from
the economic base. The other strand within contemporary theory that
Williams sought to criticize was the prioritization, amongst post-
structuralists such as Althusser, of the structural features of language
over language as a human praxis performed in social contexts (Williams
1977). Cultural practices, therefore, were both material as well as sig-
nificatory, while being dependent upon human creativity, rather than the
grinding out of social structures.

These critical elements are noticeable in Williams's (1980a) reconsideration of the media as a productive activity. By discussing the mass
media as a means of cultural production he emphasizes a sustained
historical analysis of the ways in which communicative actions are
organized into socially contingent social relations. Communicative
relations of exclusion are both historically mediated and overlain by
technology rather than directly caused by it. A fundamental division of
labour exists within communicative relations at two levels. The first is
that social communication is regulated by large media conglomerates
and the nation-state who subject cultural production to the general
conditions of political and economic organization. The other main division of labour is between those who are 'authorized' to speak and those
who are not. Williams points that there is a basic material division
between leaders, personalities and celebrities, whose actions and voices
are worthy of note, and a more passively defined public.

In understanding the social organization and regulation of communication in material terms we should investigate the ways in which

communications have been transformed by social labour. These would include what Williams terms amplificatory, durative and alternative means of transformation. The invention of human technologies such as radio, television and the telephone has meant that voices and perspectives can be amplified, thereby projecting them across huge social distances. Further, the invention of writing and other media technologies has made human cultures durative. By this Williams means that representations can be stored across time and space, disassociating cultural production from their original context. Finally, Williams argues that the history of human communications has revealed that human societies are continually inventing alternative media of communication. These have had transformative impacts upon the way we currently live. However, new technologies have to be fitted into the overwhelmingly capitalist division of labour. In this respect, a materialist analysis of the media would seek to develop a historical understanding of the media, an appreciation of the social divisions they mark, and a consideration of how technology (dead labour) has transformed communicative practice. Williams's argument, therefore, is to treat communications like any other social practice: working out its relationship with the state and the economy as well as mapping out its own specific trajectory. And yet Williams, as I have indicated, couples such concerns with more normative ethical considerations.

Williams's vision of a socialist response to communications differs substantively from that of Habermas. Radical politics would have to bring the organization of society's communicative structure into social rather than state or private ownership. The means of communication in this argument would be brought under the control of the community, thereby abolishing the previously instituted divisions of labour (Williams 1983). Properly socialist media would thereby seek to develop the communicative capabilities of the people and provide them with new opportunities to participate in public dialogue. As Williams writes:

> [S]ocialism is then not only the general 'recovery' of specifically alienated human capacities but is also, and much more decisively, the necessary institution of new and very complex communicative capacities and relationships. (1980a: 62)

Williams, in conjunction with his other writing on socialism, offers a view of a complex, participatory and planned society, where the means of production (cultural as well as economic) have been taken into common ownership. If Williams differs substantially from Habermas on what constitutes modern socialism, he shares the orientation that subjective processes of self-formation are implicated in any wider view of society. But, whereas Habermas discusses questions of moral development that encompass both self and society, Williams prefers to talk in terms of human needs and nature. Similarly with Marx, Williams (1980b) argues, human beings are material beings with certain biologically mediated needs. This relationship entails that one cannot have an expression of the biological or the cultural in a pure state; instead, human beings share a common biological structure which endows them with certain instincts. How these instincts are satisfied, and the value placed on physical characteristics, cannot be understood apart from cultural classifications. Further, Williams wishes to distance himself from the 'triumphalism' associated with the conquest of nature. While the origins of such a notion lie within capitalism and imperialism, it has also informed Marxist theory. This particular 'structure of feeling' is certainly evident within Marx's emphasis upon the indefinite expansion of production that is held to be characteristic of an 'emancipated society'. Instead, Williams emphasizes a sense of limits that recognizes our common ecological vulnerability and interconnection with nature. Human beings are both within as well as outside of nature. We are caught up with both the natural world while having developed distinctively human features, capacities and characteristics. Following Timparnaro, Williams claims that much of our experience as human beings can be appropriately termed passive whereby we are constituted through a common biological inheritance. From this recognition could spring a global materialist ethics which sought to hold in check, as far as possible, the suffering that can be associated with old age, hunger, lack of shelter, disease and infant mortality. Williams calls such a project one of 'widening happiness'.

Human beings are not only material beings but are also language users, which gives them access to a shared store of symbolic interpretations that can be drawn upon critically and reflexively. Unlike many of those who became associated with post-structuralism, Williams does not make the error of separating a concern with the structure of language from the way it is reproduced in a variety of social contexts. Yet, unlike other humanist currents, Williams maintains that subjects are born into a pre-existing structure of language that 'is at once their socialisation and their individuation' (1977: 37). In this way, Williams holds out the importance of language in such a way that seeks to balance both agency and structure. The emphasis of this argument can then be connected back to the intersubjective necessity of sharing interpretations with others, of being open to counter arguments, and of practising critique within a shared community. The final aspect of human nature pressed by Williams and the socialist humanist tradition generally is the need for culturally connected others. Community, as Williams reminds us in *Keywords* (1976), is a warmly persuasive word that is rarely used negatively. For Williams, in the broadest sense, it signifies our concerns and solidarities with others who are often interconnected with ourselves in such ways that are obscured by hegemonic patterns of individualism. In particular, Williams's novels resound with examples of individuals who are thrown into crisis, only to emerge the stronger for looking outside themselves, rediscovering and renewing their relations with others. This articulates a simple if profound truth that human beings need friendship and solidarity.

The media of mass communication, therefore, are profoundly import-ant not only because they potentially allow for wide forms of social participation but that the functioning of the media regularly reminds us of our mutual interdependency. The most powerful arguments for global socialism concern the lack of opportunities for participation in dis-cursively shaping social institutions and the failure to meet common social needs through an egalitarian distribution of resources. That we have common interests in securing human flourishing and material security is, however, often obscured by the actual content of the media. What Williams (1989) called the 'culture of distance' seeks to either naturalize social relations or obscure the connections that exist between human beings. The professional practices of the media will seek to represent global human tragedies by maintaining a safe distance between ourselves and others. This can be achieved by banishing images of the unemployed from our screen, representing the victims of wars and famines through an unthinking racism, or, as in the case of the Gulf War, consistently denying the home population any real knowledge of the suffering being experienced as the result of bombing campaigns. In such cases, for Williams, what is required is a diverse range of perspectives that continually remind us of our shared human condition. And yet the dialectical fecundity of Williams's arguments, acknowledging the com-plexities of mediated human societies, also points to the necessity of global media orders in helping make such identifications possible. Like Habermas, Williams represents mediated social practices as containing an emancipatory kernel that would find a fuller expression in a different social order.

Habermas and Williams in postmodernity

At first glance both Habermas and Williams come to a similar position by very different routes. Both would argue that the need for a globally pluralist media is connected with the capacities of the human subject. Further, as should be obvious, while Williams is willing to be more prescriptive, they mutually offer the view that a democratic society is characterized by the capacity of civil society to uphold a reflexive and participatory culture. While there is much that could be said on the similarities and differences between Habermas and Williams, here I want to concentrate on two aspects: first, the difference between discourse and materialist ethics; and, second, the relevance of these arguments in postmodern mediated contexts.

The most basic difference between Habermas and Williams seems to lie in their disposition towards morality and ethics. For Habermas we are able to use reason due to the breakdown of tradition, the rationalizing impulse of modernity, and because of our intersubjective capacity as language users. A materialist ethics, in Habermas's view, could become an important voice within the conversation, but would have a similar status to that of an ethic of care, and might more properly be thought of as a discourse of application. Further, he might also claim that Williams's materialist thesis disguises the differences between instrumental and communicative practices, and dangerously reinvents metaphysical thinking by suggesting that ethical truths can be derived from human beings' ontological condition.

The first point can be treated in a similar way to Habermas's arguments in respect of an ethic of care. Just as an ethic of care can be balanced against discourse ethics, so might a materialist ethics. That human beings continue to feel sympathy and concern for others due to their shared material condition is related to shared experiences of solidarity and concern for others with regard to bodily suffering. Both a materialist ethics, as well as an ethic of care, would emphasize human beings' shared vulnerability and dependence upon others. Again, this reminds us that maturity is not only achieved through the development of our dialogic capacities to soberly reason with others, but also through our ability to experience the others' pain. The advantage that a materialist ethics has over an ethic of care, however, is that it must be universal rather than particular in orientation. Whereas an ethic of care is oriented to specific family members, materialist identifications would have to cut across all social divisions. A materialist ethics, as Terry Eagleton (1990) has commented, recognizes that all human beings are both frail and mortal, indicating a transhistorical domain worthy of human ethical concern. The problem with discourse ethics is that they are so deontological that they miss the connection between certain facts about human existence and the values that we currently hold. A materialist ethics could provide grounds for solidarity with others irrespective of the cultural differences that are revealed within the conversation. However, these remarks do not mean, to repeat, that we have to make a choice between discourse ethics and more materialist concerns. As we have seen, Williams understood that human reciprocity, communication and understanding was a necessary precondition to the realization of our common natures. Indeed, it is probably true to say that on questions of morality both Habermas and Williams view such questions in terms of the material movement towards a more humane society. Before, if you like, we are able to enter into extended conversations with one another, certain basic human needs would have to be met. In this way, both materialist and discourse ethics ask troubling questions of the dominant capitalist order.

Where I think Habermas does score over Williams is in his resistance to the idea that the development of society's capacity to learn cannot be seen in strictly material terms. As is well known, Habermas attempts to

reconstruct historical materialism by linking the overtly material processes of production to cultural institutions which monitor moral insight
and consensual forms of understanding. To treat the cultural domain as
being as material as the economic obscures the application of the
different rationalities that have accompanied their development. Habermas's earlier distinction between work and interaction sought to point
that society was driven by the economy as well as cultural traditions,
political means that sought consensus, and practical knowledge. Yet,
given Williams's cultural Marxism, this is unlikely to have been a
conclusion with which he would have been out of sympathy. Williams,
unlike many in the Marxist tradition, clearly perceived that 'actually
existing' models of socialism had much to learn from more formally
democratic traditions of thinking. Further, Williams's central concept of
the long revolution had precisely the social creation of a learning and
reflexive society as its ultimate aim. However, it should be said, by
making culture overly material, Williams does begin to threaten these
more hermeneutic insights.

Postmodern ethics, democratic socialism and the media

Perhaps the main problem with these reflections is that they are currently
deeply unfashionable in many of the dialogues taking place within the
academy. One of the many reasons for this is that they seem unpractic-
able and riven away from the ways most people live their lives.
J.B.Thompson (1995) has argued, with Habermas in mind, that it is no
longer clear what practical relevance discourse ethics has for global
media cultures. Practically, discourse ethics seems to apply to those who
share a common social location and who are able to dialogue directly
with one another. But, under global conditions where the media are able
to recontextualize imagery into local contexts, what would an all-
inclusive conversation look like? For example, our common fate at
present is pressed by issues of nuclear proliferation, global warming and
the spread of the HIV virus. How could the millions of spatially diverse
people whom these issues affect make their voices heard? Further, it is
likely that most of those who would be affected acutely by such
phenomena will be future generations; but, again, to build a morality out
of reciprocity avoids rather than confronts these issues. In these and
other respects, discourse ethics has failed to develop along with the
changing contours of modernity. Rather than an ethics of co-presence
constructed around our ability to dialogue with others, Thompson
advocates the renewal of moral-practical thinking based upon responsibility. The emergence of global media has reminded us of the inter-
connectedness of humanity and of the necessity of breaking questions of
responsibility away from more traditional spatial and temporal co-
ordinates.

These sentiments probably find their most coherent expression in the recent social theory of Zygmunt Bauman. Bauman has sought to define a postmodern response to some of the ethical and moral problems thrown up by our current age. He defines postmodern sensibility as being aware that there are human problems with no really good solutions. For Bauman, postmodernity is modernity without illusions. Modernity offered an ethical discourse of experts who sought to legislate codified ethical responses through a universal law. This created a special cast of people whose job it was to issue binding and authoritative rules. The legislators of morality gave existential comfort in a society that was replacing the law of the divine with a human order. Unlike Habermas, Bauman argues that such attempts to ensure moral progress through law-like codes have been disastrous and have actually sapped autonomous moral abilities. There are, according to Bauman (1995: 29), two main sources that have undermined the West's confidence in its own ethical mission. The first is the link between the most morally troubling events of the twentieth century, such as Auschwitz and the Bosnian death camps, and the growth of rational bureaucratic control. These were the legitimate products of the law-like decrees of experts which sought to substitute individual moral feelings with bureaucratic codes. The second is the doubt that modernity is a civilization fit for global application. It has been the trail set by modernity that has fostered a world of economic polarization, ecological degradation, nuclear proliferation and consumptive irresponsibility. These insights, for Bauman, remove the veil from the lie that modernity has been a story of moral progress. On the contrary, the narrative told by modernity is one of history that is written from the standpoint of the victorious and the powerful. Or as Bauman puts it, 'superior morality is always the morality of the superior' (1993: 228).

These bleak remarks, however, could become the source of a considerable opportunity. The waning of the self-confidence of modernity and the detraditionalization of society generally beckons new opportunities for a morality without ethics. Rather than investing our faith in ethical experts or bureaucratic systems, Bauman reasons we should return to questions of individual responsibility and obligation. Against communitarian and universalistic commitments, Bauman contends that the moral impulse cannot be contained through accordance with community norms or universal laws, but can only be revived if we take the individual as its core. Moral responsibility must be personally owned and cannot be shrugged off onto abstract laws, community rules or traditions. We are moral to the extent to which we are able to personally own our obligations towards the other. Bauman writes:

> The readiness to sacrifice for the sake of the other burdens me with the responsibility which is moral precisely for my acceptance that the command to sacrifice applies to me and me only, that the sacrifice is not a matter of exchange or reciprocation of services, that the command is not universalizable

and thus cannot be shrugged off my shoulders so that it falls on someone else's. Being a moral person means that I am my brother's keeper. (Bauman 1993: 51)

Bauman goes on to say that not only have modernity's universal pretensions run their course but the social conditions within which moral selves operate have also fundamentally altered. The impact of new technology, such as the mass media, means that we are now aware of moral problems that are far removed from the places we inhabit. Echoing many of Thompson's concerns above, Bauman contends the mass media regularly make us aware of issues which are both worthy of our moral concern and resist technical fixes or easy solutions. The uncertain risky environment of late modernity will often mean that it is better to do nothing than to act. Indeed, first and foremost, what is required is an ethics of self-limitation. By this, Bauman means we need to become aware of the long-range and potentially long-term effects that our current actions may have for future or related communities. If modernity was about discovering with certitude an ethical order through the use of reason, postmodernity refuses any relation to the law but insists, instead, that we care for one another.

There is obviously much that is persuasive in these arguments. Bauman's concern with questions of individual responsibility is welcome in an age which has seen these questions displaced onto either the functioning of modern bureaucracies or the operation of market economies. But what is missing is Habermas's and Williams's sense that what is important is the linkage of moral and ethical questions to the provision of a pluralistic public sphere and the community in general. Habermas may indeed be mistaken, in the light of the horrors of the twentieth century, to suggest that we can talk of moral progress. Yet, missing from Bauman's reflections is the understanding that unless we find new enabling ways of talking with one another then many of the questions he opens out are likely to remain marginal. It is only through the provision of a pluralistic public sphere that the voice of the 'other' is likely to be heard. Unless, as Habermas and Williams insist, we are open to the respectful challenge and criticism of others through open-ended forms of dialogue we will be unable to decide what our collective obligations towards others should be. Moral questions are as much about personal responsibility as they are about communal provision. My concern, however, is that Bauman detaches the moral sense of the individual from that of the community. The interdependence of the individual and the community provides the grounds for rights and responsibilities in an increasingly fragile world. It is essential for our survival that there are public domains in which the voices of ourselves and others can gently, but yet insistently, interrogate one another. Of course, in a globally mediated age this is likely to take place in a multitude of contexts including where we work, care for others and take rest. However, we remain dependent upon a multitude of public spheres connecting the local and the global continuously offering different perspectives to the ones we currently hold.

To maintain that the development of the individual is the flipside for the development of the community insists upon the political importance of continuing the conversation. That this can only be achieved in shared spaces carved out by institutions and maintained by personal qualities is a line worth holding. This is an as yet unrealized ambition of modernity which is also a global necessity. To suggest that everything is the fault or responsibility of the community is a crude act of displacement; yet to reduce morality to the individual level is often to engage in the worst kind of moralism. In spite of Bauman's overly pessimistic reading, modernity has been the site where communal rights and obligations have both enabled and disabled individual and collective futures. The media, as Habermas and Williams maintain, exhibit critical possibilities despite and because of their entanglement within networks of social power. The idea of a cultural democracy whereby we can all stand in relations of mutual respect and tolerance seeking to forge relations of solidarity and hope is a continual thread that runs through modernity. To recognize the complex interdependence of the personal and the political in the mediation of modern identities highlights the unrealized potential of the times we currently inhabit.

Acknowledgements

I would like to thank Michael Kenny for his supportive and thoughtful comments on this chapter and Simon Holdaway for introducing me to the thought of George Herbert Mead.

Notes

1. I have discussed the interrelations of the three paradigms of mass communication elsewhere in Stevenson (1995).

2. A short but provocative account of Mead's writing and intellectual context is provided by Jenkins (1996).

3. A good discussion of these debates is provided by Larrabee (1993).

4. Williams's contributions to media theory are more fully discussed in Stevenson (1995).

References

Arendt, H. (1958) *The Human Condition*, Chicago: University of Chicago Press.

Bauman, Z. (1993) *Postmodern Ethics*, Oxford: Basil Blackwell.

Bauman, Z. (1995) *Life in Fragments: Essays in Postmodern Morality*, Oxford: Basil Blackwell.

Benhabib, S. (1992) *Situating the Self: Gender, Community and Postmodernism in Contemporary Ethics*, Cambridge: Polity Press.

Benjamin, J. (1996) *The Bond of Love: Psychoanalysis, Feminism and the Problem of Domination*. London: Virago.

Crossley, N. (1996) *Intersubjectivity: The Fabric of Social Becoming*, London: Sage.

Eagleton, T. (1990) *The Ideology of the Aesthetic*, Oxford: Basil Blackwell.

Flax, J.(1990) *Thinking Fragments: Psychoanalysis, Feminism, and Postmodernism in the Contemporary West*, Berkeley: University of California Press.

Gilligan, C. (1982) *In a Different Voice*, Cambridge, Mass.: Harvard University Press.

Habermas, J. (1979) *Communication and the Evolution of Society*, London: Heinemann.

Habermas, J. (1981) *The Theory of Communicative Action: The Critique of Functionalist Reason*, Cambridge: Polity Press.

Habermas, J. (1989a) *The Structural Transformation of the Public Sphere*, Cambridge: Polity Press.

Habermas, J. (1989b) *The New Conservatism: Cultural Criticism and the Historians' Debate*, Cambridge: Polity Press.

Habermas, J. (1990a) 'Morality and Ethical Life: Does Hegel's Critique of Kant Apply to Discourse Ethics?', *Moral Consciousness and Communicative Action*, Cambridge: Polity Press.

Habermas, J. (1990b) 'What Does Socialism Mean Today? The Rectifying Revolution and the Need for New Thinking on the Left', *New Left Review*, 183, September/October: 3–22.

Habermas, J. (1990c) 'Moral Consciousness and Communicative Action', in *Moral Consciousness and Communicative Action*, Cambridge, Polity Press.

Habermas, J. (1992) 'Individuation through Socialization: On George Herbert Mead's Theory of Subjectivity', in *Postmetaphysical Thinking: Philosphical Essays*, Cambridge: Polity Press.

Habermas, J. (1993a) 'On the Pragmatic, the Ethical, and the Moral Employment of Practical Reason', in *Justification and Application: Remarks on Discourse Ethics*, Cambridge: Polity Press.

Habermas, J. (1993b) 'Remarks on Discourse Ethics', in *Justification and Application: Remarks on Discourse Ethics*, Cambridge: Polity Press.

Honneth, A. (1995) *The Struggle for Recognition: The Moral Grammar of Social Conflicts*, Cambridge: Polity Press.

Jenkins, R. (1996) *Social Identity*, London: Routledge.

Jonas, H. (1985) *G.H. Mead: A Contemporary Re-examination of His Thought*, Cambridge: Polity Press.

Larrabee, M.J. (ed.) (1993) *An Ethic of Care: Feminist and Interdisciplinary Perspectives*, London: Routledge.

Mead,G.H. (1934) *Mind, Self and Society: From the Standpoint of a Social Behaviorist*, Chicago: University of Chicago Press.

Offe, C. (1984) *Contradictions of the Welfare State*, London: Hutchinson.

Said, E. (1994) *Representations of the Intellectual: The 1993 Reith Lectures*, London: Vintage.

Stevenson, N. (1995) *Understanding Media Cultures: Social Theory and Mass Communication*, London: Sage.

Thompson, J.B. (1995) *The Media and Modernity: A Social Theory of the Media*, Cambridge: Polity Press.

Walzer, M. (1994) *Thick and Thin: Moral Argument at Home and Abroad*, Indiana: University of Notre Dame Press.

Williams, R. (1962a) *The Existing Alternatives in Communications: Socialism in the Sixties*, Fabian Pamphlet, June.

Williams, R. (1962b) *Communications*, Harmondsworth: Penguin.

Williams, R. (1977) *Marxism and Literature*, Oxford: Oxford University Press.

Williams, R. (1980a) 'Means of Communication as Means of Production', in *Problems in Materialism and Culture*, London: Verso.

Williams, R. (1980b) 'Problems of Materialism', in *Problems in Materialism and Culture*, London: Verso.

Williams, R. (1983) 'Culture', in D. McLellan (ed.), *Marx: The First 100 Years*, London: Fontana.

Williams, R. (1989) 'Distance', in *What I Came to Say*, London: Radius.

4

Learning from Experience: Cultural Studies and Feminism

Ann Gray

The publication of *Off Centre: Feminism and Cultural Studies* in 1991 (Franklin et al. 1991) signalled the productive mutual exchange between the central themes in feminism and cultural studies which had developed since the publication of the first collection of feminist work, *Women Take Issue* (Women's Studies Group 1978), to emerge from the then Centre for Contemporary Cultural Studies at Birmingham just over a decade earlier. However, as the editors point out, this has not been a matter for smooth collaboration, but more one of struggle and contestation in which feminists have insisted on, amongst other things, extending the understanding of the political, of bringing the concept of power, quite literally, home and into the intimate relationships of the so-called private and domestic spheres, of the importance of representation and consumption in an understanding of cultural processes, of the need to conceptualize pleasure and desire, and, crucially, the centrality of sexuality to questions of subjectivity and identity. These interventions from feminists caused severe and lasting damage to many of the 'certainties' concerning the subject/object of cultural studies and, also, the theoretical and methodological presuppositions that had emerged through various forms of Marxism during the seventies and eighties.

Charlotte Brunsdon's (1996) recent eloquent account of the unsettling of the Centre by the Women's Studies Group, the collective authors of *Women Take Issue*, bears witness to the responses to their work which threatened to disrupt established and fiercely argued for political and theoretical positions. Surely there are many versions and formulations of these histories of sharing, of refusal, of rejection, of offence and defence, and they certainly continue: Brunsdon asks 'who in cultural studies does not pay at least token attention to gender now?' (1996: 279), whilst Celia Lury argues that 'current feminist cultural studies are repeatedly held back by the continued dominance of *ungendered* understandings of culture' (1995: 33; my emphasis).

Whilst acknowledging the importance of attending to the historical developments of both feminist work and that of cultural studies, in as complex a way possible, I am concerned here to trace another 'story' or to map out a different series of overlaps and conjunctions between and within feminist work and cultural studies, focusing on questions of methodology and method. Returning to *Off Centre*, in their introduction, the editors define some commonalities between cultural studies and feminism, or women's studies. Providing 'overviews' of intricate and complex intellectual and institutional histories is difficult and simplification is always a necessity. However, in this introduction there is a constant slippage between feminism and women's studies, where one is seemingly replaceable by the other. This needs some point of clarification, and without wishing to go into too much detail here, I think we must distinguish between those feminism(s) within the academy whose influences are far-reaching and, at least within the humanities and social sciences, cross-disciplinary, and women's studies, which has defined itself within colleges and universities as an interdisciplinary field of study in its own right. The stories of the growth and hard-won success of women's studies programmes within higher education are, to some extent, emerging as the field 'comes of age' and collections reflect on this work (Aaron and Walby 1991; Hinds et al. 1992). However, the establishment of women's studies programmes within institutions has set up particular tensions between mainstream disciplines and feminist work which is a different relationship from that which exists between feminists and non-feminists working within other disciplines. For me the difference is best expressed in the modes of intervention and interrogation which need to take place when working within disciplines such as sociology, literary studies, linguistics and cultural studies itself. I am concerned here to look at some similarities and differences between feminist work and cultural studies but at the level of ontology and epistemology, and to argue that feminist work on investigating both the 'knowledge object' and the ways of knowing as process and product structured by power relations has not fully been taken up within cultural studies.

Franklin et al. (1991), in identifying the similarities and overlaps between feminism and cultural studies, argue that whilst both are now established within the academy, this was not the origin of their formation. Both fields took root in social and political (and educational) contexts outside the university. Further, they argue, both occupy a critical position in relation to academic assumptions, having uneasy institutional placings. Certainly this is manifest in the politics of curriculum development and pedagogy within the constraints of educational institutions, but also felt by often beleaguered departments working within conventional and traditionalist institutional contexts. Much of the suspicion and distrust is brought about by the way in which both emergent fields formed critiques of existing mainstream disciplinary practices. Both identified the inability of existing concepts and theories to explore and explain the subjects of their study: women's lives and experience and emerging popular forms and ways of life. They began work on their critique of established theories and method aiming to develop and import new ones of their own. Many of the existing theoretical and methodological tools actually rendered the very subjects absent, trivial and marginal. Contrasting examples of this are the study of housework within sociology and resistance to the introduction of popular forms into the English syllabus. Ann Oakley (1974) worked hard to get her colleagues to understand this largely female activity as *work* before embarking on her own research. Similarly forms of popular culture such as romance literature, popular magazines and television did not qualify as appropriate objects for academic work, nor were the existing methods of textual analysis adequate to understand these forms, let alone the acts of reading, interpretation and consumption more generally.

Championing and celebrating

I want to go on to identify further common ground, that of the concern of both fields for marginalized and silenced groups as a strong constitutive element in their intellectual and political development. Early work in cultural studies focused on the recognition of working-class cultures and ways of life whilst feminist work has always been concerned with the systematic oppression of women within patriarchal society and culture. This shared concern with the marginalized, silenced and oppressed groups in society has given and might continue to give each field its sense of project. I see this concern as an example of the 'something at stake' which Stuart Hall (1992: 278) insists must be present, or even a necessary condition for, 'doing' cultural studies.

These concerns were imported into the academy from those earlier political formations which had sedimented and provided the basis for the growth and energy of the two fields. The acknowledgement of 'ways of being' of subordinated groups, unrecognized, rendered absent within the academy, and the need to find ways of challenging the rigidities of disciplines which ignored and silenced the very existence of these groups were central concerns. In cultural studies we hear the clarion call of Williams's 'culture is ordinary' (Williams 1958), Hoggart's rich account of his boyhood in a working-class area of Leeds in the north of England (Hoggart 1958) and E.P. Thompson's writing of history from below with his insistence on the active human agent in the, literal, making of the working class (Thompson 1963). I introduce the three authors most often cited as the 'founding triumvirate' of British cultural studies, not to repeat this refrain, but to argue that what is central to what is actually a very *disparate* group of authors and work is the notion of 'experience': experience which is drawn on, through different modes, to generate 'alternative' accounts of reality in order to question existing accounts and which itself unsettles many of the 'certainties' of intellectual practice.

Revealingly, there is no similar 'three tenors' version of feminism or women's studies and we can only hope that, as the histories of women's studies begin to be written, such notions of founding mothers will be resisted. Of course, this is indicative of feminism's critique of the 'great names' approach to any field of activity, but also, perhaps, a reluctance to 'overview' or 'map the field' which seems to drive some of the male engines. Let me then, for the purposes of this chapter, refer to feminism as a *practice* as well as a politics and a strong intellectual movement.

Accounts of the emergence in the United States and Britain of 1970s second-wave feminism, referred to at the time as the Women's Liberation Movement, draw attention to the importance of consciousness-raising groups to its broad and grass-roots development.[1] These groups were considered to be crucial in bringing women together to share experiences, to talk about their lives, but also in producing new kinds of 'knowledge' about those apparent commonalities. Thus, to invoke Friedan's (1977) portrait of women's lives in suburban developments in the United States in the 1950s, who suffered from 'the problem with no name', women's groups went about naming that problem. Friedan and the consciousness-raising groups to which her work gave rise were to some extent engaging in processes of knowledge production through the exploration of hitherto 'unspeakable' ways of being. In Foucauldian terms, this involved the 'naming' of subjugated knowledges and the identification of the dominant discourses which worked to delegitimate those knowledges.[2] As in the early work of cultural studies, central to this mechanism is the importance of experience in understanding how we and 'others' experience the social world *and* the acknowledgement of the existence of repressed or subjugated knowledges. Here then it is possible to see the shared ground of cultural studies and feminism and, further, that this shared ground is more than a concern for subjugated knowledges and experiences, but also these are ontological and *epistemological* similarities. In order to move into a more detailed discussion of these commonalities and, indeed, to look at the very different ways in which both areas have dealt with their legacies, I want to draw attention to two key terms from each field which are worth exploring. They are 'structure of feeling' and 'the personal is political'. The first was Williams's formulation, which, in *Politics and Letters*, he redescribes in this way:

> [I]t is as firm and definite as structure suggests, yet it operates in the most delicate and tangible parts of our activity. In one sense this structure of feeling is the culture of a period: it is the particular living results of all the elements in a general organisation. (1979: 48)

Williams's term expresses the articulation between the lived and those more or less determining elements in the structure which in their turn shape and inform the lived. At the very least this demands an analysis of the relationships between the different levels and sites of social and cultural activity. Taken to its extreme, human activity and agency is always and at the same time an expression of the structures. What exactly constitutes the 'structures' have been points for debate and struggle as have the ways in which we might account for human activity, but Williams's formulation can be read as a 'blue-print' for the cultural studies project.

For feminism the insistence on the validity of personal experience and the breaking down of the traditional distinction between 'objective' and 'subjective' is captured in the phrase 'the personal is political'. Stanley and Wise express it thus:

> [F]eminism argues that systems and social structures, whether concerned with the economy, the family, or the oppression of women more generally, can best be examined and understood through an exploration of relationships and experiences within everyday life. (1983: 53)

Self-knowledge, then, for this version of feminism, is the necessary starting point. It places this form of knowledge as a foundation for building and expanding and even generalizing beyond the particular into the social, and seeks to find ways of (re)theorizing the world in order to make sense of those encounters, experiences and knowledges.

I will now provide a brief outline of the ways in which 'experience' has been taken up by cultural studies and feminist work, arguing that whilst the two fields share significant characteristics, particularly in early work, there are distinct differences. These lie particularly in the extent to which 'experience' has been considered to be a basis for the production of knowledge. For feminists, epistemological issues have demanded urgent attention, whilst, as Tudor (1995) suggests, epistemology is 'Cultural Studies' murkiest intellectual pool'. My purpose, then, is to identify some of the problems associated with both areas of work and to indicate ways forward for retaining 'experience' as a central and rich category for both feminism and cultural studies.

The documenting of 'experience'

The first convergence insists on the democratizing potential of opening up narrowly defined knowledge fields to different accounts. Thus accounts were sought of 'lived experience', based upon knowledges and literal experience. How and in what ways did people account for and express the experience of living within particular sets of circumstances, particularly those limited and constrained by adverse social and cultural factors? This approach can be divined in the early cultural studies research, particularly studies of youth subcultures. Here researchers wanted to investigate and explore the 'real' worlds of working-class youth, asking questions such as: What was it like to live in that particular set of socio-economic circumstances? How did class and the changing cultures of working-class life affect that generation? What sense were young people able to make of their existence? What meanings did they invest in their worlds of work and leisure? To see the world from the point of view of these actors or agents was the main and driving force behind these studies. Methodologically they drew upon qualitative techniques, mainly participant observation and interviews with the actors involved, in order to produce rich and full accounts of these lives and social worlds. 'Telling it like it is' and allowing for the subalterns (of British and US societies) to have a voice were familiar claims made by and for this approach and this strand of study. It is, of course, important to contextualize these studies within a climate of hostility to working-class youth and a society whose powerful agencies seemed bent on constructing youth as a 'deviant' group.

Equivalent studies within feminist sociology and cultural studies sought to reveal the isolation of women within prescribed domestic lives and the entrapment of the 'feminine career' (Comer 1984; Gavron 1968) Studies explored different aspects of women's lives and experience, for example, their encounters with the medical profession, how 'house-wives' used radio and television, aspects of women's leisure, acquisition of femininity by working-class girls, and so on (Deem 1986; Graham 1984; Hobson 1980; McRobbie 1978). All these studies were empirically based and used, more or less directly, expressions of women's experi-ence. The importance of attending to women's experience was con-sidered to be a political imperative of much feminist research. Indeed, during the early 1980s, when feminism was making inroads into academia, there were fierce debates about the politics of research, and a critique of the move from the so-called 'grass-roots' of the women's movement, seen to be the site for political action (see McRobbie 1982 for a convincing argument about the politics of pedagogy). Feminist research of this period can, then, be characterized as being made up of a rich variety of interventionist projects driven by the need to pay atten-tion to and document women's lived experience.

We can see here, across these disciplinary areas, what can be described as a democratic impulse motivating researchers whose aim was to document 'hidden' lives and worlds, to 'tell different stories' and reveal different accounts. This mode of research was often politically informed, many of its practitioners were beneficiaries of a broadening of educa-tional opportunity who brought aspects of their own backgrounds and experience to their scholarship, and all were working against the grain of the constraints of traditional disciplinary paradigms.

Reflecting on the development of feminist work within the academy, Sandra Harding has identified studies adopting this approach as 'femin-ist empirical' research, which is the main response to biases and prob-lems of exclusion within traditional disciplines, those of perceived androcentric and masculinist research methods (Harding 1986). For feminist scholars working within particular intellectual and institu-tional conditions, these were necessary, and often courageous, research strategies which opened up spaces for debate and argument. Bat-Ami Bar On, for example, argues that these accumulated empirical data have supported the claim that 'experience is not gender-neutral', indeed that gender is a constitutive element of experience. She insists that 'the claim has served feminists especially well in the academy, where curricula and pedagogy alike have come under feminist scrutiny and have been found lacking because of the exclusion of women's voices' (Bar On 1993: 83).

However, this 'documentary' or 'empirical' mode has a number of serious limitations. These limitations can, in part, be traced to the core of the enterprise: the highly problematic category of 'experience'. Joan Scott (1992), a historian, usefully discusses the status of experience in historiography. Here experience is the authenticating source, what she describes as the descriptive evidence of 'the already there'. Thus, in a similar way to cultural studies and feminist work, the project is one of rendering visible hitherto hidden lives and unacknowledged experiences. However, Scott is critical of the metaphor of visibility itself, implying as it does the possibility of a direct, unmediated apprehension of a world of transparent and knowable objects. She argues that, within history, the accumulation of more evidential accounts based on this approach merely provides an enlargement of the existing picture.

This has broader consequences in the extent to which it is possible for the mainstream disciplinary practices to accommodate this body of work. For, whilst the rich documenting of people's lives and experiences broadens the picture, these data can simply by 'bolted on' to existing work more or less unproblematically. These accounts, then, become another aspect of the field of study, rather than presenting a radical challenge to the theoretical and methodological assumptions of that field. A set of more radical questions need to be asked, such as: Why have *these* accounts been rendered invisible? What is it about the established methodologies which hierarchize particular ways of knowing? Is it possible, using exisiting and 'legitimate' theoretical approaches to, in Spivak's (1987) words, 'make visible the assignment of subject positions'? For Spivak, theories and methods should be called into question unless they enable us to

> Understand the operations of the complex and changing discursive and material processes by which identities are ascribed, resisted or embraced, and which processes themselves are unremarked, indeed achieve their effect because they aren't noticed. (1987: 214)

The feminist contribution to an investigation of methodology is substantial. The philosopher Sandra Harding is one of a number of feminist intellectuals who have drawn attention to the centrality of methodology in considering a feminist social science. She takes women's experience as a starting point and argues that

> Once we undertake to use women's experience as a resource to generate scientific problems, hypotheses, and evidence, to design research for women, and to place the researcher in the same critical plane as the research subject, traditional epistemological assumptions can no longer be made. (Harding 1987: 181)

This, then, gives rise to a feminist agenda for, in this case, social science, which asks questions such as: Who can be 'knowers' and what can be known? What is considered to be 'legitimate' knowledge? What is the nature of objectivity? What is the appropriate relationship between the researcher and her/his subjects? What is the purpose of the pursuit of knowledge? (Harding 1987: 181). To paraphrase: Who can know what about whom, by what means and to what purpose?' Furthermore, if the epistemological regimes of disciplinary areas cannot accommodate research problems suggested by data generated out of women's experience, then something must be done to question and challenge those regimes. These questions and challenges are well underway (Alcoff and Potter 1993; Butler and Scott 1992; Gunew 1990) and have produced a number of epistemological positions: notably the 'feminist standpoint', which insists that women are ontologically positioned in the world as women and therefore occupy a particular viewpoint (see Haraway 1991; Harding 1986, 1987; Stanley 1990, for different versions of this, and hooks 1981, who argues that this position is multiple and, therefore, a 'site of difference'); and 'postmodern' epistemologies influenced by post-structuralist theories of postmodernity with its emphasis on 'difference' (for example, Nicholson 1990).

I signal this important body of feminist work, and direct readers towards it, but I now want to move into a deeper exploration of 'experience' and to argue that its place within feminist and cultural studies research begs the kinds of questions with which I paraphrased Harding's feminist agenda, that is, 'Who can know what about whom, by what means and to what purpose?' It is then necessary to think about how 'experience' is used, what status it is given, and the modes of interpretation employed.

Surprising 'experience'

As I have already indicated, cultural studies has only intermittently engaged in epistemological debates but it is worth looking at some of the early statements from the Centre for Contemporary Cultural Studies (CCCS) regarding their interest in 'ethnography' as a developing and appropriate method for cultural studies analysis. The authors briefly discuss phenomenology and symbolic interactionism, finding a twin tendency towards idealism in their theoretical categories, or an 'atheoreticalness which seems to suggest that theory can arise somehow naturally from the data' (Hall et al. 1980: 74). Their choice and identification of 'ethnography' as their methodological approach has left its legacy for subsequent generations of researchers, but it is made clear here that the choice was driven by this very weakness in the ethnographic enterprise, that is, its 'strength against theoretical reductionism' and, to use Willis's now famous term, its ability to 'surprise'. However, it is clear that the

CCCS researchers were addressing analytical and theoretical questions much beyond an interest in 'experience' for its own sake or for its own guarantee. They continue:

> [T]he method has been generalized now for use in the study of central and mainstream cultural forms and for the study and explication of these forms in relation to their material contexts – web of external determinations – and the contribution they make to the social reproduction of society generally and of its patriarchal and productive relations. (Hall et al. 1980: 75)

The authors call for ethnography to be 'emancipated from its Weberian or phenomenological roots' and state that:

> [F]eminist interest in 'qualitative' methods springs from no idealist concern with self-generating (or merely classified) 'horizontal' cultural forms, but from a directly theoretical interest and a concern with determinations . . . it was necessary to return to experience and the subjective plane both to record and to substantiate this reality as a firm critique of available theory. (1980: 75)

The authors are insisting on using 'experience' as a starting point to explore those 'webs of determinants'; not for its own sake, nor as the authenticating voice, but in order to integrate 'lived experience' within a broader context of the social. This, of course, requires a theory of the social which, for CCCS at that time, was an 'uneasy marriage' of conflictual Marxist (production) and feminist (patriarchal) structures.

The need to employ ethnographic methods to provide 'a firm critique of available theory' must be understood both within a context of rapidly developing theoretical work informed by structuralism, and as an anti-reductionist move in relation to Marxist theories of culture. The authors of the piece under discussion are quite clear about that. What is interesting is the way this can be seen as a key 'determinant' in the choice of method(s) and the ways in which some studies developed: that is, in order to call something of a halt to the extravagances of rapidly developing theoretical work in which the active and creative human agent was being replaced by the ideologically constructed subject. This is expressed by Paul Willis thus: 'An ethnographic method shouts at us that however persuasive and inclusive some of the theoretical arguments concerning the formation of the subject may be, they can by no means fully account for real, solid, warm, *moving* and *acting* bodies in actual situations' (1982: 78). The moving and acting bodies were certainly being theoretically evacuated in Althusserian Marxism. It follows then that the nature of the 'surprise' is that it unsettles the theory. What can then be made of this de-stabilizing of theory is somewhat unclear and much rides on the resulting analysis of ethnographic material. If we look at Willis's study of the schooling of working-class boys, *Learning to Labour*, we see that, whilst he certainly represents 'the lads' as 'real, solid, warm moving and acting bodies', the picture his study paints is a classic example of Althusser's 'reproduction' theory in action. This is in spite of the fact that he demonstrates the moments of struggle and resistance which the lads put up along their way to the shop-floor. The point is that his theoretical framework was, perhaps, less flexible than his chosen method, thus the only way he could account for the lads was by identifying pockets of resistance.

The theme of 'resistance' is a powerful one which runs through many of the 'real, solid, warm mover-subjects' of cultural studies research. Many such accounts have been made to bear the heavy weight of theory. Within cultural studies, and especially in its 'populist' mode (McGuigan 1992), this has produced some familiar characters on the landscape: the active audience member, the semiotic guerilla, the agent of 'symbolic creativity', to name but three, all of whom are resisting dominant and powerful structures, whether they be those of class, of patriarchy or the products of powerful media conglomerates. Studies of the use of media and popular culture have, perhaps, themselves borne too much of the recent weight of empirical work within cultural studies, but in some of the reflections of these studies, if not the studies themselves, 'resistance' has been interpreted in a clearly spurious way. There is confusion here as to what exactly is being resisted. Is it, for instance, that subjects are actively resisting their own particular positioning within the social and cultural hierarchy? Or is it rather that they are resisting those over-deterministic theories of the subject which disallow the active creative agent?

The sensuous active agents are, then, 'used' as, if not authenticating, then authoritative sources which enable researchers to enter into what are essentially academic debates. The expressions of living agents about their own experiences are used *carte blanche* to work with theory. Thus human beings are presented as living their lives largely unaware of their own actions, or their positionality, their utterances used to give expression to theoretical positions.

Let me return to this question of 'surprise' and frame it rather differently in terms of an extremely valuable characteristic of certain kinds of qualitative or ethnographic methods, that of 'reflexivity'. I suggest that what we might look for is evidence of these elements of surprise informing the development of the research itself. This, of course, demands that we are given access to the research as process and some knowledge of the researcher's role in its development. The role of the 'reflexive researcher' has been discussed in relation to: the impact of the researcher on the chosen 'field' or group; the dynamics of the researcher and researched; the politics of research; cultural difference; power relations between researcher and researched. These debates are relatively new and have been taken up at different times by different disciplines. However, in some traditions of research, particularly in sociology and anthropology, the researcher has often been present in written accounts. This presence can function in different ways. For example, Paul Atkinson (1990) has discussed the writing of ethnographic texts and draws our attention to the rhetorical and literary strategies which anthropologists and sociologists adopt in their writing. He suggests that the narrative of the *quest* is common in ethnographic accounts, whereby the researcher moves from 'outsider' to 'insider' as he/she is portrayed through key stages of the research encounter. This revelation, and others like it, argues Atkinson (1990: 106), simply adds weight to the authenticity of the research. But there are dimensions of the 'researcher' which do not appear. These absences are in relation to the researcher's subjectivity and, to use Stanley's (1990) term, the conditions of production of knowledge, including the politics of the academy within and from which the researcher/subject speaks. Another manifestation of reflexivity are those researchers who turn to the politics of representation in examination and analysis of texts produced, which, although interesting in themselves, tend to side-step the more challenging questions of the politics of theories of knowledge (see Bell et al. 1993 for a discussion of these moves within anthropology).

These responses to the problematization of the role of the researcher and, more broadly, the politics of power/knowledge fall short of the more radical epistemologies which are suggested by feminist work. In order to expand on this, I suggest that cultural studies' engagement with ethnography and anthropology as a way of developing methods for studying lived cultures neglected the symbolic interactionism identified with the Chicago School and especially their studies of youth. Symbolic interactionists have employed the full range of 'qualitative' methods in attending to accounts of personal experience and observations of social interaction – that is, participant observation and interviews – and, furthermore, the researchers have generally written themselves into the narrative (Whyte 1943). Norman Denzin (1992) has recently provided a very useful examination of this 'tradition' and especially its move into the terrain of cultural studies. As his stated aim is to 'shape a critical, feminist cultural studies for symbolic interactionism' (Denzin 1992: 72), it would seem pertinent to examine what this might be and how it could contribute to a future set of cultural studies methodologies. The core of Denzin's critique of symbolic interactionism and its roots in American pragmatism is its refusal to acknowledge the 'postmodern subject' in that it is wedded to an epistemological realism; thus 'the ontological status of this world, in the post-modern period, is never seriously questioned by interactionists' (1992: 120). For Denzin, this requires an acknowledgement of the production of the subject through encounters and engagement with the symbolic world. He argues that a feminist politics which is based on an understanding of the institutionalization of cultural and social difference needs to be reflected in and acknowledged by symbolic interactionist research practice. Importantly, Denzin goes a step further by calling his community of symbolic interactionists to account for their celebration of the human in their 'moving tales of the powerless' (1992: 168), to come clean and 'see how our reflective gazes have contributed to this surveillance society' (1992: 169). He asks that 'we turn to the production of progressive, reflective texts and begin the difficult task of unmasking the taken-for-granted ideologies which have for far too long justified our self-serving voyeuristic project' (1992: 169).

Reflexivity: experience and process

Denzin is putting his finger on pressure points which have long been part of a feminist pulse. However, the point of distinction which gives feminist methodologies their particular edge and their unique contribution is first, and obviously, that women have been positioned and dealt with by powerful structures which operate in complex and contradictory ways in limiting and enabling women's lives. This recognition, through intellectual and political feminist movements, has informed the areas for research and the ways in which those can be explored most effectively. Crucial, also, is an understanding of knowledge as process, one that it is produced within a concrete and practical research setting for which the researcher is accountable. And finally, as Denzin identifies, there is the necessity of speaking from somewhere. This is to say that as researchers we are positioned ourselves within institutional contexts with access to academic and intellectual discourses, but our own subjectivity, biography and commitment are a constitutive part of the research process (Gray 1995). Feminist research is not only that done by women, with women, for women, but a methodology, a mode of research, which has developed through a politics and a practice in which the political, theoretical and epistemological have been *thought together* in order to understand, analyse, explain and critique women's position in society.

What is remarkable about feminist work is that this process is continuous and responsive to changing material conditions and, through the encouragement of dialogic research, to developing theoretical work. Feminist work has built upon the earlier feminist empirical projects but has also been highly critical of them. This critique comes in part from a political intervention, from working-class and black women, who argued that a version of 'women's experience' which essentialized middle-class and white experience was inadequate. In addition, important moves in the theorizing of subjectivity and identity, and in particular gendered identity, have enabled a research practice to develop which explores the construction of identity itself. Ruth Frankenberg, whose study *The Social Construction of Whiteness: White Women, Race Matters*, I shall discuss later, suggests that the issue is not simply that black women's experience differed from that of white women, but that 'white feminist women accounting for . . . experience were missing its "racialness" '. This she argues is to do with standpoint: 'because we were race privileged . . . we were not in a structural position to see the effects of racism on our lives, nor the significance of race in the shaping of U.S. society' (1993: 9). Frankenberg describes a way of knowing (or not knowing) the world which is based on a particular standpoint or positionality. This epistemology is that of situated knowledge, and suggests that our positionality gives us a particular way of knowing about the world. My argument would be that the extent to which the intellectual is prepared to investigate his/her positionality is what is at stake for a genuinely reflexive and radical use of the category 'experience'.

Learning from experience

The difficulties involved in the use of the category are clear and legion. However, it is the very recalcitrance of 'experience' which is, in my view, the strongest argument for its retention. This is in some ways to return to its potential for 'surprise', but not as some naive and innocent expression of the authentic event or knowledge expressed by the individual who is then understood as the locus of agency; rather as representations and expressions of: direct personal participation in or observation of events; accumulated knowledge of the world in particular sets of circumstances; what it is like to live in these circumstances and the personal feelings and emotions which are engendered. This, then, is to suggest that the first step forward is to understand 'experience' as a non-unified category which can be mobilized in a number of ways, for different purposes and with different epistemological outcomes. These variant categories, and the 'data' which different methods will generate, are challenging, unwieldy and possibly intractable, but there is a need to acknowledge the nature of experience, its status, what is being drawn from this source in terms of analysis and interpretation, and how it relates to methodology and the methods employed in any study.

Surprisingly, perhaps, I want to promote the humble interview as an absolutely central discursive technology in the generation of experience, but, again, one which should be seen as a variable set of strategic methods within research, and approached with appropriate circumspection. This is in contrast to some critics of cultural studies research who have called for more properly executed ethnographies (Gillespie 1995; Nightingale 1993; Radway 1988). Here the argument is that those studies carried out in cultural studies thus far, especially those addressing the consumption of popular texts and media forms, have been inadequate as ethnographies, relying as they mostly do on one method, that of the interview. These debates are in some ways a consequence of that early methodological legacy left by CCCS and researchers like David Morley and myself who have described their research as having 'ethnographic intent' (Gray 1992; Morley 1986). However, I agree with John Fiske in his review of Virginia Nightingale's essay 'What's Ethnographic about Ethnographic Audience Research?' (1993) when he suggests that these critics, by locating their critique in the comparison between cultural studies and anthropology, miss the point of an inter/multidisciplinary cultural studies project which is, in Fiske's words, located 'between

interpretive, textualist cultural studies and [the] *social'* (1996). He goes
further and suggests that what Nightingale fails to recognize is 'that the
origin and purpose of [audience] studies lay in investigating the concept
of "the struggle for meaning" ' (1996: 370). I would concur, but go further
and insist that what cultural studies work attempts to do is to explore
these struggles for meaning in relation to the construction of social and
cultural identities. Extended time spent with groups as participant
observers would not necessarily be any more productive, in this respect
than listening to people in long conversational interviews. In fact,
extending the range of descriptive accounts might be the only possible
achievement here.[3] I suggest, therefore, that more sophisticated ethnographies are not necessarily the best direction, focused, as they would
undoubtedly be, on grounded groups and communities, placed in time
and space (Radway 1988). These spatial and temporal understandings of
'community' are being problematized in so many ways that this kind of
project is increasingly difficult to defend, even within anthropology itself
(Ferguson and Gupta 1996). I would argue that developing methods
which enable the exploration of the 'webs of determinants (and indeter-
minants)' in constructions of 'the self' as complexly constituted through
social, cultural and sexual identities is where our energies should be
placed.

In conclusion, therefore, I want to suggest some ways in which
experience can be retained as a category under three modes: testimony,
(auto)biography and life story, and suggest some of the methods which
might be employed.

Testimony

Something worth noting is that people live through particular events and
witness incidents about which they have, often urgent, stories to tell. One
very potent version of this mode of 'eye witness' account is that of
'testimony'. In one week in January 1982 Elisabeth Burgos-Debray
listened to and recorded the story told to her by Rigoberta Menchu, a
Quiche Indian woman, about her life and struggles in Guatemala.
Introducing the narrative, Burgos-Debray says of Menchu:

> [H]er life story is an account of contemporary history rather than of
> Guatemala itself. It is in this sense that it is exemplary: she speaks for all the
> Indians of the American subcontinent . . . she is a privileged witness. (1984)

This notion of privilege should be understood as that possessed by one
who is consciously speaking for a subjugated peoples. Menchu does this
through a detailed account of her own life as a Quiche Indian, a people
whose lives have been shadowed by cultural discrimination throughout
centuries of brutal regimes. Testimonies such as hers are a poignant
example of the speaking of experience which is relatable to oral traditions and the role of story-tellers within them. Walter Benjamin described

the role of the story-teller as a person who had the ability 'to fashion the raw material of experience, his [*sic*] own and that of others, in a solid, useful and unique way' (1973: 108). Burgos-Debray worked to 'faithfully reproduce' this account and not to subject it to interpretation or analysis in its published form. Clearly, this kind of account has a significance in the broader political and cultural context outside of the academy, but it should be a clear reminder that millions of people are painfully experiencing the consequences of brutal political and economic regimes and for whom the notion of 'fragmented subjectivity' is a painfully lived one. To quote Menchu's final words:

> [Therefore], my commitment to our struggle knows no boundaries nor limits. This is why I've travelled to many places where I've had the opportunity to talk about my people. . . . Nevertheless, I'm still keeping my Indian identity a secret. I'm still keeping secret what I think no-one should know. Not even anthropologists or intellectuals, no matter how many books they have, can find out all our secrets. (1984: 247)

A salutory reminder of the limits to knowledge indeed, and that, in my view, there must be a place in our work for this experiential mode.

(Auto)biography

The example taken from testimony is a very particular kind of autobiography, but this is an increasingly influential genre within the humanities and social science. It has been especially important within feminist work, and Elspeth Probyn (1993) examines the notion of the gendered self and the possibility, or otherwise, of 'speaking positions' for that self within cultural studies. She is concerned to find ways of using (our)selves and our experience in our intellectual work and critical analysis. Probyn notes how the self is 'legitimated and required' in some situations and locations and not in others. She wants to elaborate ways of tactically speaking in strategic loci where the sound of the self is unexpected and to 'reveal the self as both the possession of experience and emotion, and as a way of conceptualizing the effectivity of that possession' (1993: 87). She cites Carolyn Steedman's *Landscape for a Good Woman* as exemplary in this respect. Steedman draws on the memories of her past and, in particular, her relationship with her mother, and is able, through different theoretical perspectives, to reflect on both her (auto)biography and the adequacies of the theoretical accounts. Probyn describes this method as a kind of double move between an ontological register, a way of being in the world based on experience, and an epistemological register, through which that being/experience can become a way of knowing. Probyn's work is helpful in enabling cultural theorists and critics to find a speaking position within their own analyses, without necessarily slipping into a narrowly subjective mode. Clearly autobiography is an important form for both cultural studies and feminism, concerned to draw on our own experience as a resource, but also in thinking more analytically about how that can find its place within our epistemological projects. Similarly, the category of experience can be tremendously effective in feminist or cultural studies pedagogic practice in encouraging students to reflect on their own knowledge of the world. Probyn's insight is useful as a strategy to think beyond experience and to encourage an understanding of the intersection of the public (social-cultural) with the private (intimate-subjective).

Life story

The life story technique is a well-established method in oral history, where it has tended to be used, as Scott will attest, in order to generate 'alternative' accounts of the world, but which has great potential for the exploration of the construction of identities. A very good and recent example of the employment of a version of this method is Ruth Frankenberg's (1993) study referred to above, which draws on women's accounts of their lives as a resource for analysing racialized society. Frankenberg argues that these life stories need to be explained and understood by 'mapping' them onto broader social processes. Speaking of the women she interviewed and the interview process itself, Frankenberg states:

> [I]nterviewees were multiply positioned in relation to these life narratives. On the one hand, they were coproducers of the narratives. On the other hand, they were observers, both of their environments and of themselves as they retold and reevaluated what had gone before. This reevaluation was frequently an explicit component of the narratives. (1993: 42)

Here is a clear statement of the complexity of the life story and the intensity and richness of data which it can achieve. Frankenberg captures the shifting dynamics and positionalities adopted during the interviews, but also the self-reflexivity of the interviewees as they told their stories. It is in this self-reflexive space that the work of the production of the self takes place; the self-awareness of the subjects of her study is simply not acknowledged in more conventional uses of life story and the conversational interview. Frankenberg goes on to discuss the interview narratives:

> They are self-reflexive, and they confirm as well as contradict other accounts of the social world outside of the project. In a wider sense, they intersect with other local and global histories. (1993: 42)

Frankenberg's study, among other things, is able to '[make] explicit and tangible some of the ways in which white women's life experience is racially structured' (1993: 22).

Writing recently, Ken Plummer (1995), from a symbolic interactionist perspective, has drawn attention to the importance of stories in understanding the social, for individuals and for those broader social stories which are in circulation. Similarly, Denzin uses the concept of story as a way of exploring the ways people use publicly available stories in order to make sense of their lives. Whilst I would argue that cultural studies and feminism need to continue working towards more sophisticated methods which engage with 'lived cultures', those subjects must be allowed to be the knowledgeable and knowing subjects. Working with the life story and ideas of narrative in our analysis will enable us to conceptualize experience as, in de Lauretis's words,

> the process by which, for all social beings, subjectivity is constructed. Through that process one places oneself or is placed in social reality and so perceives and comprehends as subjective (referring to, originating in oneself) those relations – material, economic and inter-personal – which are in fact social, and, in a larger perspective, historical. (1984: 27)

Accounts of experience, as they might be given, remain a rich and necessary source for our work. Both feminism and cultural studies have, in different and similar ways, recognized this fact. It is my view that a post-structuralist feminist informed methodology, insisting as it does on the problematizing of all categories, on a clarity and openness in method and approach and a genuine reflexivity, can continue to enlighten and enrich the processes of research into cultures.

Notes

A version of this paper was presented at the Crossroads in Cultural Studies Conference, Tampere, Finland, July 1996.

1. I realize that there is a nostalgic element to this version of the early Women's Liberation Movement and would note the specificity of these groups as predominantly white and middle class.
2. See Maureen Cain's (1993) discussion of Foucault's contribution to feminism.
3. See Hammersley (1992) for a discussion of the limits of ethnography.

References

Aaron, J. and Walby, S. (eds) (1991) *Out of the Margins: Women's Studies in the Nineties*, London: The Falmer Press.

Alcoff, L. and Potter, E. (eds) (1993) *Feminist Epistemologies*, London and New York: Routledge.

Atkinson, P. (1990) *The Ethnographic Imagination: Textual Construction of Reality*, London and New York: Routledge.

Bar On, B. (1993) 'Marginality and Epistemic Privilege', in L. Alcoff and E. Potter (eds), *Feminist Epistemologies*, London and New York: Routledge.

Bell, D., Caplan, P. and Karim, W.J. (eds) (1993) *Gendered Fields: Women, Men and Ethnography*, London and New York: Routledge.

Benjamin, W. (1973) *Illuminations*, Glasgow: Fontana.

Brunsdon, C. (1996) 'A Thief in the Night: Stories of Feminism in the 1970s at CCCS', in D. Morley and K.-H. Chen (eds), *Critical Dialogues in Cultural Studies*, London and New York: Routledge. pp. 276–86.

Burgos-Debray, E. (1984) 'Introduction', in R. Menchu, *I Rigoberta Menchu*, London: Verso.

Butler, J. and Scott, J.W. (eds) (1992) *Feminists Theorize the Political*, London and New York: Routledge.

Cain, M. (1993) 'Foucault, Feminism and Feeling: What Foucault Can and Cannot Contribute to Feminist Epistemology', in C. Ramazanoglu (ed.), *Up Against Foucault: Explorations of Some Tensions Between Foucault and Feminism*, London and New York: Routledge.

Comer, L. (1984) *Wedlocked Women*, Leeds: Feminist Books.

Deem, R. (1986) *All Work and No Play? A Study of Women and Leisure*, Milton Keynes: Open University.

de Lauretis, T. (1984) *Alice Doesn't*, Bloomington: Indiana University Press.

Denzin, N. (1992) *Symbolic Interactionism and Cultural Studies*, Oxford and Cambridge: Basil Blackwell.

Ferguson, J. and Gupta, A. (1996) 'Space, Ethnography and the Question of Method in Cultural Studies', paper presented at Crossroads in Cultural Studies, Tampere, Finland.

Fiske, J. (1996) 'Down Under Cultural Studies', *Cultural Studies*, 10(2): 369–74.

Frankenburg, R. (1993) *The Social Construction of Whiteness: White Women, Race Matters*, London: Routledge.

Franklin, S., Lury, C. and Stacey, J. (eds) (1991) *Off-Centre: Feminism and Cultural Studies*, London: HarperCollins.

Friedan, B. (1977) *The Feminine Mystique*, New York: Dell.

Gavron, H. (1968) *The Captive Wife: Conflicts of Housebound Mothers*, Harmondsworth: Penguin.

Gillespie, M. (1995) *Television, Ethnicity and Cultural Change*, London: Routledge.

Graham, H. (1984) *Women, Health and the Family*, Brighton: Wheatsheaf.

Gray, A. (1992) *Video Playtime: The Gendering of a Leisure Technology*, London: Routledge.

Gray, A. (1995) 'I Want to Tell You a Story: The Narratives of *Video Playtime*', in B. Skeggs (ed.), *The Production of Feminist Cultural Theory*, Manchester: Manchester University Press.

Gunew, S. (1990) *Feminist Knowledge: Critique and Construct*, London: Routledge.

Hall, S. (1992) 'Cultural Studies and its Theoretical Legacies', in L. Grossberg, C. Nelson and P. Treichler (eds), *Cultural Studies*, London and New York: Routledge.

Hall, S., Hobson, D., Lowe, A. and Willis, P. (eds) (1980) *Culture, Media, Language*, London: Hutchinson.

Hammersley, M. (1992) *What's Wrong with Ethnography? Methodological Explorations*, London and New York: Routledge.

Haraway, D. (1991) *Simians, Cyborgs and Women: The Reinvention of Nature*, London: Free Association Books.

Harding, S. (1986) *The Science Question in Feminism*, Milton Keynes: Open University Press.

Harding, S. (ed.) (1987) *Feminism and Methodology*, Milton Keynes: Open University Press.

Hinds, H., Phoenix, A. and Stacey, J. (eds) (1992) *Working Out: New Directions for Women's Studies*, London: The Falmer Press.

Hobson, D. (1978) 'Housewives: Isolation as Oppression', in Women's Studies Group, *Women Take Issue*, London: Hutchinson.

Hobson, D. (1980) 'Housewives and the Mass Media', in S. Hall, D. Hobson, A. Lowe and P. Willis (eds), *Culture, Media, Language*. London: Hutchinson.

Hoggart, R. (1958) *The Uses of Literacy*, Harmondsworth: Penguin.

hooks, b. (1981) *Ain't I a Woman? Black Women and Feminism*, Boston. Mass.: South End Press.

Lury, C. (1995) 'The Rights and Wrongs of Culture: Issues of Theory and Methodology', in B. Skeggs (ed.), *The Production of Feminist Cultural Theory*, Manchester: Manchester University Press.

McGuigan, J. (1992) *Cultural Populism*, London and New York: Routledge.

McRobbie, A. (1978) 'Working Class Girls and the Culture of Femininity', in Women's Studies Group, *Women Take Issue*, London: Hutchinson.

McRobbie, A. (1982) 'The Politics of Feminist Research: Between Talk, Text and Action', *Feminist Review*, 12: 46–57.

Menchu, R. (1984) *I Rigoberta Menchu*, London: Verso.

Morley, D. (1986) *Family Television: Cultural Power and Domestic Leisure*, London: Comedia.

Nicholson, L.J. (ed.) (1990) *Feminism/Post Modernism*. London and New York: Routledge.

Nightingale, V. (1993) 'What's Ethnographic about Ethnographic Audience Research?', in G. Turner (ed.), *Nation, Culture, Text: Australian Cultural and Media Studies*, London and New York: Routledge.

Oakley, A. (1974) *The Sociology of Housework*, London: Martin Robertson.

Plummer, K. (1995) *Telling Sexual Stories: Power, Change and Social Worlds*, London: Routledge.

Probyn, E. (1993) *Sexing the Self: Gendered Positions in Cultural Studies*, London and New York: Routledge.

Radway, J. (1988) *Reading the Romance: Women, Patriarchy, and Popular Literature*, Chapel Hill and London: University of North Carolina Press.

Ramazanoglu, C. (ed.) (1993) *Up Against Foucault: Explorations of Some Tensions Between Foucault and Feminism*, London and New York: Routledge.

Scott, J. (1992) 'Experience', in J. Butler and J.W. Scott (eds), *Feminists Theorize the Political*, London and New York: Routledge.

Spivak, G.C. (1987) *In Other Worlds: Essays in Cultural Politics*, New York: Routledge.

Stanley, L. (ed.) (1990) *Feminist Praxis: Research, Theory and Epistemology in Feminist Sociology*, London and New York, Routledge.

Stanley, L. and Wise, S. (1983) *Breaking Out: Feminist Consciousness and Feminist Research*, London: Routledge & Kegan Paul.

Thompson, E.P. (1963) *The Making of the English Working Class*, London: Gollancz.

Tudor, A. (1995) 'Culture, Mass Communication and Social Agency', *Theory, Culture and Society*, 12: 81–107.

Whyte, W.F. (1943) *Street Corner Society: The Social Structure of an Italian Slum*, Chicago: University of Chicago Press.

Williams, R. (1958) 'Culture is Ordinary', in N. MacKenzie (ed.), *Conviction*, London: MacGibbon & Kee.

Williams, R. (1979) *Politics and Letters*, London: Verso.

Willis, P. (1982) 'Male School Counterculture', in *U203 Popular Culture*. Milton Keynes: Open University. pp. 75–103.

Women's Studies Group (1978) *Women Take Issue*, London: Hutchinson.

PART II
RESEARCHES

5

Writing the Self: The End of the Scholarship Girl

Carolyn Steedman

How has it come about that we are all of us now living and writing under the autobiographical injunction? There are commentators from many fields of inquiry to tell us that this is indeed the case. Introducing forms of self-narration from a variety of representational traditions, the editors of *De/Colonizing the Subject* suggest that 'autobiographical writing is at this historical moment a "genre of choice," for authors, audiences and critics' (Smith and Watson 1992: xviii). Anthony Giddens describes a three-hundred-year development in the West by which personhood and self-identity have come to be understood as 'the self . . . reflexively understood by the person in terms of her or his biography' (1991: 53). In *Modernity and Self-Identity* 'autobiography' is understood not so much as a form of writing, nor as a literary genre, but rather as a mode of cognition, and the process of actually writing an autobiography, getting it published and having it read is seen as a minor variant of a more general 'autobiographical thinking'. In this 'broad sense of an inter-pretive self-history produced by the individual concerned, [auto-biography] whether written down or not . . . is actually the core of self-identity in modern life' (Giddens 1991: 53).

Commenting on what she calls the 'efflorescence of personal criticism' (of which her own *Getting Personal* is certainly an example), Nancy K. Miller suggests that the current zeal for displaying yourself and your story in academic writing has something to do 'with the gradual . . . waning of enthusiasm for a mode of Theory, whose authority . . . depended finally on the theoretical evacuation of the social subjects producing it' (1992: xi). However, much recent feminist discussion of the autobiographical injunction suggests that this is simply not the case – that enthusiasm for the autobiographical act cannot be aligned with a fervour for the Real. Rather, autobiography is intellectually alluring – is 'the genre of choice' – *because* of its dizzying theoretical premise that 'all "I"s are sites where generalized operations of power press ineluctably on the subject' (Smith and Watson 1992: xiv), and *because* it stands at the confluence of many post-Foucauldian understandings that have shaped and continue to shape postmodernist thought.

When a literary genre becomes more than itself – when it becomes, variously, a cognitive form, a mode of academic writing, a way of being in the world – then the time has come to investigate its production at a particular point in time and in a limited setting; the time has come to submit large-scale claims about autobiography to some kind of historical scrutiny. To undertake this kind of investigation also suggests how sociological reductionism might be avoided in cultural history. The premise is that autobiographical texts are not to be accounted for by their author's own autobiography; rather they offer evidence of the historical relationship between stories – the circulation of particular narratives – and societies.

In Britain in the 1980s, a particular kind of women's autobiography emerged as 'a genre of choice'. Liz Heron's edited collection of 1985, *Truth, Dare or Promise: Girls Growing Up in the 1950s*, was the first of several accounts written by women born between the late 1930s and early 1950s. Originary narratives of the 1980s, which began with the Second World War and then described personal progresses through the 1950s and 1960s, they were also accounts of the effect of the 1944 Education Act and the inauguration of the National Health Service in 1948. What frames all of the disparate and different accounts to be found in *Truth, Dare or Promise*, in Sara Maitland's *Very Heaven* (1989) and in Micheline Wandor's *Once a Feminist* (1990), is the war. It is this cataclysmic historical event that shapes the everyday language and common understandings by which the children remembered in the pages of these books are socialized.

The late 1970s and early 1980s witnessed much academic and journalistic re-evaluation of the first post-war Labour government. The debate scrutinized both the 1950s welfare state and a contemporary Conservative evocation of a much earlier period of British history as a source of cultural value (see, for example, Seabrook 1978), and it may well have prompted much of this writing by women. The contributors to Liz Heron's edited collection, *Truth, Dare or Promise*, for instance, were asked to place their personal narratives of the 1950s within socio-political time. However, the 1980s' preoccupation with the 1950s as the decade that might answer the question 'What went wrong?' does not entirely explain the autobiographical form that this corpus of women's writing took. It owed at least as much to contemporary feminism, and the lessons that feminism taught about the uses of the past – personal pasts as well as public ones – in coming to consciousness of a woman's current situation (Lovell 1990a: 21–67; Steedman 1992).

People's history, oral history, the worker-writers' movement and community publishing were also manifestations of the changed status of individual stories and personal lives in the post-war period. But, if women's autobiography of the 1980s is to be considered as one of the many consequences of the People's Peace, then a historical account of it has to return to the People's War – and not just to the Second World War, but to the first one as well. War and its aftermath are made organizing critical devices in Kathryn Dodd's discussion of the large number of women's autobiographies that (along with biographies of women) were published in the 1920s and 1930s. Dodd argues that this writing and choice of genres was part of a more general assessment of the First World War and the pre-war years, so that recent conflict and death might be seen as having meaning and significance in a wider social and political context. Women's appropriation of the masculine form of autobiography was also, she suggests, connected to women's transformation into political and social subjects by the Emancipation of the People Acts of 1918 and 1928 (Dodd 1990: 127–37).

In a similar way, the Second World War also produced an auto-biographical assessment of self and social place by a number of women. This chapter is about a small number of autobiographical texts produced by women born between 1939 and 1951. They are disparate texts, pieces of fiction and autobiography, written and published and reflected on by their authors at different points in the forty years after the war. What allows them to be considered together is *not* their authors – the birthdate of the writer, her class origins, her own life story – but rather their common plot and theme. Their plot is the educational progress of a girl born into a working-class family, and her success in making a journey of educational transition that is also a journey of class transition, by entry to a grammar school and then some form of higher education during the 1950s and 1960s. Their collective theme – the shaping force of educational and welfare legislation in working-class girls' and women's lives – is important, and the literary witnessing of it in this way is of great historical interest. But the form and structure of these texts offers the more compelling evidence of the period in question, and of the shaping of psychic structure by the state in the post-war years.

This, then, is about the stories that get told in particular historical periods, the account that writers are compelled to give of certain historical events and processes, and the desire for these narratives that their audiences express in their reading of them. Who tells the story, whether or not it purports to be told autobiographically, or presents itself as a fiction, when it is written, and when it is published, are important questions to ask – but important for a different sort of inquiry from the one being pursued here. In 1964 Margaret Drabble published a fictional account of the Scholarship Girl's progress, telling a tale through the device of a heroine who arrives in the golden city from a quite different class background from the one occupied by her actually existing, historically extant author. But that's not the point; the point is the *story* that is told and listened to: the story of the post-war settlement and the dizzying educational success within it that the fictional Clara Maugham inscribes.

Why does this kind of story about the 1940s and 1950s get plotted and figured in this way? Why does it emerge when it does, and why does it stop being told in that particular way? To pose these questions demonstrates at least the negative virtue of avoiding reductionism, that is, of suggesting that the events described in *Jerusalem the Golden* are 'true', or that they tell us very much about Margaret Drabble. More positively, and even though they cannot be answered, these questions allow us to propose that the novel, the character at its centre – this particular Scholarship Girl, and what she *means*, what it is she *represents* – constitute historical evidence of the period under discussion which it is the purpose of this chapter to outline.

There are two 'Ends' to the Scholarship Girl; but to evoke her in the first place is a deliberate anachronism, my device for signalling the end of a particular social phenomenon. Strictly speaking, there were hardly any scholarship girls in the 1950s after the 1944 Education Act came into effect. With the establishment of free, compulsory secondary education for all, only that tiny number of girls who won local authority awards to attend the old endowed fee-paying grammar schools or the public day schools were technically scholarship pupils. Here I have adopted the term 'Scholarship Girl' more broadly to include and describe those children who passed the 11+ examination and went as a select band through the narrow gates to a now freely available grammar and high school education. 'End' also and more particularly refers to the end-stop of the texts discussed here. It is their structure and their particularly marked ending that allow them to be discussed together, as a kind of modern *Bildungsroman*, and also as developments of the classic 'childhood' of late nineteenth-century autobiographical writing.

What follows is also a contribution to existing historical accounts of autobiographical practices in Britain from the sixteenth century to the present day. My tale, which I tell out of other people's stories, cannot escape its destiny as a narrative of national identity, for something 'known' about the modern self is that it was forged in the reworking of men's and women's relationship to God, forced by the Reformation, and crucially mediated by writing (see, for example, Haller 1958). The self that we understand was produced in this way was a Protestant self; the accounts of it are legion, and it is one of the better known aspects of 'Our Island Story'.[1]

What is absent from this conventionally told tale is any account of the habit of self-narration as a taught and learned activity. The modern scholars quoted at the beginning of this chapter describe or celebrate 'the genre of choice' as something that people simply *do*, or as a practice that is simply available to be embraced when the spirit of modernity (or postmodernity) moves. Yet practices of writing are often the result of what is recommended, prescribed and sometimes made a matter of instruction in different historical epochs. There is a case for making connections between what the adherents of seventeenth-century sects and congregations learned from each other's written productions, and the massive programme of teaching self-expression in writing that was in operation in state schools in Britain in the forty years after the Second World War. In both cases, forms of writing were matters of instruction, and autobiographical practices were recommended and transmitted. The Scholarship Girls I discuss wrote under the influence of a twentieth-century pedagogic programme of self-expression, and of self-writing – indeed, of selfhood – taught to children in schools in the decades following the Second World War.

'Creative writing' developed in British primary schools from about 1950 onwards, and by the early 1980s was a timetabled lesson (and sometimes satirized as the structure of an entire pedagogy) for all primary school children in the society. As a practice it was promoted by 'progressive' educationalists, in training colleges and in schools, and was endorsed by Her Majesty's Inspectors of Schools; moreover, the famous Plowden Report of 1967, which was the result of a government inquiry into primary education, gave the practice unqualified support (Central Advisory Committee for Education 1967).

The Plowden Committee provided its own history of progressive education and reported on the astonishing changes that had taken place in educational practice since the end of the war. The Committee suggested that 'perhaps the most dramatic of all the revolutions in English teaching is in the amount and quality of children's writing':

> The code of 1862 required no writing other than transcription or dictation until Standard VI. . . . In the thirties, independent writing in the infant school and lower junior school rarely extended beyond a sentence or two. . . . Now . . . there is free fluent and copious writing on a great variety of subject matter . . . Its essence is that much of it is personal and that the writers are communicating something that really engaged their minds and imaginations. (Central Advisory Committee on Education 1967, Volume 1: 218–19)[2]

The Committee thought that 'creative writing' was rather a grand term for what children produced. Nevertheless, by the late 1960s it was commonly used to describe children's personal, free writing. Teachers and other educators of the 1950s and 1960s rarely used the term 'autobiography' or 'autobiographical writing' to describe this kind of practice. What they were describing by using the term 'creative writing' was a kind of ethical self-cultivation, to be achieved by children using the written word. 'What Is Good Children's Writing?' asked the journal *Use of English* in 1952. It was writing that released 'the younger child's inner creativeness' ('What Is Good Children's Writing?' 1952: 71). Formal distinctions between this kind of writing and conventionally defined 'autobiographical writing' are not very important here. It was not particularly expected that the child would write in his or her own voice, about his or her own life (though this kind of writing developed rapidly from the mid-1960s onwards). What *was* expected was that the child would be 'involved', by being presented with subjects that allowed him or her 'to draw on first-hand experiences, which are relevant to the life he lives, or which stimulate and release his imagination to a lively and sincere response' ('Creative Writing' 1964: 31). What mattered was that 'sincere response', which in the early years of the period under discussion was understood to be dependent on the teacher's gift to the children of 'vivid first-hand experience' (Stevens 1953: 126–32).

The stakes were very high and the cultural mission of the English teacher of enormous significance: one account from the 1970s of English teaching in England talks about its 'ambitious heart' (Inglis 1975: 11–18). In 1973 the Head of the English Department at a rural secondary modern school drew on the work of Lev Vygotsky, G.H. Mead and the new cultural anthropology of Jack Goody in order to express the hope:

> that in encouraging [children] to the practice of writing about things that concern them, for readers who are concerned about them, and thus helping them to find the individual selves they have become, we may also be helping to protect them from that extreme awareness of individuality that we call alienation. Thus may education compensate for society. (Thomas 1973: 74–81)[3]

Moreover, teachers and educationalists – like this Head of English – were aware of their own history, placing what they were doing with children in the tradition of English studies inaugurated by F.R Leavis in the 1930s under the auspices of the Cambridge English School, and disseminated through the journal *Scrutiny* (see Mulhern 1979). Even Ministers of Education knew this history. In the summer of 1964 Edward Boyle congratulated the journal *Use of English* on twenty-five years of existence, saying that it was 'one of the good things which we owe in the long run to the Cambridge English School' ('Twenty-Five' 1964: 243). A few years later a Head of English at a Somerset secondary school filled in the historical details:

> Although it is difficult to define, there now seems no doubt that there is a 'New English'. It perhaps took tangible form with the publication of *Reflections* in 1963, and received semi-official recognition with the Schools Council *Working Paper No. 3, English*, in 1965 (HMSO). But this was only the crystallisation out of what had been in suspension for many years. *Culture and Environment*, first published as long ago as 1933, was possibly the key book: the young men who studied this in their sixth-form days have now become heads of English Departments and writers of English books.

He went on to note that '[t]he interaction of personalities in the movement is significant: for example, it is not just chance that both Esmor Jones, the first Secretary of NATE [National Assocation for the Teaching of English], and David Holbrook . . . were both at Downing College, Cambridge, when Dr Leavis was English Tutor there' (Smith 1970: 4).[4]

Of equal importance in this history was the name of I.A. Richards, not least because of the astonishing permeation through the education system of the critical practice he inaugurated at Cambridge in the 1930s

(Thompson 1971: 3–13). Richards concluded his *Practical Criticism* of 1929 with the assertion that 'the lesson of all criticism is that we have nothing to rely upon in making our choices but ourselves' (1929: 351). He argued that 'the whole apparatus of critical rules and principles is the means to the attainment of a finer, more precise, more discriminating communication', and understood his task to be the creation of a proper reader, an adequate reader, who could respond appropriately to text. *Practical Criticism* was a university class reader and a manual for university teachers, showing examples of responses to poetry that had emerged in Richards's Cambridge seminars. There are no names and dates attached to the poems students were to study and discuss: the reader was to come to the text without preconceptions, bring only him- or herself to the poem.

Denys Thompson later attested to the very great changes that this critical practice brought about. Comparing the Cambridge English examination papers of 1963 with those of 1925, he said that 'a knowledge of history, social background, linguistic origins and Aristotle, had ceased to be tested' (Thompson 1973: 299). Thompson approved of this change, which by the late 1960s had spread far beyond the walls of ancient universities. In 1973 the University of London regulations for GCE English mentioned 'liveliness of response and sincerity of interest' as the paramount considerations in assessing sixteen-year-olds' examination answers. Pupils were expected to show evidence of 'a personal response', and examiners were often to complain about the 'lack of genuine personal response', and the 'received opinion evidenced'. Methods for assessing genuineness of response were developed:

> The evidence of a thoughtful response, of a candidate's having imaginatively 'lived through' the experiences of the text, is often provided by the careful, in some cases instinctive, choice of verbs, adverbs and adjectives with which the description of a character or an episode is presented. Such answers come alive.

Adopted as a democratic critical practice throughout the school system – for each child possessed the rich resource of his or her own critical response, and was not dependent on the unequal distribution of interpretive devices (on actually *knowing* something about history, or a literary tradition) – it simultaneously defined most responses as inadequate, for *Practical Criticism* came accompanied by other manifestos of Cambridge English. In his pamphlet of 1930, *Mass Civilisation and Minority Culture*, F.R Leavis put forward a claim for the study of literature which later became the mission statement of the journal *Scrutiny*. He wrote that:

> [I]n any period it is upon a very small minority that the discerning appreciation of art and literature depends . . . only a few who are capable of unprompted, first-hand judgement. . . . Upon this minority depends our power of profiting by the finest human experience of the past. Upon them depend the implicit standards that order the finer living of an age. In their

keeping is the language . . . upon which fine living depends. . . . By 'culture' I mean the use of such a language . . . (Leavis 1930: 3–5)

There are several accounts of the way in which 'a very small minority' was given a missionary task by Leavisite criticism, which involved sending a hand-picked band into the educational system, to organize resistance to advertisements, movies, American milk-bar culture, women's magazines and pulp-fiction (Baldick 1987: 196–234; Dixon 1991: 79–134, passim; Doyle 1989: 79–134; Mathieson 1975: 85–142). However, in the absence of any research on the movement of personnel from the Cambridge English School to the secondary schools and then into the training colleges to educate the aspiring teachers of primary school children in the period 1935–75 (though suspicions that this was the actual route the practice followed are reasonable ones), it is best to rely on the histories recounted above: of the impact of Leavis and Thompson's *Culture and Environment*, and the direct use by school teachers of *Scrutiny* and Leavisite principles of criticism in their daily classroom practice, from the mid-1930s onwards.[5]

The taught and learned practices of the self promoted through English teaching in the schools in the post-war years were connected, in as yet unexamined ways, with the reformulation of class politics in Britain, and the development of forms of political analysis and action that focused on the lived experience of working-class people. In *Poor Citizens* David Vincent explores the relationship between the poor and the state in twentieth-century Britain. He suggests that families came to be seen as poor when they could no longer keep their stories private – were forced to tell them to Poor Law Relieving Officers and Boards of Guardians (later, Social Security officials) in order to obtain state benefits, to Schools Attendance Officers, school teachers, policemen; to Uncle; to the corner shop when trying to get tick . . . to a neighbourhood that had the most sophisticated repertoire of devices for reading the marks of poverty inscribed on bodies, clothes, a way of moving through the streets (Vincent 1991: 3). A concomitant development of this enforced auto-biographical mode in the second half of the twentieth century was the encouragement of children's stories by an agency of the state, so that a recuperative selfhood might be given to the deprived.

A more or less official pedagogy of creative writing in schools has to be considered in relationship to the post-war expansion of adult educa-tion, the development of the worker-writers and community publishing movement (and thus an astonishing flowering of working-class auto-biography in the 1970s), the rapid growth of community theatre, the folk movement and its deliberate forging of community between past and present narratives of the poor, the practice of oral histories of the working class, the development of the History Workshop movement and, towards the end of the 1960s, the practice of consciousness-raising in the emergent women's movement (for instance, see Morley and Worpole 1983). All these practices operated on the assumption that the subaltern *could* speak, that through articulation in spoken or written words, the dispossessed could come to an understanding of their own story (Spivak 1988: 271–313). That story – that life – could, by various means, be returned to the people who had struggled to tell or to write it, and be used as basis for political action.

Self-writing was also used as part of the ethical preparation of intending teachers, a form of training reified in Peter Abbs's publication of 1974, *Autobiography in Education*, which he described as 'an introduction to the subjective discipline of Autobiography and of its central place in the education of teachers'. *Autobiography in Education* juxtaposes the writings of training college students with extracts from the autobiographical writings of Rousseau, Wordsworth, Coleridge, Gorky and Jung, among others. Through reading them, and then writing his or her own autobiography, the student would 'embrace parts of his childhood', and reach an 'enhanced affirmation of the self' (Abbs 1974: 22, 12).

Yet this autobiographical practice did not develop in the training colleges. It seems rather to have emerged in the schools, in the years after the Second World War. There is an extremely telling example of it at work in the school system of the 1960s and 1970s, in Valerie Avery's (1940–) *London Morning*, first published in 1964. *London Morning* was first written in 1955 when Avery was fifteen years old, in her English class at Walworth High School, at the encouragement of Harold Rosen her English teacher. Rosen later became Professor of English at the University of London Institute of Education and is best known for his militant opposition to theories of linguistic deprivation derived from Basil Bernstein's work on elaborated and restricted speech-styles, distributed by social class. In the 1950s and 1960s Rosen was a secondary school teacher and a leading member of the progressive English teachers' organization the National Association for the Teaching of English.

London Morning describes a family progress from the Old Kent Road, where Avery grew up, out to the new working-class housing estates. Interviewed in 1982, Avery remembered that 'Gran and Granddad had moved to a prefab in Peckham, and now all our neighbours were leaving the Old Kent Road to go to distant places ending in "ham" for some reason: Bellingham, Downham and Mottingham – suggesting fresh country air and grassy pavements' (Worpole 1982: 39). The book ends with that move. In its last pages it becomes a mourning for a lost way of life, and an elegy.

London Morning presents itself as fictionalized autobiography, told for the main part through dialogue recorded in dialect, and draws a good deal on a central tradition of working-class autobiography in Britain, particularly that derived from music hall: the playing of Life's Comedy, where the warm, rumbustious, disorganized life of sprawling families is told through a wealth of incidents that provoke laughter and tears, both at the same time.[6]

There is nothing surprising about *London Morning*, then, except that it was written by a girl of fifteen, in a classroom – and its subsequent publishing history. It was reprinted twice in the 1960s and in 1969 reissued as a class-reader, that is, as a text to be studied as literature alongside Jane Austen, William Shakespeare and the Georgian poets in the secondary school English class.[7] The extent of the practice was not as important as the pedagogical and political autobiographical practice it embodied: that you enabled the dispossessed to tell their story, and to come into consciousness of their self through the practice of writing, and then you returned that story, not just to the child in question, but to many other children too, so that they too might come into a sense of self.

London Morning and its publication history was the apotheosis of a common classroom practice. In 1952, a teacher working with nine-year-olds reported that he always said to the children, 'When you write, remember it is for someone to read and enjoy', and then went on to describe how 'corrected copies of some of the more interesting efforts were typed out, so as to appear more like the stuff in a printed book'. He was particularly concerned to inculcate what he called a kind of 'animism' – getting the child to imagine itself as another person or thing (Austen 1952: 147–50). Indeed, we ought to consider the proposition that an entire autobiographical pedagogy originated in the Old Kent Road, for that is where this primary school teacher was working too, a few years before fifteen-year-old Valery Avery was encouraged to produce her own book. But it was class rather than location that mattered. Whilst creative writing was an educational method recommended for all children, it was deemed particularly appropriate for the inarticulate, the dispossessed and the deprived, for what in other times had been 'the children of the poor'. It was they who particularly needed to be freed to share 'their hopes, fears, interests, needs' in this way, and through writing reveal to their teachers 'much of the social context in which they lived' (Hubbard 1970: 50–4).[8] Working-class children could be helped by being asked to draw on the resource of their own experience, their own babyhood and early childhood, in order to tell the story of the self, for lack of self was a deprivation among all the multiple ones they suffered (Walsh 1964: 91–103).[9] Once told, the story of the self nearly always had the power to move the adult reading it. As the Plowden Committee reported in 1967, 'the best writing of young children springs from the most deeply felt experience', and 'is nearly always natural and real and sometimes has qualities which make it most moving to read' (Central Advisory Committee for Education 1967, Volume 1: 220, 219).

As the epitome of these educational and autobiographical practices, *London Morning* can be read in other contexts of self-writing. Together with Maureen Duffy's *That's How It Was* (1983), Margaret Drabble's *Jerusalem the Golden* (1967), Jeanette Winterson's *Oranges Are Not the Only Fruit* (1985) and Judith Grossman's *Her Own Terms* (1989), it suggests that there could be such a thing as a sociology, or historiography, of literary forms. They prompt questions about the rise and fall of forms, about the needs and desires of writers and readers in particular historical periods that are expressed in their circulation and consumption, and about the popularity of stories told in a particular way, organized in one fashion rather than another, ending the way they do. Endings (the way the text ends, and the demise of types of text as genre of choice) may help us understand more clearly the relationship of literary forms and social forms, understand, indeed, that to write a history of literary forms even in a very partial way is to contribute to a history of societies (Moretti 1983: 1–41).

The Scholarship Girl had a mother, who also wrote autobiographically, in another mode and about another time and place. It is instructive to read Jane Walsh's *Not Like This* (1953) in conjunction with the Scholarship Girl's writing. Published by Lawrence & Wishart, this 'classic' working-class autobiography describes a childhood in unrespectable, very poor Oldham between 1905 and 1939, marriage and babies, and then the move from the north-west to Coventry, where the family is drawn by availability of work in the new light industries peripheral to car manufacture. The final move to London provides the perspective of the text. Now widowed, the narrator watches the triumphs of her daughter's progress through grammar school to teacher training college.[10]

Shelagh Delaney's (1939–) playtext of 1959 followed something of the same pedagogic route as Valerie Avery's *London Morning*. Set in Salford and Manchester, *A Taste of Honey* was originally presented by Joan Littlewood's Theatre Workshop at the Theatre Royal, Stratford East, in May 1958, transferring to the West End, to Wyndham's Theatre, in February 1959 (Littlewood 1994: 515–24). The 1961 film version, directed by Tony Richardson, moved outside the series of rooming houses to which the teenage heroine Jo and her mother Helen were confined in Delaney's script, to streets in which children run and jump and play traditional singing games. These direct references to the Opies' work (*The Lore and Language of Schoolchildren* was published in 1959) and to a past recently written up by the most famous Scholarship Boy of them all, by Richard Hoggart in *The Uses of Literacy* (1958), gives Jo a childhood that the original text seems to insist she never actually had (Lovell 1990b).

The transmogrification of *A Taste of Honey* into an O-level set text adds to the variety of forms in which it was made available. Its heroine has scarcely been schooled: she is not a Scholarship Girl at all. But the argument for discussion here is to do with the progress and fate of a text, and the way in which the heroine's story was appropriated to the school of British realism that produced *Room at the Top* (1959), *Saturday Night and Sunday Morning* (1958) and *This Sporting Life* (1963). This appropriation of one narrative to another, and the train of interpretation that ensued, has been notably discussed by Terry Lovell in 'Landscape and Stories in 1960s British Realism' (1990b). Perhaps the appropriation itself belongs to a particular historical epoch, or is at least only comprehensible in terms of what Brian Jackson, writing in 1968, called 'that debate on working-class life which blazed up, and died down so very quickly'. Its point of origin was 1958 when:

> *The Uses of Literacy* was fresh on the bookstalls, so was *Saturday Night and Sunday Morning*. On television Dennis Mitchell was showing *Morning in the Streets*. The Opies were attending to the work on family and kinship that Michael Young and his colleagues were reporting from Bethnal Green. And the whole structure of our school and university system was clarified by findings of untapped working-class talent recorded in such surveys as Floud, Halsey and Martin's *Social Class and Educational Opportunity*. (Jackson 1968: 4)

Maureen Duffy reflected on the kind of appropriation that Terry Lovell discusses, of one tale to another in 1983, in her Introduction to the reissue of *That's How It Was*. Her account of a wartime girlhood is set in Worthing and other south coast towns, where another mother (this one frail and tubercular and set to die before the end) and daughter make the move from one rooming house to another. Twenty years after its publication, Duffy was forced to insist that:

> [T]hose who ask for a sequel, have I believe, failed to grasp its purpose and structure. They believe . . . that its vividness and intensity were a welling up from memory rather than the deliberate exercise of style. In truth I couldn't repeat the book in a form that they would recognize without writing a pastiche. (Duffy 1983: x)

In *Jerusalem the Golden* (Drabble 1969), Clara Maugham escapes one of the most terrifyingly dreary mothers of twentieth-century fiction and lower-middle-class Sheffield (Northam in the text) suburbia for London University. Judith Grossman's *Her Own Terms*, which was published in the United States (where the author has lived for twenty years) in 1988, also presents itself as a fiction, in which the heroine follows the Scholarship Girl's most trodden path, to Oxford, to read the most common subject, English. All these Scholarship Girls make their brilliant progresses through the study of language and literature. This was also the journey that Jeanette Winterson described some twenty years later when at the end of *Oranges Are Not the Only Fruit* she sends her heroine to Oxford.

The Scholarship *Boy* (who is not so much a brother to the Scholarship Girl, as an organizing paradigm) came into named literary existence in 1957, the creation of Richard Hoggart in the chapter of *The Uses of Literacy* entitled 'Unbent Springs: A Note on the Uprooted and the Anxious'.[11] No anachronism he: Hoggart was writing about the 1930s, the period of his own adolescence, and about the few working-class boys who climbed the narrow ladder thrown down from the secondary schools to the elementary schools under the Free Places Regulations of 1907.

In curious language that connects the intellect to the sexual organs, Hoggart described the Boy's 'problem of self-adjustment', claiming that

[it] is, in general, especially difficult for those working-class boys who are only moderately endowed, who have talent sufficient to separate them from the majority of their working-class contemporaries, but not to go much further . . . those in the working classes who have been pulled one stage away from their original culture and yet have not the intellectual equipment which would then cause them to move on to join the 'declassed' professionals and experts. (Hoggart 1958: 293)

Now, in the 1950s,

[t]hey may be performing any kind of work, from manual labour to teaching; but my own experience suggests that they are to be found frequently among minor clerks and similarly black-coated workers, and among elementary school teachers, especially in the big cities. (Hoggart 1958: 300)

The boy had been

clever enough to take himself out of his class mentally, but not equipped, mentally or emotionally, to surmount all the problems that follow. . . . Even if he acquires some degree of culture, he finds it difficult to carry it easily, as easily as those who have not had to strain so much to get it . . . . (Hoggart 1958: 303)

But it is quite inappropriate to make the Scholarship Boy brother to the heroines discussed here. All of the girls (with the exception of Jo) are formidably successful figures: attractive, clever and bright. They read reactions to the stiff, poorly cut catalogue items that at some point all their mothers purchase for them, and that display their class origins more precisely than anything else, and, as soon as they are able, go out and buy clothes. Their sexiness (and the amount of sex they have) is presented by their authors as a gloriously intelligent thing. Uprooted, anxious and very badly dressed, inadequate in so very many ways, Hoggart's Boy is simply not in the same league.

This affective and cultural failure has a long history. One of his sadder literary manifestations was written a century before, when Matthew Arnold contemplated the waste of spirit and unbeauty of life for every-one trapped in the elementary school classrooms he visited. In 1852, in his first Report as one of Her Majesty's Inspectors of Schools, Arnold did not accuse, as he well might have done, the school managers he met and in whom the Protestant Ethic moved in such a dreary way, but rather those young men who were progenitors of Hoggart's Boy. He wrote in 1852 of pupil-teachers, of how he had been 'much struck in examining them towards the close of their apprenticeship, when they are generally at least eighteen years old, with the utter disproportion between the great amount of positive information and the low degree of mental culture and intelligence which they exhibit'. There was however, a solution to the problem of culture this young man presented:

I am sure that the study of portions of the best English authors . . . might with advantage be made a part of their regular course of instruction. . . . Such a training would tend to elevate and humanise a number of young men, who at present, notwithstanding the vast amount of raw information which they have amassed, are wholly uncultivated; and it would have the great social advantage of tending to bring them into intellectual sympathy with the educated of the upper classes. (Arnold 1910: 16–17)

It was these attributes and inadequacies that Charles Dickens divided between his two male teacher figures in *Our Mutual Friend* (1864–5), Bradley Headstone and his apprentice, Charley Hexam. As with all Scholarship Boys, the furnishings of the mind evoke awkwardness of dress. Headstone's intellect has been 'a place of mechanical stowage' from early childhood onwards, and he wears his outward clothing with equal unease, with 'a certain stiffness . . . as if there were a want of adaptation between him and it' (Dickens).

The Boy had figurative existence long before the mid-nineteenth century, as expression of a wider structure of feeling about socially mobile and newly educated lower middle-class men – teachers and clerks in particular. But no matter how far back his story stretches, it is certain that in sociological terms he no longer existed when Hoggart gave him his name. Maureen Duffy's Preface to the 1983 edition of *That's How It Was* makes much of the great divide – the 1944 Education Act – that put an end to all Scholarship Boys and Girls, and of her own relationship to knowledge, which is strikingly different from the edgy, furtive one in which Hoggart's Boy takes part. She writes about the education she was given at Trowbridge High School for Girls as being

> in the most enlightened liberal humanist tradition which exactly suited my needs and temperament. I took to it as if my family had been enjoying it for generations. . . . Above all . . . there was literature in Latin, French and English. . . . A great deal of my time was lived in a dream of verse writing, reading and learning. Much of it was spent in impersonating John Keats and imitating his odes. (Duffy 1983: viii–ix)

This is the structure of feeling that she had written into her central character Paddy twenty years before.

The same ease of learning – a kind of at-homeness with the idea of intellectual endeavour – marks Judith Grossman's *Her Own Terms*. It was her awesome facility of intellectual expression that struck Bernard Bergonzi, who remarks in *Exploding English* that 'Grossman shows in passing how formidably well-read and linguistically equipped her heroine was' (1990: 97). In a moment of deeply satisfying intertextuality, Grossman's heroine actually apostrophizes the literary figures she calls 'scholarship heroes': Paul Morel from D.H Lawrence's *Sons and Lovers* (1913), and Julian Sorel from *Le Rouge et Le Noir* (1830).

It is through their textual existence and her debate with them, the Scholarship Boys of her imagination, that she understands herself and the history that has made her. She writes that:

> [T]he Julien's of this world carry out of childhood with them an exorbitant gift and need for intimacy; they tumble about the social void with sensitive hooks outstretched, and once they find attachment the quality of attention they bring to it is close to perfect. I recognised, I *knew* that, seeing in them my own obsessive focus on the details of response, my own ecstatic compulsion to please. (Grossman 1989: 176)

The qualities of attention, the obsessive detail of response, are social as well as literary. A historically created sensibility matched an educational practice, that of Leavisism in the schools and the universities. As a historically available set of feelings that could be *personated* (by these writers, inventing their characters; by those characters in the actions they undertake), we may call the cleverness, the stunning competence of beauty and intelligence available to these Scholarship Girls, a form as well. This is something like Leopold von Ranke's 'Character, in the world historical sense': something like the 'Moment' that he described in 1823, where he wrote that 'the greatest thing that which a human being can attain is to pursue the universal while pursuing his own affairs. Then the personal existence is exalted into a world-historical moment' (Ranke 1981: 19).

When these texts have been discussed – individually, not as a corpus – they have been appropriated to the journey story (the progress, educational or otherwise, of a boy from a working-class background), to working-class autobiography in general, and to the school of British realism (the example here, already offered, is Scholarship Boy Tony Richardson's reworking of Delaney for a cinema audience). Yet these texts show formal qualities that suggest they should be considered together, and that their fragmentation under different generic headings prevents a particular kind of inquiry, into 'literary texts [as] *historical* products organized according to *rhetorical* criteria' (Moretti 1987: 9), into the history of literary forms as part of a history of society, offering evidence, in this particular case, of the post-war years in Britain, of the reformulation of class and gender in the context of welfare and educational legislation, of the post-war democratic settlement and the multifarious ways in which it was negotiated.

It was *Truth, Dare or Promise* that prompted reflection on these earlier texts, suggested indeed that they might be there to be found. Liz Heron's collection also prompts reflection on the choice of forms available to its contributors, who for the main part made a decision between 'the childhood' and 'the history'. Maureen Duffy discusses *That's How It Was* as a 'History', claiming that:

> My first book is . . . about truth and fiction, history and the selectiveness of memory. It is a political book in the sense that national and international politics govern the physical conditions of Paddy and her mother's life. . . . Those conditions aren't just a piquant backdrop to a moving image of mother and child. They are a documentary about man-made poverty and they are in the book to be remembered in the spirit in which the Great War . . . was to be remembered as the war to end all wars in *All Quiet on the Western Front*. (Duffy 1983: xi)

'The childhood', as a sub-genre of the European autobiography has received some attention as the *Jugenderinnerungan*, the recalled childhood and adolescence of the protagonist (Coe 1984; Neubauer 1992: 75–91; Steedman 1990). The childhood is often narrated in the timeless present tense, with a sudden, detailed attention paid to events and persons, brought into brief focus against the haze of memory, and a careful, dream-like attention to the relative size of things.[12]

In the longer timescales of literary history, the 'childhood' is connected to the *Bildungsroman*, which, according to Franco Moretti, is the form that above all others promotes socialization, making utterly desirable (making people *really want* to do) what it is they have to do anyway, within the context of particular societies. In Moretti's exegesis, the *Bildungsroman* is seen to focus on lively, articulate normality. His case studies are Elizabeth Bennet in *Pride and Prejudice*, Julien Sorel in *Scarlet and Black* and Dorothea Brooke in *Middlemarch*. Moretti makes comparisons between English and continental versions of the form, and suggests that in the former the end comes typically with marriage, a state of both civil society and legal structure, and of privacy, which exists somewhere between the intimate and public sphere. In the *Bildungsroman* history does not take place in the great world, in grand formulations and interpretations; rather, history lies within the confines of 'a relatively common human life'. In this way, the form cannot offer a critique of everyday life, for it is itself a culture of everyday life. It serves then to elicit consent to the social order, tempering contradiction, and allowing those aware of contradiction the means to internalize it, through the beauty and harmony of the end achieved. In this way, the *Bildungsroman* promotes 'happiness'. 'This "happiness" ', says Moretti, 'is the essence of modern "consent"; and since it is increasingly hard to obtain in everyday life a "form" becomes necessary which can in some way guarantee its existence' (1987: 22–3). The strange aspect of this happiness, and the structure that embodies it (the achievement of the heart's desire; the marriage; the end you want and have to want), is that in the novel of development and growth – of Becoming – it is the *end* of becoming that equals happiness.

If the novel of formation is about socialization, about becoming, then how the writer directs the plot towards the *end* is of very great importance. Maureen Duffy addresses this point, insisting in her Introduction of 1983 that *That's How It Was*

> is a novel rather than an autobiography because of its structuring towards [an] end, with the consequent selection among characters and events, and the heightened language used to evoke them. If I couldn't invent facts, which I couldn't because I wanted to tell a particular truth, the art must be in the style . . . (Duffy 1983: vi)

Some of her readers believed that 'its vividness and intensity were a welling up from memory', but they were rather a 'deliberate exercise of style . . . a deliberate exercise in craftsmanship': 'As with many of my books it was constructed towards its very last line, the question "And what the hell do I do now?" It is Paddy's question, not mine for when I wrote it I had already decided on my own answer . . .' (Duffy 1983: xi). She then makes some remarks about the end arrived at as a question being like Shakespearian end-stop: a form suitable to a particular historical epoch.

The End – the end-stop – of all these Scholarship Girls' stories is the move into or the triumphs of higher education. These are educational progresses, apart from everything else they are. But that end is told in opposition to another one, which hovers between the lines or just beyond the periphery of the book: there is a termination evoked that never actually takes place in the text. These heroines of the educational progress articulate with great clarity an end-that-is-evaded, that is, the Baby. Remembering the 1950s, Maureen Duffy reminds us that 'the great enemy to advancement for working-class girls was to become pregnant' (Duffy 1983: ix). In one of the most horrifying and compelling abortion scenes in modern fiction (compelling largely because it is used to structure and punctuate the entire text) Grossman's heroine avoids that end. These determinedly avoided endings are articulation of a *refusal to go back*, to be caught in any way, not just 'caught' in its particular meaning of 'fall', and 'falling for a baby'. At the end of *Jerusalem the Golden* Clara Maugham speaks not so much of pregnancy as of the whole of the old world that a baby might represent, and that she *simply will not have*. She will not be caught: 'she would survive because she had willed herself to survive, because she did not have it in her to die. Even the mercy and kindness of destiny she would survive; they would not get her that way, they would not get her at all' (Drabble 1969: 206).

The very great historical importance of post-war welfare and educational legislation for working-class girls, which is inscribed in the plot and characterizations of these autobiographical writings, should probably be taken by historians as another form of evidence for what is already well established in discussion of this period of recent British history. The particular value of the remembered and invented Scholarship Girls is the common story they tell, which raises a new set of questions not only about the social provisions made by welfare legislation of the period 1944–50, but about the particular kinds of pedagogies and presentations of sensibility that legislation brought about – in unintended ways, as teachers set their classes of eight-year-olds to write the story of the self, and O- and A-level classes learned all the gradations of rapture that responding to literature might allow. These stories also allow investigation of the large-scale affective enterprises that may, at particular points in time, be bound up with state formation. The Scholarship Girl's tale emerged from a particular pedagogical practice, in which a form of writing and a critical reading were designed to produce a particular kind of sensibility, and to bring the life stories of the previously unconsidered into the commonweal.

Once, some time ago now, what would have enthralled me about these fictions and autobiographies are all the bad, or painfully and desperately resentful, or utterly weird mothers that they contain. Seeing plain Delaney's presentation of Jo's mother Helen in *A Taste of Honey*, and

Helen's comprehensive refusal of the maternal role, has enabled Terry Lovell to ponder its appropriation to a modern mother–daughter romance. We are actually helped in B.B. Kidron's television production of *Oranges Are Not the Only Fruit* to see more plainly than the novel allows the visual connection between the heroine's extraordinary mother and the Lancashire comedy of enormous and overwhelming women (big bums and big voices, dwarfing little shrimps of fathers) and to remember the inescapable tragedies evoked by having the comedian Beryl Reid play Helen in the film version of *A Taste of Honey*. More interesting now though, I think, is use of the baby – or rather, the-Baby-That-Isn't – by many of working-class heroines of the educational process who have been discussed here. It seems more fruitful now to return to a question mapped out some years ago by a group of much younger working-class girls writing autobiographically in the 1970s, and using babies as symbols of ambivalence, conflict and resistance (Steedman 1982: 145–53). Not the least interest of the children's story of 'The Tidy House' that I edited some years ago is that it was produced by the educational paradigms discussed here, and encouraged by a belief on the part of a teacher (who was myself, in another life and long ago) that writing does indeed bring new forms of selfhood into being.

Notes

1. For the kind of history that is told in this way, see Cunningham (1991).
2. On this point, see Vincent (1989).
3. Glyn Thomas was Head of the English Department at Hunstanton Secondary Modern School, Norfolk.
4. L.E.W. Smith was Head of English at Millfield School, Somerset, and David Holbrook wrote prolifically on English as a curriculum subject.
5. *Culture and Environment* inspired many subsequent developments in English and English teaching through to the 1970s.
6. 'Miss Avery grew up in a drab London street in the years after the war. This book is a sampler of memories, deftly stitched from countless domestic details' (*Times Literary Supplement*, 22 October 1964, p. 965).
7. *London Morning* was issued in the Pergamon English Library in 1969 and in Arnold-Wheaton's Literature for Life Series in 1980.
8. D.N. Hubbard lectured at the University of Sheffield's Institute of Education.
9. The 'Breakthrough to Literacy' reading programme was an extension of this practice of the self into the field of teaching initial reading. The publishers of 'Breakthrough' estimate that two and a half million British children have been taught to read and write by this method since it was launched in 1970. See Mackay et al. (1975).
10. I wish I had known about this book when I wrote *Landscape for a Good Woman*. Walsh's discussion of clothes, food, green veg, the immense importance of 'keeping yourself clean', and a wide range of heterodox belief, from Food Reform to Socialism, operative in Walsh's childhood connects with Logie Barrow's story of plebeian striving in *Independent Spirits* (1986); and is the same kind of Lancashire tale that I tried, in a minor key, to tell.
11. Which is not to say he did not exist before 1957 in a variety of texts. A.J. Cronin, Howard Spring and Emrys Williams all described boys winning scholarships and going to the grammar in the inter-war years.

12. In the 1890s the psychologist James Sully provided most fertile insight into this form of remembering of writing (see Sully 1896).

References

Abbs, P. (1974) *Autobiography in Education – An introduction to the subjective discipline of Autobiography and of its central place in the education of teachers, with a selection of passages from a variety of autobiographies, including those written by students*, London: Heinemann.

Arnold, M. (1910) 'General Report for the Year 1852', in F.S. Marvin (ed.), *Reports on Elementary Schools 1852–1882 by Matthew Arnold*, London: HMSO.

Austen, E. (1952) 'Writing at Nine Years', *Use of English*, 3: 147–50.

Avery, V. (1964) *London Morning*, London: William Kimber.

Baldick, C. (1987) *The Social Mission of English Criticism, 1848–1932*, Oxford: Clarendon Press.

Barrow, L. (1986) *Independent Spirits*, London: Routledge.

Bergonzi, B. (1990) *Exploding English: Criticism, Theory, Culture*, Oxford: Clarendon Press.

Bratton, J.S (1986) 'Jenny Hill: Sex and Sexism in Victorian Music Hall', in J.S. Bratton (ed.) *Music Hall Performance and Style*. Milton Keynes: Open University Press.

Central Advisory Committee for Education (1967) *Children and their Primary Schools: A Report of the Central Advisory Committee for Education* ('The Plowden Report'), 2 volumes, London: HMSO.

Coe, R.N. (1984) *When the Grass Was Taller: Autobiography and the Experience of Childhood*, New Haven, Conn.: Yale University Press.

'Creative Writing' (1964) *NATE Bulletin, CSE English: An Interim Report*, 1: 30–5.

Cunningham, H. (1991) *The Children of the Poor: Representations of Childhood Since the Seventeenth Century*, Oxford: Basil Blackwell.

Delaney, S. (1959) *A Taste of Honey*, London: Methuen.

Dixon, J. (1991) *A Schooling in 'English': Critical Episodes in the Struggle to Shape Literary and Cultural Studies*, Milton Keynes: Open University Press.

Doyle, B. (1989) *English and Englishness*, London: Routledge.

Dodd, K. (1990) 'Cultural Politics and Women's Historical Writing: The Case of Ray Strachey's *The Cause*', *Women's Studies International Forum*, 13: 127–37.

Drabble, M. (1969) *Jerusalem the Golden*, Harmondsworth: Penguin. (Originally published 1967.)

Duffy, M. (1983) *That's How It Was*, London: Virago. (Originally published 1962.)

Giddens, A. (1991) *Modernity and Self-Identity: Self and Society in the Late Modern Age*, Cambridge: Polity Press.

Grossman, J. (1989) *Her Own Terms*, London: Grafton. (Originally published 1988.)

Haller, W. (1958) *The Rise of Puritanism*, New York: Harper.

Heron, L. (ed.) (1985) *Truth, Dare or Promise: Girls Growing Up in the 1950s*, London: Virago.

Hoggart, R. (1958) *The Uses of Literacy*, Harmondsworth: Penguin. (Originally published 1957.)

Hubbard, D.N. (1970) 'The Child and His Writing', *Use of English*, 22: 50–4.

Inglis, F. (1975) 'Against Proportional Representation: The Ambitious Heart of English Teaching', *English in Education*, 9: 11–18.

Jackson, B. (1968) *Working Class Community: Some General Notions Raised by a Series of Studies in Northern England*, London: Routledge & Kegan Paul.

Leavis, F.R. (1930) *Mass Civilisation and Minority Culture*, Cambridge: Minority Press.

Littlewood, J. (1994) *Joan's Book: Joan Littlewood's Peculiar History As She Tells It*, London: Methuen.

Lovell, T. (1990a) *British Feminist Thought*, Oxford: Basil Blackwell.

Lovell, T. (1990b) 'Landscape and Stories in 1960s British Realism', *Screen*, 31: 357–76.

Mackay, D., Thompson, B. and Schaub, P. (1975) *Breakthrough to Literacy Teacher's Manual: The Theory and Practice of Teaching Initial Reading and Writing*, London: Longman.

Maitland, S. (1989) *Very Heaven*, London: Virago.

Mathieson, M. (1975) *Preachers of Culture: A Study of English and Its Teachers*, London: Unwin.

Miller, N.K. (1992) *Getting Personal: Feminist Occasions and Other Autobiographical Acts*, New York: Routledge.

Moretti, F. (1983) 'The Soul and the Harpy', in *Signs Taken for Wonders: Essays in the Sociology of Literary Forms*, London: Verso and New Left Books.

Moretti, F. (1987) *The Way of the World: The Bildungsroman in European Culture*, London: Verso.

Morley, D. and Worpole, K. (1983) *The Republic of Letters: Working Class Writing and Local Publishing*, London: Comedia.

Mulhern, F. (1979) *The Moment of 'Scrutiny'*, London: Verso.

Neubauer, J. (1992) *The Fin-de-Siècle Culture of Adolescence*, New Haven, Conn. and London: Yale University Press.

Ranke, L. von (1981) *The Secret of World History: Selected Writings on the Art and Science of History* (ed., with translations, by R. Wines), New York: Fordham University Press.

Richards, I.A. (1929) *Practical Criticism*, London: Routledge & Kegan Paul.

Seabrook, J. (1978) *What Went Wrong?*, London: Gollancz.

Smith, L.E.W. (1970) 'Creative Writing and Language Awareness', *English in Education*, 4: 4–9.

Smith, S. and Watson, J. (eds) (1992) *De/Colonizing the Subject: The Politics of Gender in Women's Autobiography*, Minneapolis, University of Minnesota Press.

Spivak, G.C. (1988) 'Can the Subaltern Speak? Speculations on Widow Sacrifice', in C. Nelson and L. Grossberg (eds) *Marxism and the Interpretation of Culture*, Urbana: University of Illinois Press.

Steedman, C. (1982) *The Tidy House: Little Girls Writing*, London: Virago.

Steedman, C. (1990) *Childhood, Culture and Class in Britain: Margaret McMillan, 1860–1931*, London: Virago.

Steedman, C. (1992) 'La Théorie qui n'en est pas une, or, Why Clio Doesn't Care', *History and Theory*, 31: 33–50.

Stevens, F. (1953) 'What is Good Children's Writing? (A Report on Some Representative Work Sent from Nine Primary Schools in Different Parts of England and Scotland), Part II', *Use of English*, 4: 126–32.

Sully, J. (1896) *Studies of Childhood*, London: Longman.

Thomas, G. (1973) 'The Process of Writing', *English in Education*, 6: 74–81.

Thompson, D. (1971) 'The Relevance of I.A Richards', *Use of English*, 23: 3–13.

Thompson, D. (1973) 'Teacher's Debt', in R. Brower, H. Vendler and J. Hollander (eds), *I.A Richards: Essays in His Honour*, New York: Oxford University Press.

'Twenty-Five' (1964) *Use of English*, 15: 243.

Vincent, D. (1989) *Literacy and Popular Culture 1750–1914*, Cambridge: Cambridge University Press.

Vincent, D. (1991) *Poor Citizens: The State and the Poor in the Twentieth Century*, London: Longman.

Walsh, J. (1953) *Not Like This*, London: Lawrence & Wishart.

Walsh, J.H. (1964) 'Writing about "Experiences" ', *Use of English*, 16: 91–103.

Wandor, M. (1990) *Once a Feminist*, London: Virago.

'What is Good Children's Writing? (A Report on Some Representative Work Sent from Nine Primary Schools in Different Parts of England and Scotland), Part I' (1952), *Use of English*, 4: 66–75.

Winterson, J. (1985) *Oranges Are Not the Only Fruit*, London: Pandora.

Worpole, K. (1982) 'Class of '55', *City Limits*, Jan./Feb. 39.

6

Relocating Location: Cultural Geography, the Specificity of Place and the City Habitus

Martyn Lee

Within the field of social geography, cultural geography is in its infancy. For this emerging field of study the 'convergence of interests between those with an historical interest in the evolution of geographical land-scapes and those with a contemporary interest in cultural studies and social theory' (Jackson 1989: 1) clearly represents an exciting and potentially illuminating sphere of social investigation. Whilst the theoretical and methodological compatibility which exists between the established investigative paradigms within human geography and cultural studies is by no means unproblematic, my primary contention in this chapter is that particular assumptions about the significance of location and locality within this expanding field have become prevalent. In particular I want to suggest that these assumptions are in the process of establishing a certain paradigmatic hegemony which is defining the character of the intellectual field; a hegemony, moreover, which runs the very real risk of marginalizing precisely one of the central issues which cultural geography would claim to address, namely the *specificity of location*. Briefly my argument here is that whilst contemporary cultural geography often seeks to explore the tripartite relationship between human agency, social process and spatial location, it is precisely the last dimension, spatial location, which is indeed in danger of assuming a subordinate status in terms of its input into a general methodological framework for cultural geography.

The question I want to pose, therefore, is how can we begin to think about location and locality as a dynamic, rather than incidental or secondary, social component within any analysis which considers space as important to its concerns? I believe that to do this involves conceiving of location culturally. Here I am not simply referring to the cultural orientations of human agents (individuals, social groups, classes, and so on) who happen to exist upon a particular geographic terrain, or necessarily to the cultural consequences of certain generalized social processes upon those human agents. Put simply I want to think about *the culture of place itself*. This is to say that places (towns, cities, regions, nations) have cultural characters which transcend and exist relatively autonomously, although by no means independently, of their current populations and of the consequences of the social processes which may be taking place upon their terrain at a given historical juncture. The culture of a location, I want to suggest, is the cumulative product of the collective and sedimented history of that location, and like any history cannot be readily or easily dissolved but manifests a certain durability, marking its presence onto the contemporary social and physical land-scape of the location in question. In arguing for this position I want to deploy Bourdieu's concept of *habitus*, suggesting, in this particular case, that cities have a habitus: that is, certain relatively enduring (pre)disposi-tions to respond to current social, economic, political or even physical circumstances in very particular ways, ways in which other cities, with different habitus formations, may respond to very differently.

Modernity, globalization and the marginalization of location

Fundamental to the 'project' of cultural geography is the recognition that geography, be that the object of social or physical space, or concrete geographical features, be treated culturally. In this respect it is critical to our comprehension of what properly constitutes geography that, as Jackson has argued, it 'is conceived of not as a featureless landscape on which events simply unfold, but as a series of spatial structures which provide a dynamic context for the processes and practices that give shape and form to culture' (1989: 48). Shurmer-Smith and Hannam have echoed this sentiment in somewhat bolder terms: 'if mountains, rivers and weather are not approached culturally there is a terrible lie uttered every time the word "environment" is used' (1994: 216). In short, space is to be seen not as mere neutral ground – a convenient, unquestioned location upon which things happen, people live and work and social processes develop and transform, but as a historically determined site upon which the effects of prior social relations produce a complex array of meanings. The assertion that I want to explore here, therefore, is the idea that space, when taken culturally, represents a relatively coherent and autonomous social domain which exercises a certain determinacy upon both the population and the social processes located upon its terrain, and as such should be seen as far more than the mere aggrega-tion of the actions and activities of those populations and processes. This is not necessarily to subordinate populations and social processes to the determinacy of space, but rather to situate them within an already historically configured cultural zone which exerts its own particular cultural logic, momentum and dynamism.

The implication, then, which emerges from such an assertion should be relatively clear: that if space represents the historically constituted embodiment of particular social meanings, values and attitudes, then the *precise specificity of location matters* and, in the first instance at least, should not be regarded as reducible purely to the functional product of general or universal processes or phenomena. Yet I believe that all too often the specificity of location tends to go unscrutinized, posited, albeit implicitly, only as a setting, site or, at worst, a mere backdrop to events or social processes.

At first glance the assertion that there is a tendency within cultural geography to neglect the proper scrutiny of location might appear to be a somewhat peculiar claim given that almost by definition the concern of cultural geography is indeed the notion of location itself. I clearly do not mean by this that location is absent in cultural geography, rather that the emphasis for investigation typically is situated elsewhere. For instance, attention might focus upon human agency and space: that is, the relationships between people (defined by their class position, gender, age, racial or ethnic origin, and so on) and their geographic environments, how they use or are used by these environments, how notions of 'identity', 'belongingness' or 'alienation', for example, are forged through these environments, and so on. Alternatively, concerns might settle on the effects of certain social processes, such as capital, ideology, modernity, postmodernity, globalization, consumption, Fordism, post-Fordism or gentrification on space, or the consequences of the siting of such processes within the boundaries of a particular space. Finally, we might consider the interaction between human agents and social processes situated within a particular spatial frame or type of space: for example, the use and 'abuse' of shopping malls as sites of popular resistance to contemporary consumer capitalism (see, for example, Presdee 1986; Shields 1992), or de Certeau's (1984) work on the resistive practices of everyday life where physical geographies, as the concrete embodiment of certain dominant ideologies, become sites of struggle over the determination of cultural meanings.

Whilst I am not suggesting that any of these approaches are, in their own terms, necessarily inherently flawed, I do want to argue that any study which chooses to see space, location or geography as somehow central to its concerns needs to consider their precise specificity. In this context the term 'specificity' explicitly does not refer to *types of space* (shopping malls, modern or postmodern cities, flexible specialization districts, and so on), but to *actual, unique locations* (the Metrocentre at Gateshead in the United Kingdom, Glasgow, Los Angeles, the Veneto in northern Italy, and so on). Whilst it is of course true that real locations figure prominently in a great deal of literature, it is deeply unfortunate that relatively few studies actually begin to acknowledge the precise uniqueness of those locations. In many cases the cultural significance of location lies hidden and unexplored, either because location is abstracted from its broader historical significance and treated simply as a set of physical and social features with which people interact, or because the analysis wishes to treat location as somehow merely an exemplary site of the particular characteristics of a more general social process. In short, studies in which it is implicit that space is seen as somehow significant actually tend to neglect the proper scrutiny of space, or, as Sayer (1985) puts it, 'the difference that space makes'.

This latter tendency surely represents one of the fundamental intellectual legacies of modernity. For when seemingly all spheres of social endeavour, from Newtonian physics and systems of jurisprudence to architecture and aesthetics, sought to identify the universal structuring principles by which the whole of the world could be organized and made intelligible, then notions of difference, heterogeneity and uniqueness necessarily become the prime casualties of such a totalizing project. For modernity what matters most are the connections, the similarities and the lines of continuity across space, rather than the distinctions and differences which may separate particular spaces, whether these be engendered by the universalizing tendencies of capital and the market or the imposition of national or international systems of governance and polity on localities and regions. It is arguably, then, from this tradition that locality and the specificity of place, as the embodiment of uniqueness, is sacrificed.

The apogee of this generalized process towards universalization and the equalization of difference surely emerges during modernity's highest and most refined stage in which the supremely organized power of Fordist capital combines with the modernist's narratives of emancipation and progress to produce an irresistible force. Strangely, however, it is during this period of Fordist modernity that, in an important sense, the notion of the universal is perhaps replaced as *the* leading modernist discourse by the ideas of standardization, uniformity, conformity and homogeneity. In the name of economic expediency these ideas come to characterize the age in which we live. As Zukin puts it:

> The spread of national and even global cultures (especially those that emanate from Hollywood and Disney World) tends to weaken local distinctiveness. So do cheaper transportation costs, which encourage the long-distance diffusion and consumption of industrial products. The use of new technologies, moreover, equalizes conditions of *producing* goods in different regions of the world. The same standardized motors or jeans can be produced anywhere from Oshkosh to Singapore. And the job of manufacturing them can be shifted from North Americans to Mexicans and Chinese, or from middle-aged men to young women. . . . All in all the net effect of these technological and organizational changes is to make places 'more equal'. (1991: 12–13)

Thus when faced with a world characterized by such an apparently overwhelming sameness it is small wonder that attempts to make intelligible and interpret space, place and location are almost inevitably drawn towards the investigation of those general social forces and processes which produce these effects. True, recent assaults on modernity's universalizing tendencies in both theory and practice have begun to refocus attention on the specificities of the local and to reassert heterogeneity and diversity as significant themes of everyday life. However,

against this the full-scale emergence of a dominant or hegemonic discourse of globalization serves only to reaffirm established attitudes about
the insignificance of location. Hence, the theme which typically achieves
pre-eminence in much of the literature about globalization is the idea of
the flattening out or eradication of spatial differences – cultural, economic, political and geographical – by the unstoppable process of capital
as it strides roughshod over national boundaries in its attempt to
colonize the world (see, for instance, Featherstone 1990; Harvey 1985,
1989; Ritzer 1991; Soja 1989). It must be said, however, that in the face of
such approaches there have been some notable attempts to retain the
idea of the specificity of place as in some way significant (see, for
examples, Davis 1990; Lash and Urry 1987; Urry 1990; Zukin 1991). In
this context some of the ideas suggested in Massey's influential essay
'Power-Geometry and a Progressive Sense of Place' (1993; see also
Massey 1991) are briefly worth considering.

Massey's ideas in this essay are important, not least because she
clearly wishes to retain and emphasize the notion of the specificity of the
local. However, she also suggests that in many ways to speak of the
significance of the local is also to run the risk of assuming a conservative
or even reactionary intellectual position. Hence: 'it is certainly the case
that there is at the moment a recrudescence of some problematic senses
of place, from reactionary nationalisms to competitive localisms, to
sanitized, introverted obsessions with "heritage"'. The question, she
continues, 'is how to hold on to that notion of spatial difference, of
uniqueness, even rootedness if people want that, without it being
reactionary' (Massey 1993: 64). This problematic notion of location, she
argues, in many approaches, including ultimately that taken up in
Harvey's writing (see, for example, Harvey 1989), derives from the
Heideggerian dialectic of space/place as *being*, and hence static or fixed,
against the progressive and dynamic qualities of time which is *becoming*.
This approach has tended to produce several problematic assumptions
about place, most notably that places have 'single essential identities'
which derive almost exclusively from 'an introverted, inward-looking
history based on delving into the past for internalized origins' (1993: 64),
and the mistaken assumption that it should be incumbent upon those
analysing space and place to draw boundaries or indicate the limits of
spaces and places. Not surprisingly, then, the combination of these two
assumptions if applied to specific locations tends to yield a depiction of
place as an isolated and somewhat insular domain in which the culture
of place can be easily characterized and quantified, its 'legitimate'
population defined (that is, those who share its officially sanctioned
heritage), and foreigners or 'aliens' quickly identified. This, then, is a
particular depiction of place which in many ways is ideally attuned to
the fostering of the sort of extreme prejudices found in those assertions
of locality adopted in many regions by the far right. Against such
representations of place Massey suggests it is possible to imagine a

'progressive sense of place' in which notions of uniqueness and specificity need not be lost or given over as the property of conservativism. Using the example of Kilburn High Road in London she describes in detail a specific place which, whilst clearly having a particular 'character of its own', is none the less composed of multiple and complex identities of which Kilburn itself is only one amongst many other global contributors. As a consequence:

> It is from this perspective that it is possible to envisage an alternative interpretation of place. In this interpretation what gives place its specificity is not some long internalized history but the fact that it is constructed out of a particular constellation of relations, articulated together at a particular locus. . . . The uniqueness of a place, or locality, in other words is constructed out of particular interactions and mutual articulations and social relations, social processes, experiences and understandings are actually constructed on a far larger scale than what we happen to define for that as the place itself. . . . Instead then, of thinking of places as areas with boundaries around, they can be imagined as articulated moments in networks of social relations and understandings (Massey 1993: 66)

Now in a curious way, and despite her claims to restore the importance of the specificity of location, Massey's disavowal of the significance of the history of the local forces her to adopt a position in which the local is effectively subsumed, if not by the global, then at least by determinants other than the local. This is not to suggest that she is arguing that locations are not without their specificities: on the contrary, her depiction of Kilburn High Road is so vivid that it could be nowhere else in the world:

> It is a pretty ordinary place, north-west of the centre of London. Under the railway bridge the newspaper-stand sells papers from every county of what my neighbours, many of whom come from there, still often call the Irish Free State. The postboxes down the High Road, and many an empty space on a wall, are adorned with the letters IRA. The bottle and waste-paper banks are plastered this week with posters for a Bloody Sunday commemoration. Thread your way through the often almost stationary traffic diagonally across the road from the newsstand and there's a shop which, for as long as I can remember, has displayed saris in the window. Four life-sized models of Indian women, and reams of cloth. In another newsagent I chat with the man who keeps it, a Muslim unutterably depressed by the war in the Gulf, silently chafing at having to sell the *Sun*. (Massey 1993: 64–5)

My point is this, the specificities described by Massey can be seen to derive from the unique mix of wider social processes and experiences which originate largely from outside the particular location in question: Irish nationalist, English, Muslim identities, global capital and communications, and so on. This again begs the fundamental question: does location matter? In the attempt to avoid conservative and reactionary representations of places are we forced to marginalize their particular histories and treat them as mere loci, points of intersection for social relations and processes, or can we conceive of a way of treating the history of location in a manner which is itself genuinely progressive and contributes to a sensitive understanding of the place in question?

The habitus of location

In attempting to address this question I want to suggest that locations, in this case cities, have relatively enduring cultural orientations which exist and function relatively independently of their current populations or of the numerous social processes through which the location in question may be moving. This is not to deny the significance of these populations or processes as instruments of social action within a location, but precisely to *reassert the determinacy which is contingent on the history of that location itself*. In making this assertion I want to move away from a conception of local history which is effectively nothing more than the accumulation of particular historical events, facts or incidents, and likewise a notion of 'heritage' as merely a particular, institutionally sanctioned public display of socially disembodied artefacts from the past. Instead, it is vital to see the history of a location as a set of, sometimes contradictory, social processes from which complex, but often relatively coherent, place-specific cultural orientations are forged. A very similar approach to this is taken by Taylor et al. (1996) in which the UK cities of Manchester and Sheffield are analysed according to Raymond Williams's notion of 'structure of feeling'. Whilst the evidence presented and the arguments developed in this work are compelling and genuinely original, I believe such an approach is perhaps better served by the adoption of Bourdieu's concept of habitus rather than that of structure of feeling, although the two terms do share several important character-istics. Here, then, I want to suggest that it is productive to speak of the *habitus of location*: that is, a set of relatively consistent, enduring and generative cultural (pre)dispositions to respond to current circumstances, or 'the outside world', in particular ways. In this sense we can describe a city, for example, as having a certain 'cultural character', a cultural character which clearly transcends the popular representations of the populations of certain cities say (for example, the 'Liverpudlian charac-ter', the 'cockney character', and so on), or that manifestly expressed by a city's public and private institutions.

Essentially Bourdieu develops the concept of habitus as a way of theorizing the complex determinants of social action in both individuals and social groups or class fractions. In transposing this concept to the field of space I initially want to build upon a conception of habitus as Bourdieu defines it in the following ways. First, the habitus exists 'as a system of acquired dispositions functioning on the practical level of categories of perception and assessment or as classificatory principles as well as being the organising principles of action' (Bourdieu 1990: 13). Likewise, 'the habitus is an endless capacity to engender products –

thoughts, perceptions, expressions, actions – whose limits are set by the historically and socially situated conditions of its production' (Bourdieu 1977: 95). Elsewhere Bourdieu describes the habitus as 'necessity intern-alized and converted into a disposition that generates meaningful prac-tices and meaning-giving perceptions; it is a general transposable disposition which carries out a systematic, universal application – beyond the limits of what has been directly learnt – of the necessity inherent in the learning conditions' (Bourdieu 1984: 170).

In essence, then, the range of certain objective conditions of existence, or social and material 'facts', as these confront social actors who share the same social space *through time* give rise to particular cultural disposi-tions or ways of viewing the world which appear to those actors as entirely spontaneous or natural forms of cognition. The habitus is thus, I have suggested elsewhere, a 'perception-enabling prism' (Lee 1993: 31), a conceptual lens through which particular understandings or interpreta-tions of the social world are generated and as such invite particular forms of response or action to the social world.

Although the habitus is here conceived as a cognitive mechanism it should be stressed that it does not function mechanistically; it is therefore properly adopted as an intermediary concept in order to describe the particular negotiations which take place between a set of real-life material or objective conditions and a set of relatively structured concrete actions. Consequently whilst the habitus functions according to an 'organizing principle', its outcomes are most appropriately characterized as *dispositions*: that is, a propensity or inclination, rather than a compul-sion, towards certain types of action. Likewise whilst the habitus is a stable phenomenon, it would certainly be wrong to conceive of it as a static or 'completed' state of being. Hence it is precisely because the habitus moves through time in response to changing objective conditions of existence that it too is forever in an ongoing state of evolution or development. Continually readapted, the perceptions it generates are themselves always modified versions, however slight these may be, of the previous perceptions of the habitus. To express this somewhat more simply, whilst the habitus is the product of a history, that history is always in the process of being made, or, to return to a particular dialectic referred to earlier for a moment, the habitus is always in a state of becoming and never one of simply being.

Now let us try to imagine for a moment that a city embodies a habitus: bundles of relatively coherent social dispositions in an ongoing state of generation and regeneration. These dispositions result in *place-specific actions*, the *practice* of the city or, one might almost say, the way a city behaves. This practice appears as the product of the *necessity* to respond to and treat the objective world in particular ways and thus presents itself as a sort of axiomatic logic from which practice is grooved into well-defined responses of habituation, although these are adapted and adaptable to the individual requirements and necessities of different social fields. How a city chooses to spend its budget, the ways in which it uses its land space and the way it tends to envisage its physical landscape, how it sees fit to preserve and depict its history and heritage, the emphasis it places on the collective welfare of its citizens, the choices it makes over styles of civic and public architecture, and so on, all are conditioned by a sort of governing logic which is not merely reducible to the actions of say a particular local government but actually constitutes the outcome of the 'guiding hand' of habitus. But of course this logic, this habitus, is not a disembodied or free-floating 'spirit' which hangs over the city; it is not, for instance, to be seen as some metaphysical presence or as the 'city's unconscious' acting independently of the city, for it is precisely a sometimes conscious, reflected upon and debated cultural disposition which is lived through and expressed concretely in its citizenry and public and private institutions (the city council, business and community groups, local media, city fathers, and so on).

We may therefore summarize: the objective conditions of existence, or the social and material 'facts' which confront a city through time, give rise to the formation of a particular habitus which manifests itself as distinct, durable and adaptive dispositions which in turn generate the place-specific practices of the city. This practice or set of concrete actions will over time adjust the original objective conditions of existence of the city, thereby leading to the modification of the original habitus in response to these changes, which accordingly will generate changes in practice (see Figure 6.1). It is from such a theoretical basis that we can begin to imagine a genuinely productive way of conceiving of local history, namely as the *movement of the city habitus through time*. In this way local history is seen not as the simple aggregation of historical facts pertaining to a place but as the cumulative product of the dialectical interaction between the objective conditions of existence and the city habitus as each form and re-form in response to the other. Such an approach I believe allows us to retain the notion of the 'agency of place', to see a city for instance as generating relatively autonomous practices which are consistent with its collective history but not necessarily the inevitable outcomes of that history. Likewise this approach does not

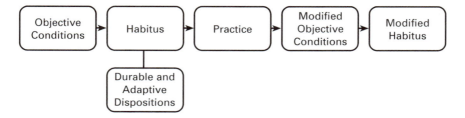

Figure 6.1   *The Dialectic of Habitus and the Objective Conditions of Existence*

force us to choose between a view of the city as either the sovereign decider of its own destiny, or the mere product of 'other' or 'outside forces' (such as national government or the impact of global capital), but allows us to see it as the result of the mediation of these two extremes.

Let me now try to concretize some of the above ideas. What, for instance, might the objective conditions of existence of a city refer to? In short the objective conditions of existence indicates all those material and social facts that any city is confronted with and has to negotiate at any given moment in its history. These material and social facts may be 'internal' or 'external' in their origin. So-called 'internal' facts may include: the city's physical geography; its climate; the demographic composition of its population (class ratios, ethnic and racial mix, gender balance and age composition of its inhabitants, and so on); the status and types of industrial and commercial activity; the character of civic, legal and political regimes that are currently or were recently imposed upon a city (for example, whether a city council is liberal or conservative, radical or reactionary in its orientation). 'External' facts, meanwhile, are composed of all those 'outside forces', whether deriving from regional, national, international or global origins, that a city has to negotiate (national government funding, the character of contemporary capital, the character of contemporary labour, and so on).

Again, what needs to be stressed here is the temporal as well as spatial dimension to the city habitus, for it is to miss the point to see a city habitus simply in terms of some functional outcome of the contemporary objective condition of the city. The habitus is not born out of the contemporary objective conditions of existence but is in fact the product of the effects of the history of the habitus which has itself been constituted by the shifting balance and significance of objective conditions over time. Therefore the city responds to the contemporary objective conditions of existence according to the pre-existing logic of habitus, but these contemporary conditions subsequently sediment to form another layer of the city's collective history from which a modified version of habitus emerges which is different from but consistent with the character of the previous habitus. In a general sense, then, we can begin to perceive this axiomatic logic of necessity, that is, the habitus, of a city as the embodiment of very particular clusters of dispositions, for example 'enterprising', 'independent', 'flexible', 'adaptive', 'nostalgic', 'reactionary', 'industrious', 'radical', 'conservative', and so on. Nowhere are these dispositions more manifest than in the ways a city perceives, treats and uses its own space. In order to demonstrate this I now want to consider how the argument that I have been developing may be applied to a particular case: that is, how certain objective conditions of existence led to the formation of a specific habitus type and how this habitus type exercises a logic which ultimately leads to its own reproduction through time.

Coventry: an open city

The city I want to examine is Coventry, an industrial city in the West Midlands, United Kingdom, with a current population of approximately 300,000. A glance at the standard sources of local history tells us that the settlement of Coventry has historically been associated with a diverse variety of trades and industries: wool, cloth, ribbon weaving, metal goods, leather, clocks and watches, soap, sewing machines, industrial components, bicycle and automobile manufacture, machine tools, military goods, being amongst the most prominent of these. Such sources also stress the early historical importance of Coventry as a market or trading centre. Likewise contemporary local history of the city inevitably focuses on its devastation by the German bombers during the Second World War, its emergence as a post-war 'boom town', its internationally renowned status as a manufacturer of automobiles and its position as a pioneer of urban modernism (great emphasis is often placed, for example, on the fact that Coventry was the first UK city to develop a fully pedestrianized city centre following the war).

On their own these facts contained within the routine vignettes of Coventry's local history tell us practically nothing about what the character of the local habitus might be. Indeed such accounts often misrepresent or even mythologize the history of Coventry: for example, post-war Coventry is often characterized as a phoenix rising from the flames (the corporate symbol used today, for instance, by the city's university). It is characterized, in short, as a city entirely reconstructed from the irresistible cast of modernism: that is, simply the inevitable consequence of the German bombing of the city. Such an account presents the emergence of post-war urban modernism in Coventry as purely the functional response to the city's war-time destruction. This is deeply problematic, for this explanation, such as it is, fails to recognize, for instance, that a systematic urban modernism 'project' had been underway within the city at least ten years prior to the Second World War, that as a mature project Coventry's urban modernism focused only on particular areas of the city's life (most notably production and commodity consumption rather than, for example, social welfare), and why there was relatively little popular resistance, as there was in other cities for example, to the modernist project. To begin to address these sort of issues requires us to explore the longer historical trajectory of the city habitus.

The habitus of the city of Coventry is inevitably the result of a complex weave of historically shifting objective conditions of existence and social relations. Without doubt, however, these can be traced to a quite particular origin: the city's geographical location. Situated in the centre of England with easy access to other regional and national centres, and close to important natural resources (the Forest of Arden, the particular quality of local water and good pastoral land), the original settlement of the space which is now Coventry depended on its precise location for the formation of the future habitus of the city. This location gave rise to two crucial and interrelated activities: specialization in textile production and the development of the site as a centre of exchange and distribution. These activities in many ways set the character for the future industrial development of the city: as a producer of valuable contemporary commodities and as a marketplace and progressive economic centre. More than this, however, the early crystallization of Coventry's industrial activity in this way triggered the development of a very distinctive habitus type which I want to describe in the following terms: Coventry as a city which was 'enterprising', 'flexible', 'open' and geared largely to the contingencies of the often short-term time horizons required by capital. My argument is that Coventry's early formation as both a producer of commodities and a marketplace led it to develop a disposition which in many ways was perfectly attuned to the rapid cognition of and response to the requirements of contemporary capitalism. This, allied to the particular consistency of its historical population, has marked Coventry as a city which was positioned at the forefront of national and international economic activity.

The early prosperity of Coventry, which dates back to at least the eleventh and twelfth centuries, derived from the interaction of a dynamic wool and cloth trade, based on an abundance of grazing land for sheep, and its position as an important regional and national point of distribution and exchange. As a marketplace locked into an established network of roads such as the Fosse Way and Watling Street, Coventry had always been defined primarily as a site of traffic, and hence a place which had both access to and knowledge of other places and people. In this sense Coventry has always been an 'open' city, and it is significant for instance that, unlike other cities, Coventry had rarely seen the need to build defences against the outside world (the nearby, and misnamed, Lunt 'fort' was in fact never a true fort but functioned primarily as a staging post for trade and travel). This status, combined with a fiercely independent and highly productive textile industry, led to the recognition of Coventry as a medieval 'enterprise zone' in the latter part of the twelfth century by the Crown, a status maintained and reinforced some two hundred years later when, in 1334, the city's traders and merchants were granted special privileges by the Crown, including tax and toll exemptions. The guild of Coventry merchants founded in 1340, again recognized by the Crown, had an important function in the process of standardizing the then non-standard systems of measurement for cloth, wool and other commodities. By the end of the fourteenth century Coventry's privileged status as an industrial and commercial centre had situated it as one of the most important, and now self-governing, cities in England.

The fact that textiles, rather than any other form of industrial activity, lay at the heart of Coventry's early prosperity is not insignificant. Textile production is notable for being an *extremely fragmented mode of production.* Cloth, for instance, needed to be cleaned, pounded, thickened, measured, finished, dyed and tailored. All of these functions required very specialized forms of labour which were often spatially dispersed throughout the city. Moreover, each of these crafts had its own distinct guild with its own particular rules and regulations. For this reason the city drapers were keenly aware of the need for a highly integrated, coordinated and choreographed system of overall industrial organization and management which could be fed into and supported by municipal government.

By the fourteenth century it is possible to describe Coventry almost in terms of being a medieval 'flexible specialization district', and it is this which marks out Coventry's distinctiveness as an English city during this period. This status derives from the combination of Coventry as a site of exchange and distribution, both of commodities and of knowledge, its national prestige as a producer of textile goods and the manner by which the decentralized, spatially dispersed and highly specialized departments of this production were skillfully coordinated, and the city's sponsorship by the Crown as a form of encouragement in spreading standardized systems of measurement and quantification of goods. Along with these factors we can also add another crucial element, itself a key feature of flexible specialization districts, which, to this day, continues to play an important role in defining the character of the city and the reproduction of the city habitus, namely the largely migrant composition of the city's local population.

The fact that highly specialized forms of labour were, and continued to be, required for Coventry's industrial activities should not be seen as merely incidental to the long-term historical trajectory of the city habitus. For it is precisely this demographic character that reasserts Coventry's status as a highly flexible and adaptive space for production and makes it extremely fertile ground for the relatively swift establishment of new industrial activities. Aside from wool and cloth, therefore, Coventry has historically gained national and international recognition in the following areas of production: metal trades (pins, needles, small metal goods such as buckles) (1300–1800), leather (1300 onwards), clocks and watches (1600–1800), ribbon weaving (1600–1800), sewing machines and bicycles (1860s–1900s), automobiles and military hardware (1900 to the present day), and latterly financial goods and services. In this respect the city's migrant population, continually renewed with each new wave of industrial development, embodies several significant characteristics. Primarily it tends to hold a view of the city which is essentially utilitarian. By this I mean that Coventry has historically been regarded by its population chiefly as a place of work and a site for wage gathering. This feature still dominates the demographic character of Coventry today, with the city having significant Irish, Scottish, Welsh, Tyneside, Polish, Ukrainian, Indian, Pakistani and West Indian communities. As a consequence one of the striking features for anyone arriving in the city to live or work is the remarkable lack of a sense of shared, stable and permanent city-wide community. For many of its inhabitants, Coventry does not represent 'home', for home is somewhere else, the place that one has temporarily left for work and one day will be returned to. In this sense the idea that Coventry exists as a more than convenient, and often extremely lucrative, staging post represents not just a description of the physicality of the city but, it could be argued, as the imaginary construction of place which exists in people's heads; that is, as a staging post in people's life-cycles or careers. The point I am making here is that the population's relatively weak historical links with the city, the absence of a general psychic affinity to Coventry, other than as a place of work, this refusal to see Coventry as a place of permanent settlement, feeds directly into and helps reproduce the city habitus. It is striking, therefore, to see just how little popular resistance there has been historically to the inevitable upheavals caused by the various rounds of urban development and redevelopment in Coventry, a fact which has certainly helped to ensure that Coventry has always been ideally placed to react and respond to the immediate needs of capital, and allowed it to define itself as a 'city which can turn its hand to anything'.

This latter fact, of course, has been particularly marked during the twentieth century, where, from the 1930s onwards, Coventry was situated at the forefront of urban modernist redevelopment. In this respect it is striking just how unencumbered the city appears to have been by nostalgic notions of 'heritage' and attitudes towards the preservation of its historical landmarks. Whilst such attitudes were clearly in keeping with the general political sensibilities of the period, Coventry was still notable for the alacrity of the manner in which it embraced the modernist ideal of a total urban reconstruction based upon a complete disavowal of the past. Of course popular mythology has since tended to represent this phase of Coventry's urban development as merely the functional response to the city's war-time devastation by the German bombers. Yet such a view is ignorant of the fact that substantial redevelopment plans for the city were being drawn up several years before the outbreak of war and that these plans had actually been completed as early as May 1940, a full six months before the city was bombed. Moreover, the City Architects Department, clearly heavily influenced by the revolutionary rhetoric of figures such as Le Corbusier, had envisaged a city that would be completely reconstructed according to modernist designs. With the exception of a handful of the many ancient buildings within the city which were dismantled and placed into storage until after the war, Coventry was to be effectively demolished. A pamphlet, published by the City Architects in 1940, entitled 'Coventry of Tomorrow: City of Desire' makes this clear:

> How are we to build when so much is to be destroyed? Can we afford to cease work for a creative end, even though we are at war? If we do not, the open

gate of defeat lies ahead, and behind it the declining path of civilisation and decadence. . . . Here is the challenge! If we do not take it up we are indeed decadent, defeated. (Quoted in Drake 1995: 5)

From this perspective the bombing of the city, whilst brutal in the extreme, none the less provided an extremely powerful *alibi*, rather than the cause, for the city's reconstruction, with the city council able to acquire compulsorily the large tracts of bombed land for rebuilding. As Drake reveals: 'A pamphlet of 1941 entitled "Disorder and Destruction: Order and Design" [depicts] an aerial photograph not of the blitzed ruins but of the pre-war city, subtitled "This must not happen again"' (1995: 6).

The brief evidence that I have presented here is not intended in itself to demonstrate conclusively the nature of the habitus of the city of Coventry, for clearly it is inconceivable that several centuries of complex and sedimented urban history can be analysed in anything other than a somewhat schematic manner in a few pages. Rather, this material should be seen merely as illustrative of the types of evidence required to be examined in order to investigate systematically how the city habitus originates, develops and reproduces. Such analyses should be, almost by the nature of their focus, extensive, detailed and necessarily empirically grounded (in this respect Taylor et al. 1996 remains exemplary), for, unless we are to succumb to the easy but ultimately inadequate view that cities are either simply spaces upon which things happen or the mere loci of intersection of social processes and relationships, such an approach is, I believe, essential and indeed inevitable.

Acknowledgements

I am indebted to Jim McGuigan for his extremely helpful and constructive comments upon the ideas developed in this paper, and to Patrick Canning for sharing his knowledge of Coventry with me and making me look afresh at the city I have lived in for sixteen years.

References

Bourdieu, P. (1977) *Outline of a Theory of Practice*, Cambridge: Cambridge University Press.
Bourdieu, P. (1984) *Distinction*, London: Routledge.
Bourdieu, P. (1990) *In Other Words*, Cambridge: Polity Press.
Davis, M. (1990) *City of Quartz*, London: Verso.
de Certeau, M. (1984) *The Practice of Everyday Life*, Berkeley: University of California Press.
Drake, M. (1995) 'The Corruption of Vision: The Postwar Reconstruction of Coventry', unpublished conference paper, British Sociological Association, University of Leicester.
Featherstone, M. (ed.) (1990) *Global Culture: Nationalism, Globalism and Modernity*, London: Sage.
Harvey, D. (1985) 'The Geo-politics of Capitalism', in D. Gregory and J. Urry (eds), *Social Relations and Spatial Structures*, London: Macmillan.

Harvey, D. (1989) *The Condition of Postmodernity*, Oxford: Basil Blackwell.

Jackson, P. (1989) *Maps of Meaning*, London: Unwin Hyman.

Lash, S. and Urry, J. (1987) *The End of Organized Capitalism*, Cambridge: Polity Press.

Lee, M.J. (1993) *Consumer Culture Reborn*, London: Routledge.

Massey, D. (1991) *Spatial Divisions of Labour: Social Structures and the Geography of Production*, Basingstoke: Macmillan.

Massey, D. (1993) 'Power-Geometry and a Progressive Sense of Place' in J. Bird, B. Curtis, T. Putnam, G. Robertson and L. Tickner (eds) *Mapping the Futures: Local Cultures, Global Change*, London: Routledge.

Presdee, M. (1986) 'Agony or Ecstacy: Broken Transitions and the New Social State of the Working-class Youth in Australia', Occasional Papers, South Australian Centre for Youth Studies, S.A. College of A.E., Magill, S. Australia.

Ritzer, G. (1991) *The McDonaldization of Society*, London: Pine Forge Press.

Sayer, A. (1985) 'The Difference that Space Makes', in D. Gregory and J. Urry (eds), *Social Relations and Spatial Structures*, London: Macmillan.

Shields, R. (ed.) (1992) *Lifestyle Shopping*, London: Routledge.

Shurmer-Smith, P. and Hannam, K. (1994) *Worlds of Desire, Realms of Power: A Cultural Geography*, London: Edward Arnold.

Soja, E. (1989) *Postmodern Geographies: The Reassertion of Space in Critical Theory*, London: Verso.

Taylor, I., Evans, K. and Fraser, P. (1996) *A Tale of Two Cities: A Study in Manchester and Sheffield*, London: Routledge.

Urry, J. (1990) 'Lancaster: Small Firms, Tourism and the "Locality"', in M. Harloe, C. Pickvance and J. Urry (eds), *Place, Policy and Politics*, Boston: London and Sydney: Unwyn Hyman.

Zukin, S. (1991) *Landscapes of Power*, Berkeley: University of California Press.

7

Dancing: Representation and Difference

Helen Thomas

This chapter builds on an earlier essay (Thomas 1993), which emerged from a nine-month study of a youth and community dance group in south-east London in 1990–1. That essay set out to explore the grounds for doing ethnographic research in the area of dance, gender construction and identification. The substantive focus was upon certain aspects of the relations between dance and femininity that were based on the analysis of one-to-one interview transcripts and participant observation of classes and rehearsals. The argument was that although the body in dance for both the men and women in the study was an 'active doing body, . . . there was a disjucture between the active doing female body and the passive appearing body in the women's talk' (Thomas 1993: 89). This asymmetrical relation did not seem to come through in the case of the men. Rather, in their discussions, both the dancing body and the representing body were located in terms of activity and strength, not in terms of surveillance by others and/or themselves.

Although the context here is the same, that is, the youth and community dance group, the present chapter draws on additional research material,[1] namely a filmed and recorded *group* interview with the dancers after the initial essay had been written, which, in turn, provided illuminating talk about how the dancers themselves perceived of differences between women and men dancing and between typical attitudes towards black women dancers and black men dancers. This chapter, then, calls attention to the importance of considering the relations between gender and race that the earlier essay alluded to but could not address in any detail. The major concern is to locate the different images – female/male, black/white – that the dancers themselves invoked in terms of traditional and pervasive Western images of black sexuality, particularly in this instance with regard to female sexuality.

A further related concern is to celebrate ethnography as an intellectual pursuit for the analysis of cultural forms and practices. By this I do not mean the textbook sense of ethnography (see, for example, Hammersley and Atkinson 1995) but, rather, an understanding of the kind of enterprise that it constitutes, or, in the words of Clifford Geertz (1975: 5), 'what doing ethnography is'. Ethnography for Geertz (1975: 6), following the linguistic philosopher Gilbert Ryle, is 'thick description':

> What the ethnographer is in fact faced with . . . is a multiplicity of complex
> conceptual structures, many of them superimposed upon or knotted into one
> another, which are at once strange, irregular, and inexplicit and which he must
> contrive somehow first to grasp and then to render. (Geertz 1975: 10)

Ethnography, from this perspective, is not about making truth claims. Geertz and those who follow in his footsteps, like James Clifford (1988), challenge the principles of philosophical realism upon which much ethnography was founded. Instead they advocate a relativist stance in which ethnography is viewed as an interpretive act. Ethnographic writings in themselves, being based on second- or third-hand constructs, are also treated as interpretations. Hence, the interpretations of culture that ethnographic writings offer are 'fictions' in the sense that they are 'something fashioned', not in the sense that they are 'false' or 'unfactual' (Geertz 1975: 15). Geertz's illuminating essay 'Thick Description' (1975: 3–30) maintains that ethnographic formulations of 'other people's symbol systems must be actor-oriented' and that the construction of ethnographic descriptions is an imaginative act which should bring us into touch with the lives of 'strangers'. It is this sense of ethnography that I wish to celebrate.

Although ethnography was a visible strand in the early stages in the development of cultural studies (see, for example, Hall and Jefferson 1975), it came to be superseded by more metatheoretical considerations and textual analyses of popular cultural processes and artefacts in the 1980s. Nevertheless, some of the earlier ethnographic work raised interesting methodological issues that are perhaps worth revisiting and revitalizing. Paul Willis's (1977) influential study of working-class 'lads', for example, despite its noted limitations of 'going native' (see Hammersley and Atkinson 1995), was an important contribution to the field. Ethnography, for Willis (1977), is the study of 'lived meanings', in this case the counter-school culture, which is used 'to make theoretical points about wider cultural issues' (Brake 1985: 64). Willis's recent contribution to the field, *Common Culture* (1990), has good intentions, which he sets out in the first chapter of the book, but the majority of the case studies in this 'collective enterprise' fall far short of the theoretical and methodological insights of studies like *Learning to Labour* (1977) and *Profane Culture* (1978). Although Willis sees the method as 'broadly ethnographic', the resulting case studies in *Common Culture* may be described in terms of 'thin description' as opposed to the 'thick description' that Geertz (1975) advocated and subsequently demonstrated in his case study material. Nevertheless, Willis does raise some useful critical points regarding the consequences that ensue from high culture separating itself off from everyday 'common' cultural life. It is important to note that he does not advocate a kind of 'Adorno in reverse' (see Huyssen 1986) and seek to examine popular culture as a sort of equivalent to high culture, as a number of textual approaches have done. Rather than beginning with 'objects and artefacts', the concern is to begin with people and then move on to objects. The task is to understand popular representations through their 'creative' *usage* in everyday life, not to confine understanding of the everyday to the study of popular media texts: the aim is to demonstrate the importance of ethnographic work in drawing out the lived meanings.

In the introductory essay to *Common Culture*, Willis (1990) argues that young people have been systematically excluded and, for the most part, have excluded themselves from the 'institutionalization' of art. This is High Art with a capital A, whose 'existence, reproduction and appreciation depends on institutions, from art galleries, museums, theatres, ballet companies to the Arts Council itself' (Willis 1990: 2). With the establishment of *institutional* art, 'aesthetic value' comes to reside in the formal characteristics of art as opposed to its relevance to *real* life, leading to the possibility of the 'complete dissociation of art from living contexts', an 'internal hyperinstitutionalization of art' (Willis 1990: 2). Appreciation of art, according to Willis, becomes stultified and hollow. Those who are not a part of hyperinstitutionalized art, and that means the majority, are not 'in' simply or only because they lack the codes, because they have not learned the language. The outsiders, the mass, are often seen by the insiders – that is, those who have the cultural capital, as Bourdieu (1984) called it – as being ignorant or lacking in artistic sensibilities.

Despite the fact that the majority of young people are not involved in 'the arts', Willis (1990: 1) maintains that there is life out there in the streets and that young people's lives 'are actually full of expressions, signs and symbols through which individuals and groups seek to creatively establish their presence, identity and meaning; the task that *Common Culture* (1990) sets itself is to 'literally re-cognize' this.

The democratization of culture that was part of the social reformist ethos which led to the establishment of the Arts Council after the Second World War was short-lived according to Willis (1990: 4–5). The residue of the ideal of democratization of culture is still promoted by community arts projects through their attempts to make the arts more relevant to everyday life experiences. Nevertheless, the institutionalization of art is often encoded within these democratizing movements to the extent that they operate implicitly on the basis of the institutional conventions and practices of what counts as art. The youth and community dance project which provides the backdrop for this discussion both attempts to draw on the young people's creativity and to offer them experience of contemporary theatre dance practices in a 'good' dance space.

The youth and community dance project under discussion is supported by Lewisham Council, a local inner-city authority in London, with the Laban Centre for Movement and Dance providing the space for classes and rehearsals. There are two open classes every week, for young people between the ages of fourteen and twenty-five, and these are led by a teacher who is white and male. The classes can be best described as jazz-based movement to popular contemporary music. The aim of the classes is to provide a space for young people who live and work in an inner-city multicultural environment to experience the pleasures of and gain skills in the area of performance-based dance. The classes attract a number of young black men and women who seem to come in by word of mouth (see Thomas 1993).

Keith, the teacher, invites individuals from the class to join the Dance Group. They stay on after the class to rehearse and work up new dances. At any one time there are around twenty members of the Group with varying levels of dance experience, and as individual dancers drop out, so other new ones are brought in from the classes. The Group has a programme of dances that lasts about one and a half hours and they perform regularly throughout the year to audiences in the local community and sometimes outside of the area. Some dances stay in the programme for a long time because they are popular with the audiences, the dancers or Keith, who choreographs most of them. Occasionally, Keith invites one of the more experienced dancers to choreograph a piece for members of the Group.

As part of the research process and as a means of thanking the dancers and Keith for allowing me to sit in on classes and to video the classes and rehearsals, we spent a day filming six dances in the television studios at Goldsmiths' College, University of London. Keith insisted that two of the dances should involve all of the Group so that everyone could enjoy the experience, which was in keeping with the community spirit that he sought to generate in the classes and the Group. The other four dances were chosen for the following reasons: I had sat in on the rehearsals and/or had filmed them being worked through to performance and could perform the direct editing from the four different camera shots on an informed basis of this stock of 'knowledge at hand' (Schütz 1967: 208). Nine of the dancers in the dances had been interviewed on an individual basis and it was anticipated that the group discussion might generate further insights into gender relations and prevalent notions of femininity and masculinity in dance. Moreover, the dances covered a range of material and the dancers performed them well.

Four volunteer undergraduates worked the cameras, one of the college technicians worked the sound, the other the lighting and the editing equipment, and I directed it. The camera crew and the editor were women and the two technicians were men. The concern was to create an atmosphere which would not completely replicate the structure of (male) looking (Mulvey 1989: 14–29) by having 'real' women work the cameras and take control of the production of the images. But the 'voyeuristic-scopophilic' (Mulvey 1989: 25) character of using the cameras and the editing suite on the surface of dancers' bodies in action seemed to ensure that this would remain a vain hope. I would reluctantly agree with Laura Mulvey (1989: 29), who argues that the concept of the 'male gaze', which she developed in relation to cinema spectatorship, is contingent not on the 'actual' sex of the spectator but, rather, on the 'masculinization' of the spectator position.[2] Moreover, ethnography, as Clifford (1986) points out, has traditionally privileged 'sight', and the paradigm of visualism has been a key device in the domination and surveillance of 'others'. A further related concern worth noting was the fact that all of the crew, except for the sound technician, were white (despite efforts to recruit black students to join the camera crew), while most of the dancers were black. There was apprehension in case we were simply replicating the stereotype of blacks as performers which has been prevalent in the history of film and the musical stage (Dyer 1989; hooks 1992). Moreover, as bell hooks (1992: 62–5) argues, when analysts discuss the experiences of racism through the sexual stereotyping of the represented 'Other', more often than not they are speaking about themselves, not the 'Other'.[3]

The concern to maintain an interactive approach in the research that would enable the dancers voices to be heard in the discourse (Thomas 1993) led to the proposal that I should take part in a videoed group interview with the dancers at the first viewing of the video, and thus the researcher would also be put into the 'actual' research frame under the gaze of camera. Two of the students who operated the cameras in the television studio agreed to video the interview. Later the dances were edited with the interview so that when the research was presented both the dances and the discourse of the dancers, at the very least, could be partially seen and heard. It could be contested that this cutting and editing reduces further the 'reality' of the dancers' experiences, practice or talk and, in so doing, invalidates the work. Clifford (1986), however, advocates an analytic shift away from the ethnographic gaze towards a more discursive paradigm that enables a multiplicity of 'voices' to be heard, in which the ethnographer is simply one voice among many others. Thus, from this perspective, all ethnographic accounts are partial. As such, it becomes important to reveal the ground(s) and processes that inform the discussion in the first instance, through the practice of reflexivity.

The discussion that follows centres on some of the talk that took place in relation to three of the dances over two screenings and interviews with seven members of the Group (two men and five women). The first is a *pas de deux* with Errol and Dawn in two sections. The dance is episodic in form and centres on the coming together and break-up of a (hetero)sexual relationship. The first part of the dance contains a long, sustained, almost 'slow motion', section beginning with the dancers lying on the floor and spatially close to each other. There is a great deal of close physical contact, holding, touching, one lying on top of the other, and rolling over each other. The oneness of the two bodies is fragmented by the woman resisting the touch of the man and attempting to avert her gaze and her body from the presence of his touch. Both dancers are dressed in white: Errol in loose-fitting trousers, with bare torso, and

Dawn in a halter-neck dress with fitted bodice and three-quarter length flared shirt.

The second piece is a lyrical 'pure' dance *pas de trois* with Juliet, Maxine and Carol that contains both unison movement in time or in canon form, and individual motifs. Their costumes are the same but in contrasting pastel shades: calf-length dresses with leotard tops with three-quarter length sleeves, and flared handkerchief skirts. The spatial relationships between the dancers provided an interesting stylistic contrast to the first dance. The dance begins with the dancers standing with heads bowed and arms at their sides in a line at the top right side of the stage facing the other side of the stage, so that their bodies are side-on to the audience. Although the distance between them is so small that the breath of the third and second dancer could be felt on the back of the neck of the one in front of them, there is little sense of a relationship here: they seem to be on their own, almost like the queue at a bus stop. Throughout most of the dance they remain apart from each other so that even when there is unison movement, the dancers appear to be individuated by spatial difference. The effort quality of the movement is light and fluid, with a flexible and open upper body. The dancers seem to glide across the floor, and when they transfer their body weight to the floor they appear to slide onto it with a minimum of effort.

The third dance is a large group piece for seven or more people that Michael, a Group member, had choreographed after he had been on a visit to Jamaica. In the version under discussion, there are five women and two men. The women are dressed in black leotards and black drawstring calf-length skirts; the men in black tights with bare torso. Although it does not contain an extended narrative, it is, according to Michael, a dance about 'roots'. The movement quality is rhythmical, wide, grounded, strong and encompassing. Although not all of the dancers are on stage throughout the dance, unlike the previous dance, there is a sense in which each dancer is part of a larger whole. The strong sense of a group is generated through the use of core motifs which appear at points throughout the piece, the forming of group movement shapes and patterns, or unison movement with a common spatial focus.

The group discussion dwelled on issues of identity and difference in terms of representations of: heterosexuality/homosexuality in dance; femininity/masculinity in dance movement; black/white, Afro-Caribbean/European dance; black women dancers/black men dancers. The dancers talked very easily, and on occasions I had to interrupt to ask them to speak one at a time so that we could catch the sound on the video.

After showing the first duet with Errol and Dawn, I asked Michael if he and Errol could perform this dance together. They both said that they could, if they had to, but they would not be able 'to show any emotions'. Both were concerned that if they performed a 'couple' dance 'like that' on the stage it would have ramifications for how they were viewed in their ordinary everyday lives. Said Michael:

> The way things are with society now, if they see two men do that on the stage they would say – gay! homosexual! You'll come out and people will be thinking that you're gay!

The problem seemed to be that they could only show a limited range of emotions on the stage if they were to be seen as 'real' (heterosexual) men off-stage:

> As a man you can show emotions, but it can just be about *brotherly love*, people would look at you unless the movements say this is not a sexual relationship, it's a *brotherly love* relationship. (Michael)

One of the key considerations here is the 'feminization' of theatrical dance in the West. The feminine connotations of dance stand in binary opposition to the masculine connotations of physical sports like rugby and football.[4] In terms of male ordering (Rutherford 1988: 26), the female constitutes a prominent negative 'dangerous' Other to heterosexual masculinity. As Jonathan Rutherford argues:

> The dominant meanings of masculinity in our culture are about producing our bodies as instruments of will. Flesh, sexuality, emotionality, these become seen as uncontrollable forces and a source of anxiety. We live within a culture that alienates men from their bodies and sexuality. We learn to repress these because they are the antithesis of what it means to be masculine.
>   The dark illicit secrets and fantasies of heterosexual masculinity are projected onto the property of others: our images of women, homosexuals and black people are created by the fleshy fears of heterosexual men. (1988: 26)

Dance is viewed as a predominantly feminine activity and the men who engage in it are always in 'danger' of being classed as effeminate alongside the denigrated female Other. The pervasiveness of this conception (among others) in popular culture is expressed clearly in the Foster's Lager advert which features Paul Hogan (as an uncultured Australian male chauvinist), watching the ballet from an opera box (probably at the Royal Opera House) with a woman (high-class, white, English) in an evening dress and tiara, who is viewing the spectacle through opera glasses. When Hogan catches his first sight of the principal male dancer leaping onto the stage in tights, he jumps up and covers the woman's eyes with his hand, exclaiming to the viewer, 'Struth! there's a man down there with no strides on!' – in other words, women should not look at scantily clad men (that is what men do to women) and 'real' men do not leap around in tights.

That pervasive representation of men in dance was highly problematic for both Michael and Errol. They were working in a cultural form which clearly they loved but they were on guard against common-sense perceptions of men who danced, which ran counter to their sense of their (hetero)sexual identities. There were certain kinds of movements between two men 'like rolling all over each other' that were burdensome for them to perform because they perceived that their sexual identities would be called into question by others. Thus, their talk brought into play negative representations of men in dance that were absent in the previous paper (Thomas 1993).

According to Michael:

> The society always sees dance as feminine . . . and men as not manly . . . when they see a man dressed up on stage in tights and all that, they actually see it as feminine and they think that you are 'bent'. Therefore, it would be difficult for us to do something like that [the first couple dance] without feeling distressed!

For Errol and Michael there was another set of paradoxes at play. They were not only (heterosexual) men taking part in a feminized cultural form who did not want to be contaminated by the association of femininity; they were, at the same time, black men of Afro-Caribbean descent who were aware of and to some extent took on board the representations of black male sexuality (the stud with a large penis) which have been constituted historically through such institutions as Christianity, slavery and colonization (Shilling 1993: 55–9). In the arena of popular culture, as bell hooks's (1992) study of race and representations shows, black performers have often become embroiled in the negative stereotype of black sexuality and have used it as an attribute. Some dancers, like Bill T. Jones, for example, have sought to question the prevalent images of masculinity in contemporary culture in their dance works by deconstructing the dominant body politic (Boyce et al. 1988).

When I asked the women if they would encounter the same problems as the men if they performed this dance with another woman, Veronica considered that the problem would probably be similar 'but not [felt] so strongly as [by] the men'. Kate went further and said that it could be seen as a dance of 'camaraderie or friendship' if women performed it. This led me to enquire how the same dance performed by two men together or two women together could be interpreted differently, the first as expressing camaraderie and friendship and the second as symbolizing some kind of sexually dangerous involvement or intimacy. The key to this, according to Veronica, can be found in the relationship of everyday movement to dance movement: 'You don't often see a man walking down the street arm and arm with another man but it's different with women – you see them hugging and kissing – it looks normal.'[5]

For Errol and Veronica, it is not simply about the movement itself, rather it is 'what lies behind it'. Thus, the distinction is locatable in terms of intentionality and the relatedness to and/or transformation of the conventions of everyday movement. It may also speak to the silence on lesbianism in our culture at least until quite recently (Ruehl 1986), which, in turn, can be linked back to the historical construction of masculinity and its fear of 'dangerous others' (Shilling 1993: 55).

When we moved on to discuss the second dance for three women the focus was directed towards trying to tease out further perceived differences between women and men dancing. I asked the men how they would feel about performing this particular dance, which, as indicated above, is lyrical with apparently effortless, soft and flowing movement, particularly in the upper body. The men indicated, and the women agreed, that they could do this piece, although the dynamics would not be quite the same. 'It would be feminine, but it would be done with a certain coarseness' if the men performed it, 'whereas the girls would have a softer quality' (Errol). I asked Errol if, given the earlier discussion, 'feminine' was the right word, and he responded in terms of stereo-typical notions of the distinction between the feminine and the mascu-line that is underscored by the power of masculinity:

> The female dancer, her extreme is like a Tinkerbell where she can be as soft and as petite as she wants to be and males are naturally expected to be strong, strong physically – looking strong the way they dance. To do a piece like that would be a challenge. I wouldn't be thinking, that's too feminine or too gay!

When I asked what were the most significant differences between the two dances, the dancers commented on the fact that they varied in degree of physical contact and that they were structured and fashioned in a different manner. Although the second dance was performed by (real) women, it had a certain individual 'quiet strength' about it that did not pose a problem for the men. Moreover, its 'pure' dance form meant that the representation of emotions was kept to a minimum and, therefore, it was less 'dangerous' for them:

> In the second dance each of them are individuals, but yet there is something about them that they all feel and they all portray . . . despite the fact that they are individuals, they dance as one. (Michelle)

In our discussions of the third dance that Michael choreographed, two related issues emerged: 'the fact of blackness' (Fanon 1992); and the qualitative distinctions between representations of black male dancers and black female dancers.

The dancers loved performing Michael's dance. They considered that it related to them on a cultural level as black British dancers. Kate, the only white dancer in the discussion group, said she did not ask to be in the dance because she thought that her presence would have dissipated its power – 'the message was stronger because it was all black' (Kate). The inspiration for the dance came, as mentioned above, after Michael had been to Jamaica on holiday for the first time:

> I saw how black people live in everyday life and I thought this is my culture this is where my roots are. I wanted to bring this out in the dance. [Black culture] over here gets distorted and over there [life] seems more natural and I wanted to bring out the best side of it.

The dancers felt that it was sometimes difficult to achieve the earthbound movement quality that Michael required because they have been trained in a European style, which advocates a high bodily attitude. As Michael wanted the 'dance to be more African', he said that he had to keep reminding them in rehearsals 'to get down and be more earthy' (see Oyortey 1993 on African people's dance).

The dancers were not, I think, implying there is one homogeneous African dance,[6] or that their dance was genuinely 'African', but, rather, they were seeking to locate themselves, as black British dancers trained in a European style, to the African diaspora. The dance did give them a sense of pride in being of Afro-Caribbean descent in a culture which did not appreciate their difference and in which they were almost invisible. They considered that it had a spiritual quality for both the dancers and the audience and it made them feel as if they were united in some kind of bond:

> The reason we like doing this dance is that we are not often allowed to portray ourselves as we are as black people in this western world, and when we do it [this dance], it brings us out, it makes us feel real good. (Veronica)

When asked to explain a little more about what they meant by this, Juliet responded:

> We're born with black skin right, and no matter whether you want to go for a job or to go to certain schools – we can't go to certain schools. Deep down we are all cast on the same level. Whatever we want to get or to undertake – we have to get through white supremacy – and once we have got what we want we have to maintain it – but it's really hard – we have always got to be strong! All we are asking for is equality!

Thus, the differences between the representation of men and women in dance that had informed the discussion over the first two dances seemed to be overtaken by their coming together in their knowledge of the consequences of the 'fact of blackness' (Fanon 1992),[7] and the celebration of their identities and differences in and for themselves. This unity, however, was interrupted for a time. As the discussion turned towards their understanding of the ways in which black dance and black dancers did not have the same status as European dance and dancers,[8] the issue of difference between the media representation of black men and black women in dance began to emerge. According to Juliet:

> In terms of the media, black guys are classed on the same level as white dancers; white male dancers and black male dancers are treated the same. But black female dancers are not treated in the same way, unless you are of a particular shape, have European features, or have long flowing hair. Black female dancers are not treated as attractive enough to be seen on a television screen. To white supremacy or to other nations of the world, we are sort of built physically on a hideous [bodily] structure.

I indicated that there had been a long history of struggle for black dancers to be accepted in theatre dance, most particularly in classical ballet, and that this lack of acceptance by the establishment had been the driving force behind Arthur Mitchell's quest to establish the Dance Theatre of Harlem. Juliet thought that things might be slightly better in America, but, 'over here black female dancers do not have a chance unless you go' – at which point, Juliet moved from her crossed-legged position on the floor onto her knees, arched her back and pushing her upper body outwards and parallel to the floor, she began to shake her shoulders and gyrate her hips, saying, 'That is the only way you can get work. You have to shake your hips and your breasts!'

Juliet's vivid interpretation of the typical image of a black female dancer, which caused a considerable amount of laughter among the Group, can be linked to the representation of black women in popular culture (hooks 1992: 61–77) and to nineteenth-century iconography (Gilman 1992). These representations are underpinned by nineteenth-century racist interpretations of black female sexuality (hooks 1992: 62). In nineteenth-century iconography, as Sander Gilman (1992: 176–80) demonstrates, the black female was defined in terms of her genitalia. The genitalia were deemed to be abnormal and this, in turn, was offered as a sign of her rampant sexuality and the place of the black on the 'great chain of being'. The theory of the great chain of being rejects the idea that all human beings are created in the eyes of God and in his Image, in favour of the view that humankind is made up of diverse types of species who take up their place on the evolutionary ladder. The black was perceived to constitute humanity at its origins while the European variety at the top constituted the fully formed rational type. The poly-genic view of the innate differences between the races was applied to numerous aspects of humankind, including sexuality. The black, occupy-ing the base position of humanity, was seen as having animal-like sexuality and physical appearance in contrast to the high sexual mores and beauty embodied in the European. The essential black was repre-sented by the Hottentot female. Sarah Baartmann, ironically named the 'Hottentot Venus', was put on display in 1810, largely to show her protruding buttocks. Her naked body was put on show on numerous occasions over the next five years before she died. After she died an autopsy was performed and was written up so that her 'primitive' genitalia could be investigated. In her life and death, Sarah Baartmann, as an icon of black female sexuality, as Gilman argues, 'was reduced to her sexual parts. The audience that paid to see her buttocks and had fantasized about the uniqueness of her genitalia when she was alive could, after her death and dissection, examine both' (1992: 172).

Thus, Juliet's talk and actions (emphasizing the bottom and the breasts through arching her back and shaking her hips and shoulders), along with the dancers' discussions of how black dancers are perceived as having a different physical structure ('black people are seen as too big boned', according to Errol) from that of white (European) dancers, seem to substantiate Gilman's (1992) and hooks's (1992) claim that the negat-ive images of black female sexuality in the discourses of nineteenth-century iconography still shape perceptions in contemporary culture. Although bell hooks points out that contemporary 'thinking about black female bodies does not attempt to read the body as a sign of "natural" racial inferiority' (1992: 63), the black women especially and the men in this study stressed that they were still seen as 'naturally' inferior in dance in particular and in the culture in general. From their perspective, however, Michael's dance enabled them collectively to feel like *them-selves*, not as they felt they were *seen by others*. In that dance, as Veronica put it: 'Everyone is together. It *is* such a power.'

Notes

1. I would like to thank the dancers of the South East London Community Dance Group and Keith O'Brien for allowing me to conduct the research. I am grateful to my students, Janet and June, for the time they spent recording the interview and the dances in the television studios at Goldsmiths' College and to Tony and Jonathan for their technical advice and help in the television studios and in rehearsals.

2. The term 'male gaze' has been much used, abused and criticized in film studies and cultural studies since it was used in Mulvey's essay 'Visual Pleasure and Narrative Cinema' in 1975. In recent years, several of the new wave of dance scholars, influenced by cultural studies and feminist studies, have also been drawn to the term when considering the dominant representations of women's bodies in Western theatre dance. I have argued elsewhere (Thomas 1996) that the term has often been used without consideration of the theoretical framework in which it was generated, namely a psychoanalytic semiotics. With the result, as Mary Anne Doane (1987) has noted with regard to its use in film studies, the psychic subject is often collapsed into the social subject in an unproblematic fashion without recognizing the distinction between the two. Hence, my concern to use the term without qualification.

3. This is not the place to pursue the problems of conducting research on difference and representation in any detail. For a more detailed account in relation to dance and feminist research see Helen Thomas (1993) and Christy Adair (1992). For accounts and critiques of the relation between feminism and racism see Caroline Knowles and Sharmila Mercer (1992).

4. I am grateful to Don Slater for making this point.

5. For a fuller discussion of the relation of everyday movement to dance movement see Helen Thomas (1995).

6. In 'The Fact of Blackness', Frantz Fanon (1992) demonstrates how the socio-historical construction of the opposition between blackness and whiteness takes on the character of an indisputable fact of nature. By revealing the mechanisms, Fanon opened up a space for an awareness of racial categorization that was non-essentialist.

7. See Zagba Oyortey's (1993) useful discussion on the diversity of African people's dance on the one hand, and his schematic approach to the grouping of dance types and movement, pattern on the other.

8. See Lynne Fauley Emery (1988: 219–72) and Christy Adair (1992: 160–81) on this issue.

References

Adair, C. (1992) *Women and Dance: Sylphs and Sirens*, London: Macmillan.

Bourdieu, P. (1984) *Distinction: A Social Critique of the Judgement of Taste*, London: Routledge & Kegan Paul.

Boyce, J., Daly, A., Jones, B.T. and Martin, C. (1988) 'Movement and Gender: A Roundtable Discussion', *The Drama Review*, 32(4) (Winter): 82–101.

Brake, M. (1985) *Comparative Youth Culture*, London: Routledge & Kegan Paul.

Clifford. J. (1986) 'Introduction: Partial Truths', in J. Clifford and G. Marcus (eds), *Writing Culture: The Poetics and Politics of Ethnography*, Berkeley: University of California Press.

Clifford, J. (1988) *The Predicament of Culture: Twentieth-Century Ethnography, Literature, and Art*, Cambridge, Mass.: Harvard University Press.

Doane, M. (1987) *The Desire to Desire: The Woman's Film of the 1940s*, London: Macmillan.

Dyer, R. (1989) *Heavenly Bodies: Film Stars and Society*, Basingstoke: Macmillan.

Dyer, R. (1992) *Only Entertainment*, London: Routledge.

Emery, L. (1988) *Black Dance from 1619 to Today*, 2nd edn, London: Dance Books.

Fanon, F. (1992) 'The Fact of Blackness', in J. Donald and A. Rattansi (eds), *'Race', Culture and Difference*, London: Sage.

Geertz, C. (1975) *The Interpretation of Cultures*, London: Hutchinson.

Gilman, S. (1992) 'Black Bodies, White Bodies: Towards an Iconography of Female Sexuality in Late-Nineteenth-Century Art, Medicine and Literature', in J. Donald and A. Rattansi (eds), *'Race', Culture and Difference*. London: Sage.

Hall, S. and Jefferson, T. (1975) *Resistance Through Rituals*, Birmingham: Centre for Contemporary Cultural Studies.

Hammersley, M. (1992) *What's Wrong with Ethnography?*, London: Routledge.

Hammersley, M. and Atkinson, P. (1995) *Ethnography: Principles in Practice*, 2nd edn, London: Routledge.

hooks, b. (1992) *Black Looks: Race and Representation*, London: Turnaround.

Huyssen, A. (1986) *After the Great Divide: Modernism, Mass Culture, Postmodernism*, London: Macmillan.

Knowles, C. and Mercer, S. (1992) 'Feminism and Antiracism: An Exploration of the Political Possibilities', in J. Donald and A. Rattansi (eds), *'Race', Culture and Difference*, London: Sage.

Mulvey, L. (1975) 'Visual Pleasure and Narrative Cinema', *Screen*, 16(3), Autumn.

Mulvey, L. (1989) *Visual and Other Pleasures*, Basingstoke: Macmillan.

Oyortey, Z. (1993) 'Still Dancing Downwards and Talking Back', in H. Thomas (ed.), *Dance, Gender and Culture*, Basingstoke: Macmillan.

Ruehl, S. (1986) 'Inverts and Experts: Radcliffe Hall and the Lesbian Identity', in R. Brunt and C. Rowan (eds), *Feminism, Culture and Politics*, London: Lawrence & Wishart.

Rutherford, J. (1988) 'Who's That Man?', in R. Chapman and J. Rutherford (eds), *Male Order: Unwrapping Masculinity*, London: Lawrence & Wishart.

Schütz, A. (1967) *Collected Papers 1: The Problem of Social Reality*, The Hague: Martinus Nijhoff.

Shilling, C. (1993) *The Body and Social Theory*, London: Sage.

Thomas, H. (1993) 'An-Other Voice: Young Women Dancing and Talking', in H. Thomas (ed.), *Dance, Gender and Culture*, Basingstoke: Macmillan.

Thomas, H. (1995) *Dance, Modernity and Culture: Explorations in the Sociology of Dance*, London: Routledge.

Thomas, H. (1996) 'Do You Want to Join the Dance?: Postmodernism/Poststructuralism, the Body and Dance', in G. Morris (ed.), *Moving Words: Re-Writing Dance*. London: Routledge.

Willis, P. (1977) *Learning to Labour*, London: Saxon House.

Willis, P. (1978) *Profane Culture*, London: Routledge & Kegan Paul.

Willis, P. (with Jones, S., Canaan, J. and Hurd, G.) (1990) *Common Culture*, Milton Keynes: Open University Press.

8

Irish Cultural Studies and the Politics of Irish Studies

Sabina Sharkey

Introduction: Here comes anybody

In a recent issue of the *New Statesman* (29 November 1996) a short piece on Irish studies appeared under the dubious title 'A Fine Old Irish Stew' (Maddox 1996: 21–2). The argument is directly stated in the subtitle: 'Irish studies may be a popular university course. But as an intellectual discipline it is largely bogus' (1996: 21). I muse on this as I set about writing on the subject, wondering about the high levels of antagonism and inaccuracy contained in the article. To begin with, to my knowledge, Irish studies does not present itself as a discipline; rather its delivery is structured either in a multidisciplinary or occasionally in an inter-disciplinary way. 'Step forward, then, Irish studies', orders Ms Maddox as prosecuting counsel and introduces her first piece of incriminating evidence. Irish studies is 'not quite Irish literature nor Irish history, but rather a stew of these with geography, sociology, politics, feminism, and, inevitably, media thrown in' (1996: 21). So the problem appears to be that Irish studies does not limit itself to a single discipline. Maddox notes that there is no 'harm' in studying things Irish 'for their inherent interest', a point upon which she does not elaborate, preferring instead to bestow an apparently beneficent general legitimation of knowledge acquisition: 'There is no reason why anybody should not study any subject that passes muster as an academic discipline' (1996: 21). Dream on, sister. Seemingly unaware of influencing factors such as increasing commodifi-cation of university education in recent years, she confidently delimits the proper process of study as one which occurs where a subject can pass muster as a discipline. In this erroneous interchange a confusion, between subject and discipline, is made to pass muster as method. Furthermore, her interpretation of 'any' subject/intellectual discipline is reduced to those which are traditional and long-established. At the outset of the article she positions herself in antipathy to 'studies', media and cultural studies and, most recently, Irish studies. There are the bins wherein myriad products and phenomena in contemporary cultural circulation and consumption, not previously studied within history or literature, may be consigned as of no 'inherent interest'. The apparent all-inclusiveness of those who may partake in her prescribed organizational field of study is suggested by her use of the term 'anybody'. But anybody, it seems, is also subject to a selective cull, for she immediately modifies her remarks:

> But there is something unlovely about young people seeking academic degrees in how the world has done them wrong. Irish studies are particularly popular in the new universities [the former polytechnics] and in areas with large immigrant populations. Not all Irish, by any means. Greek Cypriots and West Indians are drawn to the subject in significant numbers. This is where the worry comes in. (1996: 21)

Who is worried is not altogether clear in this quotation. But the uptake of Irish studies by a range of migrant unlovelies clearly involves their expressing a quality of interest in the subject distinguishable from the harmless 'inherent interest' which she so values and which presumably is palpable to 'anybody', other than them. Just what 'the worry' is can be identified in the opening of her next paragraph: 'Irish studies is riding the crest of the larger, more sinister wave known as "post-colonial studies". This is a politically correct vogue for elevating the grievances of newly independent nations to academic status' (1996: 21). From vague to vogue, an unaccountable but sinister conspiracy is afoot, to advance whingeing students of whingeing nations by the devious ploy of curriculum development. What is being eroded by these sinister waves is left unspoken, perhaps as too 'inherently' obvious to need stating, to *anybody*. Why the designation 'post-colonial' is so inappropriate to Ireland is then rehearsed, and again we may assume that the basis of these assumptions is inherent since it is not stated. Her complaints are threefold: it denies the Irish role in colonizing and administering the British empire; it emphasizes the Irish as exiles, rather than Europeans; and it leads to rough-shod riding over the complexities of recent Irish history for political ends.

Having taught Irish studies at both undergraduate and postgraduate levels within a variety of third-level institutions, I am conscious of the frequency with which the range of debates on terminology is addressed, where the genealogy of the term 'post-colonial' and the variety of ideological stances taken in relation to this term (including that presented by Maddox) are themselves subject of study. So too within core courses is the process of Irish incorporation within British imperialism. This regularly involves specific study of the interactive range of responses, of assimilation, cooperation, collusion and/or resistance by Irish agents over time. The axiology of Irish identity, 'mere' Anglo-, European, migrant, exilic, diasporic and nativist, is a key subject of study, as is the highly complex recent political history. That phenomena are studied rather than avowed or negated is the moot point of which Maddox is either unaware, or perhaps she is just unwilling to allow such knowledge to modify an inherent conviction. In any case, she is not the first long-term American resident in Britain (exile, European, diasporic, British?) to express a cultural conservatism by declaring things in America to be far worse, and so it proves in relation to Irish studies: 'It is hardly surprising that, in the harsher American environment, Irish studies should have joined black studies, Hispanic studies and the rest as a manifestation of aggressive ethnicity' (1996: 21). *The New York Times* is accused of viewing Ireland 'only in post-colonial terms' since it avers that the 'Irish are ascendant again' and lists a range of recent cultural output – Riverdance, U2, Jordan's *Michael Collins* and Seamus Heaney – to prove this 'new kind of tribal pride' (1996: 21). Particularly offensive to her is the *NYT*'s closing quotation from Roddy Doyle's *The Commitments*, 'the Irish are the blacks of Europe'. But why this American appreciation of yet another resurgence of Irish cultural vitality may be interpreted as exclusively post-colonial, or even particularly so, remains unexplored. However, the Doyle quotation neatly facilitates the introduction of Maddox's next *bête noire*, women and women's studies: 'And women are the blacks of Ireland. One of the marvels of Irish studies is how easily it makes common cause with women's studies' (1996: 21). The 'common cause' is not adumbrated. Rather she lunges ahead, dispatching doctoral research pertinent to Irish women as a journey 'into the heart of darkness' (1996: 21), scorning a Californian Professor of Literature and then taking issue with an Irish one:

> Kiberd maintains that all imperial powers infantilise their colonies. He detects in W.B. Yeats's 'Easter 1916', an Anglo-Irishman's diminution of the sacred martyrs by portraying them as 'children whose limbs had run wild'. 'In it,' he says, 'the Irishman is still a child.' (1996: 22)

It may be worth noting that Kiberd does not actually valorize those involved in the 1916 Rising as 'sacred martyrs'. Maddox's commentary on Kiberd is terse and baffling: 'Exactly. Infantilising. Divisive. Redundant' (1996: 22). Exactly? What, exactly? one is tempted to ask. But she has now begun to vent her indignation broadly: 'It is bad news when the defiant exile James Joyce can be turned into an ardent nationalist', and bad too when Bloom's definition of a nation is quoted 'in a nationalist context' (1996: 22). Against such heinous deviation she offers her own magisterial assurances:

> The last thing that either the Jewish Bloom or European Joyce wanted was for their words to be enlisted to support a narrow nationalism. The point of *Ulysses* is that Irish is universal. The danger in Irish studies is that the clarity of that truth is reduced. (1996: 22)

Thus she completes her condemnation of Irish studies. But how appropriate is it to call James Joyce and Leopold Bloom as independent witnesses at the trial of Irish studies? Understandably biographers sometimes fight shy of the now infamous death of the author. But, regardless of how energetically the minutiae of their subject's everyday lives may be acquired by a biographer, their meanings cannot be

accordingly retained. Although Maddox has undeniably penned a biography of James Joyce's wife, Nora, her confidence as to what either
Joyce or Bloom may have wanted is hardly thereby justified. No text
slots so completely into context that it cannot generate further open-
ended chains of effects in addition to their source of utterance. To put it
another way, traditionally literature has been regarded in part as one of
the persuasive arts collectively understood as rhetoric, and that is before
we even begin to consider the complex matter of the reception of a
literary text. We are familiar enough with the phenomenon of recycling
little bits of the English canon, particularly Shakespeare, as sententious
nuggets for the party conference sound-bite, the company after-dinner
speech or the school prize-day. Our responses to this may be varied but
few worry about such citation being out of context. Why should Maddox
assume that in the particular case of Joyce's *Ulysses* readers or auditors
will be unable to detect a politically motivated citation and be duped
into remarkable singular credibility? Why should the common knowledge that texts function in contexts to discernible effect be abandoned in
this instance?

Maddox professes to heartily dislike 'studies', presumably including
cultural studies. Thus she is likely to have missed one of the fundamental theses of cultural studies, namely, 'that no object, no text, no
cultural practice has an intrinsic or necessary meaning or value or
function, and that meaning, value and function are always the effect of
specific (and changing, changeable) social relations and mechanisms of
signification' (Frow 1995: 144–5). What Clifford says of culture may also
be ascribed to texts, that is, that they have a relational aspect. This
involves the idea that 'communicative processes continue to exist, historically, between subjects in relations of power' (Clifford and Marcus
1986: 15). Against the possible introduction of such unwelcome issues as
politics and power Maddox offers the stalwart, universal truth: 'The
point of *Ulysses* is that Irish is universal' (1996: 22); a point which again
receives no further elaboration. But universalism may be deemed hypo-
critical where it is located 'in a system founded both on the permanence
of inequality and on the process of material and social polarisation'
(Balibar and Wallerstein 1991: 230). Many of those students identified by
Maddox as the unlovely – black, Irish, ethnic and women – engage
closely with universal truth, examining protocols of reading and regimes
of value, tracing processes which universalize and totalize the cultural
field in the course of their studies. Maddox's categorization of the
collective unlovely raises the related issue of the student cohort she
would consider acceptable (all those anybodies) to undertake study in
those subject/disciplines which pass muster, such as literature or history.
For many of the black, ethnic, Irish or female student populace, among
others, it has been difficult to complete a programme in English literature
or British history without registering processes of selection of materials
and canon formation. It is arguable that the development of post-colonial

writing programmes, social history and 'studies' courses arose in part from a rejection of the hierarchy of criteria which organized those aforementioned 'traditional' fields of study. Maddox appears oblivious to these issues of power relations. Instead she prefers to rail against the advent of 'studies', to dismiss an unlovely student population and by inference to promote an ideal student body, 'anybody', providing of course that it is Lovely. The Lovely are those for whom the 'inherent interest' of their subject is quite literally self-evident, whose relation to the canons of traditional disciplines is never eccentric, and who may currently experience a decentring by these new studies. In short she attempts to recuperate an academic regime of (D)WEMs for WEMs disguised under the mask of the universal. Her collapse of any distinction between subject and discipline begins to make sense at this point of purported disinterest.

The hostility and misinformation in Maddox's article regarding Irish studies might appear less surprising had it appeared in a conservative magazine. Maddox has contributed over a number of years to the right wing *Daily Telegraph*. That it appears in the left wing *New Statesman* is remarkable, although perhaps not to the range of Irish commentators in Britain who have noted that when it comes to Ireland, the British left is not always distinguishable from the British right. Maddox's article is an interesting text not least because it shows clearly just how political are the issues surrounding interdisciplinary formations such as Irish studies and cultural studies.

**An incorrect political ABC of Irish studies, beginning with U:
U is for *Ulysses***

Cyclops, the one-eyed monster, is the episode from Homer's *Odyssey* which Joyce deemed the analogue for the ninth section of his own work, *Ulysses*. The novel was serialized in America between 1918 and 1920 and was first published in Paris in October 1922, six years after the Irish general uprising, a year after the treaty partitioning Ireland and a few months after the outbreak of the resultant civil war. The ninth section explores in anti-heroic and comic fashion the excesses of nationalist construction and in doing so asks serious questions about nationhood, nationalism, race and racism. A central figure in the section is known to us only as 'the citizen'. Our eponymous hero is accompanied by a dog, Garryowen, whom the citizen fondly addresses from time to time in the Irish language (*gaeilge*/Gaelic). Located in a snug in Barney Kiernan's public house these two figures guard the hostelry with a lazy belligerence which seems not to bother the local clientele unduly. Much of this ninth section is narrated by one such member of the clientele, an unnamed Dublin punter:

There he is, says I, in his gloryhole, with his cruiskeen lawn and his load of
papers, working for the cause. The bloody mongrel let a grouse out of him
would give you the creeps . . .
– Stand and deliver, says he.
– That's all right, citizen, says Joe. Friends here.
– Pass, friends, says he. Then he rubs his hand in his eye and says he:
– What's your opinion of the times? (Joyce 1985: 293)

In describing the citizen, Joyce departs from the punter's narration and
appropriates the conventions within old and middle Irish epic, such as
the provision of lists (ornamental and descriptive 'runs' which form part
of the epic story-telling tradition) and the early practices of chroniclers
and genealogical historians who trace events and lineage back to pre-
historic biblical, classical and mythological sources. Nineteenth-century
nationalists (including revivalists and celticists), in Ireland, as in other
European countries, found early historical and mythological source
materials a resource in their own oppositional constructions of a nationalist culture and history. In some cases, notably as in MacPherson's
'discovery' of Ossianic poetry, the materials could be invented, thus
duping a British public temporarily for a Scottish cause. Where the
materials existed, a process of selection from a represented past could aid
in the projection of an imaginary future for a disparate group of
individuals imagined in the present as *a/the people*, who are then represented as the key players in a national, grand narrative (Anderson 1983).
With the construction of this narrative underway one can then move
backwards as well as forwards to reinforce its teleology (Balibar and
Wallerstein 1991). Thus in an age of post-Enlightenment a celtic twilight
could still have purchase.

And so to the citizen, the description of whom begins merely anach-
ronistically: 'he wore a long unsleeved garment of recently flayed oxhide
reaching to his knees . . .' (Joyce 1985: 294). The citizen we are told carries
'tribal images' upon his person, and as these are listed, decorum sags,
strains and finally gives up the burden of epic grandeur, collapsing in a
mock-epic heap: 'from his girdle hung a row of seastones which dangled
at every movement of his portentous frame and on these were graven
with rude yet striking art the tribal images of many Irish heroes and
heroines of antiquity, Cuchulin, Conn of hundred battles, Niall of nine
hostages, Brian of Kincora . . .' The list begins promisingly enough with
figures well known to the average school child, but goes on to include
Dante, Charlemagne, Paracelsus, Goliath, Captain Moonlight, Jack the
Giant Killer, Thomas Cooke and Son, Adam and Eve, Cleopatra, the first
Prince of Wales, the man that broke the bank at Monte Carlo, Patrick W.
Shakespeare and Lady Godiva among the ever-swelling ranks of full-
blooded Irish heroes. Joyce's genius is to invoke the slow burn: fired by
the consideration of Cleopatra as an Irish heroine, the grey cells can then
warm sufficiently to recall that one of Pharaoh's daughters, Scota, was
indeed believed to have brought the Irish language to the island,

according to early Irish mythological sources. Even at his most expansive, Joyce's scorn is well directed.

List-making occurs again towards the end of the section in a different context. Leopold Bloom, the central figure of the novel, enters the pub, smokes a cigar, departs on an errand (he is an advertising canvasser) and returns. Unlike the punters, apathetic to the point of agreement, Bloom has been in lively discussion with the citizen and others on subjects ranging from capital punishment, past Irish rebellions and new language policy. Antagonism towards Bloom builds up, not on an ideological issue, but on the misapprehension that he has left the pub not to deliver a message, but rather to place a bet and collect the winnings. Seen as a man lucky with horses and unwilling to spend his imagined gains on providing more 'wine of the country' (served black and frothy and by the pint) for his compatriots, the ensuing personal hostility is articulated in a discourse on patriotism. They begin by noting that in previous pub conversations Bloom has provided a prominent nationalist editor with a number of hypothetical proposals for Irish, independent development which subsequently found their way into print in the local republican newspaper. From this an average response might be to suppose that Bloom was a nationalist, a republican or a patriot, but the group instead are led to speculate on the interrelations of patriotism and race, taking in a few anti-semitic stereotypes en route:

> – Where is he? Says Lenehan, defrauding widows and orphans.
> – Isn't that a fact, says John Wyse, what I was telling the citizen about Bloom and the Sinn Fein?
> – That's so, says Martin, or so they allege.
> – Who made those allegations? Says Alf.
> – I, says Joe. I'm the alligator.
> – And after all, says John Wyse, why can't a jew love his country like the next fellow?
> – Why not ? Says J.J., When he's quite sure which country it is.
> – Is he a jew or a gentile or a holy roman or a swaddler or what the hell is he? No offence, Crofton.
> – We don't want him, says Crofton the orangeman or presbyterian. (Joyce 1985: 335)

As it happens, just a few minutes prior to Bloom's temporary departure his own views on the relation of an individual to his/her country had been delivered, as noted by one of the drinkers:

> Bloom was talking and talking with John Wyse and he was quite excited . . .
> . . .
> – Persecution, says he, all the history of the world is full of it.
> Perpetuating national hatred among nations.
> But do you know what a nation means? says John Wyse.
> – Yes, says Bloom.
> – What is it? Says John Wyse.
> – A nation? Says Bloom. A nation is the same people living in the same place.
> – By god, then, says Ned, laughing, if that's so I'm a nation for I'm living in the same place for the past five years.

> So of course everyone had a laugh at Bloom and says he, trying to muck out of it:
> – Or also living in different places.
> – That covers my case, says Joe.
> – What is your nation if I may ask, says the citizen.
> – Ireland, says Bloom. I was born here. Ireland.
> The citizen said nothing only cleared the spit out of his gullet and, gob, he spat a red bank oyster out of him right in the corner. (Joyce 1985: 330)

Bloom is clear about the potential dangers of promoting strong national consciousness, the fostering of hatred of others (whether these be other nations, or just other people, foreigners or immigrants). The citizen, by contrast, has been exhibiting rather than analysing those same symptoms, referring disparagingly to other European countries and in particular to the 'bloody thicklugged sons of whores gets!', that is, the British. Bloom offers an initial definition of a nation which, from a sociological point of view, could be applied to any loosely collective cultural unit: 'the same people living in the same place', that is, a group sharing a common relation to the territory and as a same people, presumably sharing some common experiences accreting into memories – an ethnie in other terms (Smith 1995). It is the work of the nation-state to incorporate ethnically different groups into an imagined unit, a nation, to fuse, as Bloom does, what defines several collective units into one. For these purposes, distinctions between ethnic minorities and a core ethnie (where it exists) disappear, so although Bloom is well aware that he has multiple identities, '– and I belong to a race too, says Bloom' (Joyce 1985: 331), he is equally sure to which nation he belongs and why: '– Ireland, says Bloom. I was born here. Ireland.' Nation-states, whether they be ethnic (formed around a core ethnicity) or civic (formed around immigrants, as in the USA), are often assessed by their representation of ethnic minorities: Do they have equal citizenship? Access to political, social and economic development? Parity of esteem? Do they experience multiculturalism rather than mere pluralism? The citizen as representative of his nation fails on all points. Here his immediate response to Bloom's assertions foreshadows a more aggressive approach towards him later, again as told by the unnamed drinker who sees the citizen about to leave the pub:

> I was just lowering the heel of a pint when I saw the citizen getting up to waddle to the door, puffing and blowing with the dropsy and he cursing the curse of Cromwell on him . . . and begob he got as far as the door and they holding him and he bawls out of him:
> – Three cheers for Israel! . . .
> . . . And all the ragamuffins and sluts of the nation round the door and . . . [he] starts singing *if the man in the moon was a jew, jew, jew* and a slut shouts out of her:
> – Eh, mister! Your fly is open, mister! (Joyce 1985: 340)

In the face of hostility Bloom is spirited in defence. And says he:

– Mendelssohn was a jew and Karl Marx was a jew and Mercadante and Spinoza. And the Saviour was a jew and his father was a jew. Your god. He had no father, says Martin. That'll do now. Drive ahead.
– whose god? Says the citizen.
– Well, his uncle was a jew, says he. Your god was a jew. Christ was a jew like me.
Gob, the citizen made a plunge back in to the shop.
– By Jesus, says he, IÕll brain that bloody jewman for using the holy name. By Jesus, IÕll crucify him so I will. Give us that biscuit box here . . .
. . . Where is he till I murder him? (Joyce 1985: 341)

The citizen's aim is impeded by his eyepatch as well as his bellyfull of porter and his missile (the biscuit tin) shoots past Bloom. The latter escapes, given chase by the citizen's Gaelic-speaking mongrel, Garryowen.

Joyce's brilliantly comic text identifies two key functions of listing in the process of identity formation. Initially one seems constructive and the other defensive. The citizen promotes a nationalist construct wherein the listing of Irish heroes and heroines proves useful. Bloom, facing racial harassment resorts to the strategy of listing. In fact both are essentially defensive strategies. One defends by aggrandizement against the imperial hegemony of the British, listing Irish grandeur and simultaneously asserting that the British had 'no music and no art and no literature worthy of the name. Any civilisation they have they stole from us' (Joyce 1985: 323). The citizen's bravado is directed against the hated Sassenach. Bloom defends against gentile racism, anti-semitism.

L is for Listing, as happened in *Ulysses*

Listing as an activity seems to be unavoidably reactive and defensive, and not just in novels. I recall that when I was growing up in Ireland it was a strategy used in relation to other forms of identity too, including sexual identity: Proust was gay and Wilde was gay (and they jailed him) and Roger Casement was gay (and the British assassinated him and the Irish couldn't add him to the list of republican martyrs because he was a gay patriot), and so on. The subtext to this list is still a sense of being under attack, of being victims. Because listing occurs in a context of hierarchical power relations its articulation often reaffirms that hierarchy and reinforces the subalternity of the speaker. Implicitly there is an appeal to an imaginary addressee who is positioned as dominant, acknowledging that they are the arbiters of mainstream taste or value, the major holders of cultural capital, or status or power or justice. (If only they could realize what a worthy list this is! Why can't they just accept us?) Unsurprisingly, then, the gay movement in Ireland as elsewhere has ditched this as a strategy, and now prefers the tactical like-it-or-lump-it 'in your face' approach as a way of addressing identity and issues of asymmetrical power relations. Curiously part of the movement has also chosen to use the term 'queer nation' as a way of articulating its mass (presumably using the sort of definition Bloom offered of a nation as people 'also living in different places'). As many gay people have had an ambiguous relationship to the nation-state, based on the latter's failure regarding parity of esteem, the term strikes me as an unfortunate choice. But the main point is that listing as a strategy has been consigned by many gay activist groups to the filing-cabinet, if not the dustbin, of history, as gay pride has been succeeded by Act Up.

Brecht is often quoted for the axiom 'pity the land that needs heroes', to which we could add: and be cautious also of those who purport to be proud of something; they are often in a state of defence or purveyance. I want to write about Irish studies, by which I mean the interdisciplinary formation of studies of Ireland, which, as we noted at the outset of this chapter, has a strong relationship with other interdisciplinary formations such as cultural studies. And I want to write about Irish studies without attempting to defend or to sell it. One question which immediately faces me is how does one communicate what in many countries is a minority subject of study without compromising the material or the reader? Often when this newly emerging area of study is mentioned in Britain, in particular, the question mark at the end of the phrase is sometimes distinctly audible. It is the same sort of question mark that can be heard occasionally when the name of the country is mentioned: *Ireland? Irish* studies? The issue then arises as to whether one addresses the raised eyebrow and curled lip, informing their owners as to who was a Jew and who was an Irishman, and giving a sample list of cultural or political grandees. A few decades ago Irish community activist groups, such as the Irish in Britain Representation Group, inaugurated precisely such measures, in part defensively ('How dare you assume that we are bereft of cultural capital') and in part as positive models for a second-generation Irish community growing up without information regarding the same. The agendas of Irish in Britain groups have developed and expanded over recent decades, though in many cases they are still having to negotiate the sneer which accompanies the articulation of the term 'Irish' and are still battling with lexicographers. Given a history of Anglo-Irish relations conducted within the British empire it may be clear that Britain is a highly particular case in terms of its reception of Irish studies. However, even more generally because academic culture is prone to conservatism we may be faced with the analogous reflex action when Irish studies is mentioned; a sneer not unfamiliar to those engaged in other interdisciplinary formations. This type of response has been experienced by a number of crucial subject areas of curricular develop-ment already: women's studies, gender studies, black studies, cultural studies, subaltern studies. Interestingly, the methodology within many of these interdisciplinary studies has not maintained validatory listing, either defensive or promotional. Indeed it is more frequently the state-funded studies of a national culture (often within Foreign Affairs Budget headings), such as Canadian, American or British studies, which adopt a benign listing of cultural capital, in their overseas pursuit of influence.

But Irish studies in Britain is neither a diplomatic nor a missionary project, nor does it operate an easy exchange wherein ignorance is reduced and affirmation increased. This latter methodology has had a place in 'well-meaning' statutory-funded extramural education wherein areas of study loosely understood as multicultural or as awareness training were thought to propagate better community relations. Attractive though this may be to a liberal consciousness, such an exchange also nurtures a Whiggish teleology wherein the area of study is placed in a trajectory of assimilation to something which has traditionally consistently disparaged it. Had women's studies started out in response to the infamous question 'What do women want?', the development of the subject would have been jeopardized from the outset. For the response to a question posed thus: 'What do women/gays/Irish people want?' may result in the continual servicing of dominant needs which coopt the particular group's agency towards an established agenda and which then in turn compromises their interests with increased subtlety. Hegemony. Thus some questions are rhetorically great and strategically disabling. Irish studies might rather be to *open the question as to what* types of knowledge about Ireland have been previously and are presently in circulation amidst different identity groups in different parts of Britain and how these knowledges have been formulated and regulated at specific points. The objective may be to undertake the study in a way that is relational and provisional, as opposed to what Gilroy calls the 'ethnically absolutist' (1993: 24).

This may be regarded as a cussedness, not unlike that of some schools of cultural study who resolutely refuse to define the subject monologically or with fixity and who remain unwilling to provide a definitive canon of cultural studies texts. But while unwilling to offer a single definition of Irish studies, it may be useful to indicate the emergence of its positioning in Britain, to offer one among many provisional mappings of its terrain, and finally to note some basic aspects of its methodology which are informed by cultural studies.

D is for Definition, at least local ones

Irish studies in Britain is a minority subject located within a culture that has oscillated between habits of ignorance and of incorporation. Both positions held by that culture have helped reproduce a climate of denial with regard to Ireland, offering merely a trajectory of assimilation to a British culture which has discredited what it recognized as 'Irish'. The history of the emergence of Irish studies in Britain, therefore, involves issues of visibility, and the pioneering agents of this history are worth noting. The Irish in Britain are a long-resident community and Irish studies has been a subject which has evolved in recent decades as part of their struggle against the dominant narratives towards other forms of awareness (Curtis 1984a, 1984b; Hillyard 1993). The formal recognition of Irish studies as an area of study within A-level programmes and third-level institutes (as well as extramurally) has arisen in large part from the efforts of these Irish community groups since the 1960s. Their demand for and organized delivery of Irish studies at extramural level created a foundation in Britain upon which the more recent programmes were developed. Here Irish studies seems to share a similar history to the establishment of cultural studies in Britain, where the impetus began within Workers' Educational Associations and the adult education sector generally, and where, as the subject gained increased recognition, it then developed within academic contexts. One can now study for a diploma, undergraduate degree or an MA in multidisciplinary Irish studies programmes within British universities. Additionally, some single subject areas, such as history or English, now offer integral units specializing in Ireland. While this may read as a success story in terms of institutional access, it is worth noting that these courses may currently be adversely affected by contemporary developments in increased fees at undergraduate level and in the introduction of chequebook graduate education.

While any number of outline programmes of Irish studies are potentially available to the student, I proffer some elements which I currently include in my mapping of the terrain. In terms of representations there are a number of available readings.

P is for Post-colonial, R is for Revisionist

At present, valuable work is being carried out in the process of national de-mythologizing, uprooting fixed stereotypes. Noting a refusal to buy into a representation of ourselves as museum artefacts or theme park personae, for commodification either at home or abroad, contemporary academics have been concerned to analyse these refusals. Most crucially writers such as Deane (1991), Eagleton (1995), Gibbons (1988) and Lloyd (1993) have identified these developments in contemporary cultural activity as post-colonial. Other aspects of contemporary historical study termed 'revisionist' have provided valuable contributions by Boyce (1991) and Foster (1993). Sometimes where historical study questions received versions of political history in Ireland, this has become known as revisionism within the discipline of history. However, it is worth bearing in mind that there are many forms of revisionist history in process in Ireland: cultural and social history (Brown 1985; Cairns and Richards 1988; Carlson 1990; Curtin et al. 1987; Curtis 1984a; Kearney 1988), labour history (Connolly 1910; Keogh 1982) and gender history (Luddy 1995a, 1995b; Luddy and Murphy 1989; MacCurtain and

O'Corrain 1978; MacCurtain and O'Dowd 1991; Walter 1989; Ward 1983), to name a few. Within interdisciplinary Irish studies the term 'revisionist' refers to the various ways in which the dominant narratives about Ireland, including those produced within the ideology of the Irish as well as the British state, at historically specific points, are subject to deconstruction. Much of Irish studies, from post-colonial to gender studies, is a revisionist practice.

As an example of the process of reappraisal integral to Irish studies, we can consider the way in which, in general, the failure of multiculturalism in Ireland up to the 1970s was perceived to result from nationalist and national hegemonies. The lack of secularization was attributed to a chauvinism on the part of nationalist politicians which fused the elements of Catholicism, Gaelic ideology and conservatism into an essentialist notion of Irishness. The resulting impact on social legislation and culture has been well documented by critical and cultural commentators (Brown 1985; Connelly 1993; Curtin et al. 1987; Farrell 1988; Scannell 1988; Sharkey 1993a), and there is a well-established consensus that the agency accorded to the Catholic Church in Irish politics retarded processes of modernization and of liberal pluralism. Though this is irrefutable, it is also to be recognized as presenting an incomplete picture, offering only a partial representation of Irish society. First, it can be stated that a strain of Christian fundamentalism has never been absent from the other Christian denominations in Ireland. This is why in areas such as Northern Ireland, although they are linked to Britain under the Union, social legislation has differed on a range of issues from more limited abortion rights to the regulation of public houses and children's playgrounds. These differences were directly linked to Northern Protestant, Presbyterian and Methodist influence. Second, in Ireland as a whole, legislation generated by nascent Christian fundamentalism was considerably at odds with cultural practice and was often unenforceable. But, enforceable or not, such legislation was offensive in itself to many and was circumvented by large numbers from all the constituent communities in Ireland. This may be stressed because in previous representations of 'Southern' Catholic/nationalist hegemony, it was assumed that the intervention of the state, particularly in the regulation of the family, was injurious to the tiny minority Protestant community alone and that the Catholics there were willing recipients, indeed celebrants, of this paternalistic and pietistic authoritarianism. Quite unproblematically, this previous account assumed that the majority culture in the Republic was a univocal, homogeneous group. Irish studies now, while resisting wholesale acceptance of this dominant narrative, corrects the former erasure of the opposition to nativist hegemony from within the Catholic community in the Republic and restores to visibility the agency of those who resisted the state (among whom we can include women, lesbian and gay and working-class movements – see Conroy Jackson 1986; Prendeville 1988). It is also interesting that when the liberal pluralist position in Ireland attributes blame for the nativist strand in recent history, it looks only across the Channel for models of better practice and overlooks positive examples within Ireland.

I was brought up in border territory, growing up in the sixties in the north-west of Ireland, County Donegal, thirty miles away from Derry, but on the other side of the border, thus rendering it still Ulster but in the Republic, still the most northern point in the country but deemed part of 'the South'. The cultural characterization of the Southern community seems to me unrecognizable and at a remove from our experience. The area was mixed, roughly equally, 50 per cent Catholic, 50 per cent Protestant, and both sides smarted from the restrictions imposed on personal freedoms through social legislation. Thirty miles away Catholics and Protestants were locked in combat over what began as a civil rights movement for the minority culture in Northern Ireland. In Donegal our co-existence as neighbours, school-mates, work associates and partners was long-established and continued beyond the onset (again) of the war in Northern Ireland. For us, although social legislation was indeed inspired by a Catholic, nativist strain in Irish politics, it failed both communities and was resented and, where possible, circumvented locally. Moreover, unlike Northern Ireland, we did not feel the weight of a state-supported system of economic and political discrimination, whereby religious affiliation determined chances of employment, housing or the basic right to vote. This may have something to do with why we freely exhibited cultural differences and expressed the popular forms of cultural nationalism with seasonal gusto, the Green contingent travelling into the more urban centres like Strabane to engage in a *Feis* (a celebration of Gaelic culture, through dancing, song, poetry, and so on), or to a Saint Patrick's day parade, and the Orange contingent donning bowler hats and sashes and going the same route, travelling to Strabane for the Twelfth of July. It didn't occasion us to stop speaking, much less choose violent opposition. Memories of difference from my childhood have little to do with religion compared with other factors such as class, and opportunities regarding employment were most obviously gender-linked. Interestingly, County Donegal is a corner of the Republic often forgotten when the representation of 'the South' as a Catholic, nationalist monolith is offered. I am not proffering it as a progressive Utopia; far from it. But the conservatism of life there was not attributable merely to Catholicism, and this community embodied and embodies an easy co-existence of differing cultural groups, a pluralism which mitigates against the caricature of a chauvinist totality labelled 'the South'. Against the dominant liberal narrative wherein the retardation of secularism and pluralism in Ireland is attributable to a Catholic nationalism there needs to be an account taken of the border experiences. These latter both complicate the picture and by contrast throw into sharp relief the experience under a Northern state, experiences which raise that taboo word unspoken by revisionists, sectarianism.

G is for Gender, W is for Women

For women in particular, post-colonial Ireland has attracted a degree of critical attention and in gender terms it has been ideologically located within stereotypes which fix women in fairly easily identifiable and negative ways. It is arguable that the ways in which women were constructed, with a view to their containment and a need to regiment and police their agencies, in particular their sexual agencies, provide an eloquent gloss on the failure of the post-1937 state to attain a post-colonial status, aligning it with the nativist attitude in representation to which I have already referred (Connelly 1993; Conroy Jackson 1986; Prendeville 1988; Sharkey 1993b; Smyth 1993). The dominant narrative here points to familial law, issues of abortion, divorce and contraceptive provision. But it is possible to tire of this dominant narrative and the relish with which this stereotype is purveyed. One might then point to developments in gender related matters which complicate the picture-advances in secularizing the state, the lowering of the age of consent for young gay men, the provision of exemplary employment legislation which protects lesbian and gay people from discrimination in the workplace, the level of provision of publicly funded child care and of course the fact of a feminist head of state (all of which compare favourably with the case of Britain for example). The divorce referendum where the yes vote was carried by a 1% majority is a recent subject requiring careful study.

N is for Northern Ireland

Again, a revisionist perspective on Northern Ireland may form a component part of Irish studies. For interestingly, while the study of Northern Ireland has become a significant area of academic study in its own right, within recent accounts some critical aspects have received scant attention. Sectarianism as upheld by the state in Northern Ireland, has merited little comment, as I have stated earlier, though it is in fact a major inhibitor of multicultural development. Instead there have been glib dismissals of Northern Irish 'atavism' and 'tribal loyalties', thus obfuscating an examination of sectarianism which exists there as part of a colonial legacy. Brewer (1992) points out that Northern Ireland is a settler society in which two communities through a range of social practices have managed to self-perpetuate easily. However, he stresses that this is not an example of 'benign ethnicity' (Rex 1986: 95) since 'the colonial background which originally forced the two communities together also left a legacy of inequality and conflict into which current

stratification patterns fit' (Brewer 1992: 354). When Britain established
the government of Northern Ireland in 1920, it attempted to write in
assurances that religious discrimination would not occur. But, as evidenced in the range of government commissions throughout the sixties
and seventies, it was precisely the widespread discrimination against
Catholics which precipitated the Civil Rights Movement in 1968. In the
domain of culture, from a range of sociological analyses (Buckley 1982;
Jenkins 1984; both quoted in Brewer 1992). Brewer concludes that
sectarianism is relatively low key. 'Catholics and Protestants share significantly in a common culture, certainly more so than in inter-racial
situations . . . at a cultural level Catholics and Protestants have as much
in common with each other as not' (Brewer 1992: 357–8). The distinction
between the two communities is equally apparent:

> [W]hat they do not have in common is a consensus on the legitimacy of the
> state. . . . [R]eligion is invoked as a market of difference despite other aspects
> of shared culture because it represents different socio-economic and political
> interests. Religion articulates the conflict between the relative economic
> privilege of one community and the relative economic dispossession of
> another . . . [s]ectarianism operates whenever religion is invoked to draw
> boundaries and to represent or reproduce patterns of inequality and social
> conflict. . . . [R]eligion is situationally appropriated to represent other conflicts
> and inequalities. (Brewer 1992: 358)

Brewer is unequivocal on the issue of sectarianism in Northern Ireland,
viewing it as experienced on three levels – of ideas, individual action and
social structure. The first two are commonly experienced, the third less
so:

> A major difference on this plane is that Catholics in the working-class ghettoes
> (as distinct from those in the middle-class suburbs) are subject to intimidation
> from a source which Protestants do not experience: namely, the security forces,
> whose presence in working-class Catholic areas in many of the large towns
> approaches saturation. The Royal Ulster Constabulary [RUC] espouses
> religious impartiality as one of its principles, but in day-to-day confrontations
> on the streets of the hard-line Catholic council estates, some members of the
> force, both male and female, do not practise it to the same degree, any more
> than do some members of the British Army. . . . At the level of the social
> structure, sectarianism is experienced solely by Catholics, because it expresses
> itself in the patterns of indirect or institutional discrimination that Catholics
> alone experience and in their greater social and economic disadvantage.
> (Brewer 1992: 363)

As Mike Tomlinson (1995: 15) points out in a seminal article, the
British government still has a central political conflict over its role in
Ireland. At issue is the legitimacy of the state in Northern Ireland
and sectarianism within the forces which uphold that state. To invoke
religion as the explanatory factor in Northern Ireland is a misunderstanding which bypasses the necessary political study of the issues and
the practical problem of sectarianism. To involve all parties in restructuring that state and to introduce policing and other forces which operate
with parity and non-sectarianism may be on the agenda in terms of

rethinking Northern Ireland. Interestingly, while these potential developments are afoot in the realm of politics, new political developments have
been introduced into the study of Northern Irish culture.

In her recent book *The Living Stream*, Edna Longley regards herself as a
'revisionist' literary critic, revisionism being 'a shorthand and quasi-
abusive term for historical studies held to be at odds with the founding
ideology of the Irish state' (1994: 10). Longley is a pluralist who dislikes
those for whom she can find no place in her version of pluralism. These
include nationalists, post-colonialists, would-be pluralists (that is, those
she regards as covert nationalists), counter-revisionists, neo-republicans,
Marxist republicans, 'cultural materialists from England and post-
colonialists from America' (1994: 67) who have all made the grievous
error in her opinion of commenting on Northern Ireland. The Irish
diaspora is dismissed with contempt: 'Ireland goes float about again'
(1994: 47), and those with whom she disagrees are represented as
militant and outside the bounds of legitimacy. Lloyd's (1993) attempt in
literary texts to 'recover subterranean or marginalised practices' is read
by her as an activity which 'mystifies the illegal organisation', and she
accuses him of exhibiting a 'sinister purity' ('Marxist-Republicanism' no
less) in his discussion of the collusion between 'imperial ideology' and
'bourgeois nationalism' (1994: 31). Seamus Deane, the general editor of
The Field Day Anthology, is accused of 'sniper attacks on empiricism'
(1994: 26) and the entire three-volume anthology is reduced to 'a Derry
meta-narrative' (1994: 39). The sniper attack metaphor points to her
tendency to introduce a discourse of terrorism into the realm of cultural
production just at the period when it may be receding in the realm of
political activity. And, just when the advocacy of an unchallenged
unionism and an upheld sectarianism is being downplayed in the realm
of politics, she attempts its introduction into the realm of culture, where
it has until now had less purchase. Longley has a double argument to
make. First, that the literature of Northern Ireland should be seen within
the context of the British Isles and that the literary influences from
mainland Britain be emphasized; a matter of opening up 'the Britannic
unconscious, exposing much that has been repressed by the Anglo-Celtic
archipelago as a whole' (1994: 49–50). Second, that 'the relation of all
writing to Protestantism and Catholicism, an issue masked by homogenizing "Irishness", should be opened up. "Irishness" with its totalit-
arian tinge ought to be abandoned rather than made exclusive. To
include/exclude the Ulster Protestants is a false and sterile alternative'
(1994: 179–80).

She has already avowed that she is 'concerned with the relations of
literature to the academy and to the body politic' (1994: 66) and is aware
that the realms of culture and politics are frequently interactive, noting
that 'poetry has sometimes lent itself to the construction of national
meanings' (1994: 50). Therefore, one can only assume that as a revisionist
and a liberal pluralist in Ulster she is consciously introducing this

methodology wherein texts should be read within a British context and may be categorized as British-influenced and Protestant or, alternatively, they may be regarded as that binary other: Catholic and Irish. This essentialist categorization of texts by the marker of religion is a process of cultural sectarianization presented by one who identifies as a cultural 'revisionist'. As a phenomenon it is an interesting one to juxtapose with the contemporary political developments which aim to begin de-sectarianizing the realm of political agency.

R is also for Religion and Race, C is for Colonialism

The marker of religion has proved extremely useful for a long time in the field of Anglo-Irish relations. A tradition of racial denigration which was formerly established by such figures as Gerald of Wales and Stanihurst aided early attempts to colonize the country. The racialization of the Irish in English discourse from the medieval period has been recognized and well discussed (Gillingham 1990, 1992; Jones 1971; Lennon 1978). From this medieval base position a new British discourse pertinent to sixteenth- and seventeenth-century colonial expansion developed which cohered around the Reformation categorization by religion. This had the advantage of further reinforcing the subordinate status of the 'Irish' (a category which was then made to include the old English in Ireland, that is, previous settlers who adhered to Catholicism), and could represent British appropriation of lands and reallocation into the hands of English, Scots and Welsh as part of a Protestant, providential narrative. It is important to note how Ireland has been specifically positioned over many centuries as an Other against which a British state formulated itself. Although the general debates about the rise of the state and of nationhood are often set very late, most usually from the Enlightenment period and preferably from the nineteenth century onwards, it can be argued that the late sixteenth and early seventeenth centuries be re-garded as the early modern period in which a new awareness of concepts such as nation and state arose in Britain, informed in part by experiences of colonial expansion. As the start of empire coincides with that of national self-awareness, the colony provides an interesting site in which ideas about state and nation, and myths of formation relating to the same, were projected and consciously discussed. Given that the state and nation often appear a more coherent entity precisely in their external and international relations, an examination of the practices in operation in the colonial site often reflects lucidly on the national self-consciousness in the colonizing country.

The relevance of Ireland in any discussion of early modern colonialism is no longer disputed. Historians such as Andrews et al. (1979), Bradshaw et al. (1993), Brady (1986, 1989), Canny (1973, 1987) and Quinn

(1945, 1966) have stated the case and it has recently achieved a more general recognition in comparative studies of colonization. Loomba (1994: 30), for example, notes that several studies have now pointed out that the case of the Irish provided a model for slavery and colonialist discourse in Africa and India. Boose on the subject of racial discourse in early modern England offers the following:

> If 'race' originates as a category that hierarchically privileges a ruling status and makes the Other(s) inferior, then for the English the group that was first to be shunted into this discursive derogation and thereafter invoked as almost a paradigm of inferiority was not the black 'race' – but the Irish 'race'. In tracts such as Spenser's *A View of the Present State of Ireland*, the derogation of the Irish as 'a race apart' situates racial difference within cultural and religious categories rather than biologically empirical ones. But when that discourse then places the Irish into analogy with what twentieth-century Americans would call 'people of colour', within what category do these claims of difference belong – the biological, the cultural, or the theological? In early modern English treatises on New World 'Indians' the Irish frequently appear as analogous because similarly primitive/barbaric. In *The White Devil*, John Webster repeatedly associates the black Zanche with the Irish. (Boose 1994: 36–7)

O is for Othering

In the grand narrative of relations between Britain and Ireland it is notable that the othering of the Irish was mobilized in specific ways over historical periods for the purposes of constructing aspects of the British state and of British nationalism. Demonized and the butt of anti-Catholic riots, they were mobilized as representational resources in consolidating a nineteenth-century British working class, and a British nation (Belchem 1985; Best 1967; Cahill 1957; Holmes 1988; Kirk 1980). In the twentieth-century era of new Commonwealth immigrants and new racisms, the strategy changed from one of ostracism and othering to one of enforced assimilation. The Irish were to be undifferentiated as an ethnic minority, part of an undeconstructed whiteness (Hickman and Walters 1995), despite clear signs in landlords' windows indicating the contrary: 'No Irish, No Blacks.' The strategy for the British state at this point involved shifting the axis of absolutist othering onto exclusively colour lines so that new and conveniently exclusivist 'British' selves could be produced. British anxiety about the category of the Irish still has a currency, as evidenced in the February 1995 neo-facist football riots, which stopped the Ireland–England game in Dublin, or the press response to the Commssion for Racial Equality research initiative into anti-Irish racism. While *The Sunday Times* merely disapproved, *The Sun* (22 January 1994: 9) dismissed the exercise as 'codswallop' and printed a page of anti-Irish jokes to aid the researchers. Such data also need to be investigated and processed within Irish studies in Britain.

I is for Irish studies, P is for Politics

The excitement of these studies is in part that they can potentially integrate the experiential and draw upon a local, urban and national constituency as both subjects and agents of knowledge. The accessing of the experiential as a legitimate resource within the academy is a link between the subjects of cultural study and of Irish studies, and in this and other ways the methodology of Irish studies may relate to other interdisciplinary studies rather than taking any ethnically absolutist approach. Where an Irish studies programme is interdisciplinary, it can provide a set of methodological tools pertinent to key disciplines and, at the same time, position the learner on border territories where the specific strengths and limitations of specific methodologies are apparent. It may adopt some key tenets (however disparate may be their delivery) of other cultural studies too. Culture may be read as the maps of meaning whereby a particular group of people make sense of everyday practices (Hall and Gieben 1992: 233), and a culture may therefore be studied through the historically specific interrelating of identity factors such as age, gender and generation with social institutions, employment, leisure and education. If cultures are composite, involving dominant, residual and emergent elements (Williams 1977: 121–8), then within that schema uneven developments and contradictions held in a particular locale can be identified and explored. Finally, considering that 'tradition', like history, in Irish studies as elsewhere, is always a selective construct (excluding as well as privileging), a reflexive mode of analysis of the specific maps of meaning currently in production and circulation may be adopted. In pursuing Irish studies we might invite our own and others' conscious participations in working with the processes of formations and deconstructions of the maps of meaning in a culture. That this may also prove politically empowering is, as we have seen, a 'worry' that can niggle conservative critics.

Acknowledgements

My consideration of how the field of Irish studies is organized here is an expansion of some issues raised in a conference paper delivered to the Northern Ireland: What Next? Conference (Centre for Irish studies, University of North London, March 1995) and in 'A Present View of Irish Studies' in Susan Bassnett (ed.), *Studying British Cultures* (London: Routledge, 1997).

References

Anderson, B. (1983) *Imagined Communities: Reflections on the Origin and Spread of Nationalism*, London: Verso.

Andrews, K.R., Canny, N. and Hair, P.E. (1979) *The Western Enterprise: English Activities in the Atlantic and America 1480–1650*, Detroit: Wayne State University Press.

Balibar, E. and Wallerstein, I. (1991) *Race, Nation, Class: Ambiguous Identities*, London: Verso.

Belchem, J. (1985) 'English Working-Class Radicalism and the Irish, 1815–50', in S. Gilley and R. Swift (eds), *The Irish in the Victorian City*, Beckenham: Croom Helm.

Best, G.F. (1967) 'Popular Protestantism in Victorian Britain', in R. Robson (ed.), *Ideas and Institutions in Victorian Britain*, London: Bell.

Boose, L.E. (1994) 'The Getting of a Lawful Race', in M. Hendricks and P. Parker (eds), *Women, 'Race' and Writing in the Early Modern Period*, London: Routledge.

Boyce, D.G. (1991) *Nationalism in Ireland*, London: Routledge.

Bradshaw, B. (1988) 'Robe and Sword in the Conquest of Ireland', in C. Cross, D. Loades and J. Scarisbrick (eds), *Law and Government under the Tudors: Essays Presented to Sir Geoffrey Elton on His Retirement*, Cambridge: Cambridge University Press.

Bradshaw, B., Hadfield, A. and Maley, W. (eds) (1993) *Representing Ireland: Literature and the Origins of the Conlict, 1530–1660*, Cambridge: Cambridge University Press.

Brady, C. (1986) 'Spenser's Irish Crisis: Humanism and Experience in the 1590s', *Past and Present*, 111: 17–49.

Brady, C. (1989) 'The Road to the View: On the Decline of Reform Thought in Tudor Ireland', in P. Coughlan (ed.), *Spenser and Ireland: An Interdisciplinary Perspective*, Cork: Cork University Press.

Brewer, J.D. (1992) 'Sectarianism and Racism, and Their Parallels and Differences', *Ethnic and Racial Studies*, 15(3): 352–65.

Brown, T. (1985) *Ireland: A Social and Cultural History 1922–1985*, London: Fontana.

Cahill, G.I. (1957) 'Irish Catholicism and English Toryism', *Review of Politics*, 18: 62–76.

Cairns, D. and Richards, S. (1988) *Writing Ireland: Colonialism, Nationalism and Culture*, Manchester: Manchester University Press.

Canny, N.P. (1973) 'The Ideology of English Colonization: From Ireland to America', *William and Mary Quarterly*, XXX: 575–98.

Canny, N.P. (1987) 'Identity Formation in Ireland: The Emergence of the Anglo-Irish', in N.P. Canny and A. Pagden (eds), *Colonial Identity in the Atlantic World, 1500–1800*, Princeton, New Jersey: Princeton University Press.

Carlson, J. (ed. for Article 19) (1990) *Banned in Ireland: Censorship and the Irish Writer*, London: Routledge.

Clifford, J. and Marcus, G.E. (eds) (1986) *Writing Culture: The Poetics and Politics of Ethnography*, Berkeley: University of California Press.

Connelly, A. (ed.) (1993) *Gender and the Law in Ireland*, Dublin: Oak Tree Press.

Connolly, J. (1910) *Labour in Irish History*, Dublin: Colm O Lochlainn.

Conroy Jackson, P. (1986) 'Women's Movement and Abortion: The Criminalization of Irish Women', in D. Dahlerup (ed.), *The New Women's Movement: Feminism and Political Power in Europe and the USA*, London: Sage.

Curtin, C., Jackson, P. and O'Connor, B. (eds) (1987) *Gender in Irish Society*, Galway: Galway University Press.

Curtis, L.P. (1984a) *Nothing But The Same Old Story: The Roots of Anti-Irish Racism*, London: Information on Ireland.

Curtis, L.P. (1984b) *Ireland and The Propaganda War: The British Media and the 'Battle for Hearts and Minds'*, London: Pluto Press.

Deane, S. (ed.) (1991) *The Field Day Anthology of Irish Writing*, 3 vols, Derry: Field Day and Faber & Faber.

Eagleton, T. (1995) *Heathcliff And The Great Hunger: Studies in Irish Culture*, London: Verso.

Farrell, B. (1988) *De Valera's Constitution and Our Own*, Dublin: Gill and Macmillan.

Foster, R.F. (1993) *Paddy and Mr. Punch: Connections in Irish and English History*, London: Penguin.

Friel, B. (1981) *Translations*, London: Faber & Faber.

Frow, J. (1995) *Cultural Studies and Cultural Value*, Oxford: Clarendon Press.

Gibbons, L. (1988) 'Coming Out of Hibernation? The Myth of Modernity in Irish Culture', in R. Kearney (ed.), *Across the Frontiers: Ireland in the 1990s*, Dublin: Wolfhound.

Gilley, S. and Swift, R. (1985) *The Irish in the Victorian City*, Beckenham: Croom Helm.

Gillingham, J. (1990) 'The Context and Purposes of Geoffrey of Monmouth's *Historia Regum Brittaniae*', *Anglo-Norman Studies*, 13: 99–118.

Gillingham, J. (1992) 'The Beginnings of English Imperialism', *Journal of Sociology*, 5: 392–409.

Gilroy, P. (1993) *Small Acts: Thoughts on the Politics of Black Cultures*, London: Serpent's Tail.

Hall, S. and Gieben, B. (eds) (1992) *Formations of Modernity*, Cambridge: Polity Press.

Heaney, S. (1983) *An Open Letter*, Derry and Belfast: Field Day.

Hickman, M. and Walters, B. (1995) 'Deconstructing Whiteness: Irish Women in Britain', *Feminist Review*, 50: 5–19.

Hillyard, P. (1993) *Suspect Community: People's Experience of the Prevention of Terrorism Acts in Britain*, London: Pluto Press.

Hoggart, R. (1957) *The Uses of Literacy*, London: Chatto & Windus.

Holmes, C. (1988) *John Bull's Island: Immigration and British Society, 1871–1971*, London: Macmillan.

Jones, W.R. (1971) 'England Against the Celtic Fringe: A Study in Cultural Stereotypes', *Journal of World History*, 13: 155–71.

Joyce, J. (1985) *Ulysses*, Harmondsworth: Penguin.

Kearney, R. (ed.) (1988) *Across the Frontiers: Ireland in the 1990s*, Dublin: Wolfhound.

Keogh, D. (1982) *The Rise of the Irish Working Class*, Belfast: Appletree Press.

Kirk, N. (1980) 'Ethnicity, Class and Popular Toryism, 1850–70', in K. Lunn (ed.), *Hosts, Immigrants and Minorities*, Folkestone.

Lennon, C. (1978) 'Richard Stanihurst and Old English Identity', *Irish Historical Studies*, 82: 121–43.

Lloyd, D. (1993) *Anomalous States: Irish Writing and the Post-Colonial Moment*, Dublin: Lilliput.

Longley, E. (1994) *The Living Stream: Literature and Revisionism in Ireland*, Newcastle upon Tyne: Bloodaxe.

Loomba, A. (1994) 'The Color of Patriarchy: Critical Difference, Cultural Difference and Renaissance Drama', in M. Hendricks and P. Parker (eds), *Women, 'Race' and Writing in the Early Modern Period*, London: Routledge.

Luddy, M. (1995a) *Women in Ireland 1800–1918: A Documentary History*, Cork: Cork University Press.

Luddy, M. (1995b) *Women and Philanthropy in Nineteenth-Century Ireland*, Cambridge: Cambridge University Press.

Luddy, M. and Murphy, C. (1989) *Women Surviving: Studies in Irish Women's History in the 19th and 20th Centuries*, Dublin: Poolbeg Press.

MacCurtain, M. and O'Corrain, D. (1978) *Women in Irish Society: The Historical Dimension*, Dublin: Arlen House.

MacCurtain, M. and O'Dowd, M. (eds) (1991) *Women in Early Modern Ireland*, Dublin: Wolfhound.

Maddox, B. (1996) 'A Fine Old Irish Stew', *New Statesman*, 29 November: 21–2.

Maley, W. (1994) 'Cultural Devolution? Representing Scotland in the 1970s', in B. Moore-Gilbert (ed.), *The Arts in the 1970s: Cultural Closure*, London: Routledge.

Prendeville, P. (1988) 'Divorce in Ireland: An Analysis of the Referendum to Amend the Constitution, June 1986', *Women's Studies International Forums*, 2(4): 355–63.

Quinn, D.B. (1945) 'Sir Thomas Smith (1513–1577) and the Beginnings of English Colonial Theory', *Proceedings of the American Philosophical Society*, 89: 543–60.

Quinn, D.B. (1966) *The Elizabethans and the Irish*, Ithaca, New York: Folger Shakespeare Library, Cornell University Press.

Rex, J. (1986) *Race and Ethnicity*, Milton Keynes: Open University Press.

Roston, B. and Waters, H. (guest eds) (1995) *Race and Class*, 37(1) (July–September).

Scannell, Y. (1988) 'The Constitution and the Role of Women', in B. Farrell (ed.), *De Valera's Constitution and Our Own*, Dublin: Gill and Macmillan.

Sharkey, S. (1993a) 'Frontier Issues: Irish Women's Texts and Contexts', *Women: A Cultural Review*, 4(2): 125–36.

Sharkey, S. (1993b) 'Gendering Inequalities: The Case of Irish Women', *Paragraph: A Journal of Critical Theory*, 16(1): 5–23.

Sharkey, S. (1995) 'And Not Just for Pharaoh's Daughter: Irish Language Poetry Today', in H. Ludwig and L. Fietz (eds), *Poetry in the British Isles*, Cardiff: University of Wales Press.

Smith, A.D. (1995) *Nations and Nationalism in a Global Era*, Oxford: Polity Press .

Smyth, A. (1993) *Irish Women's Studies Reader*, Dublin: Attic Press.

Tomlinson, M. (1995). 'Can Britain Leave Ireland? The Political Economy of War and Peace', *Race and Class*, 37(1) (July–September): 1–22.

Walter, B. (1989) *Irish Women in London*, London: Ealing Women's Unit.

Ward, M. (1983) *Unmanageable Revolutionaries: Women and Irish Nationalism*, London: Pluto Press.

Wiener, C.Z. (1971) 'The Beleaguered Isle: A Study of Elizabethan and Early Jacobean Anti-Catholicism', *Past and Present*, 51: 27–62.

Williams, R. (1977) *Marxism and Literature*, Oxford: Oxford University Press.

PART III
REFLECTIONS

9

Thin Descriptions: Questions of Method in Cultural Analysis

Graham Murdock

Elective affinities

The century-long contest between empiricist and interpretive visions of social and cultural inquiry has a number of affinities with Britain's first-past-the-post electoral system. Two major contenders command the field, pushing minor players to the periphery. Both are prepared to accommodate internal debate on priorities and procedures, but each insists that the central differences between them are unbridgeable. For the faithful, a vote for one is a vote against everything the other stands for. Like contemporary political parties, the main methodological camps have their roots in nineteenth-century reactions to High Modernity. Whilst empiricism pursues 'the Enlightenment urge to categorise and count' in the service of prediction and control, the interpretive tradition's desire to recover authentic experience 'harks back to the romantic movement' and its rejection of routinization and instrumental rationality (Silverman 1993: 197).

Supporters of empiricism have laboured long and hard to present themselves as the 'natural' party of intellectual government, arguing that only they can deliver a 'science' of social and cultural life, comparable in reach and status to the natural sciences. Faced with this imperialism, advocates of interpretive styles of work were quick to claim leadership of the opposition, insisting that investigations of contemporary life belong alongside the study of history and literature, as integral contributions to a 'human science', radically different in kind from a 'social science' modelled on the aims and procedures of physics. Like supporters of the rival medieval claimants to the papacy – one in Rome the other in Avignon – true believers in both camps insist on the evident superiority of their case. The Swedish communications scholar Karl Eric Rosengren, for example, sees it as a 'really sad thing' that some researchers insist 'on staying within the fold' of ethnographic work in their studies of every-day responses to popular media, because they miss 'the potentially rich harvest bound to come in, once the necessary transubstantiation of . . . valuable qualitative insights into quantitative descriptions and explana-tions based on representative samples from carefully defined popula-tions has been carried out' (1996: 40). He is adamant that true 'science' must trade in 'hard' facts. Qualitative materials are seen as too 'soft' from this position, 'too imprecise, value laden, and particularistic to be of much use in generating general or causal explanations' (Lindlof 1995: 10). It is no accident that Rosengren uses a religious metaphor. For devotees in empiricism, counting is a kind of communion, revealing truths and insights through the benediction of statistics. This arrogance has been met with an equally truculent rejection of any kind of calcu-lating on the part of many interpretive researchers. And for the last two decades or so they have enjoyed steadily increasing levels of support as social and cultural inquiry has been swept by a generalized 'turn' towards interpretation. The party, so long relegated to the opposition benches, has found itself within shouting distance of forming a govern-ment.

As with many shifts in the political arena, this intellectual movement has been fuelled as much by the governing party's declining credibility as by the attractions of the alternative platform. Growing recognition of the environmental and other costs of instrumental rationality has severely dented the Enlightenment equation of empiricism and 'pro-gress'. Faced with nuclear contamination and acid rain, the physical sciences no longer seem such a desirable model of inquiry and respons-ibility. In any case it is now clear that biology, not physics, will be the decisive science of the next century (Castells 1996: 13). The rise of ecological studies has weakened the appeal of laboratory experimenta-tion as a master template for 'scientific' method. Though it continues to attract loyal support, particularly among psychologists, and those sociologists who see the systematic control of confounding variables in analysing large-scale sample surveys as a surrogate form of experimenta-tion, its critics have became more vociferous. There has been growing unease, even in the ranks of those generally sympathetic to the empiricist project. The small band of early doubters, like the eminent American sociologist Robert Merton, have found a more receptive audience. As Merton later recalled, his work on the impact of military training films during the Second World War persuaded him that 'the rigour of the controlled experiment had its costs since it meant giving up access to the phenomenological aspects of the real-life experience and invited mis-taken inferences about the sources of that experienced response'. He was careful to add, though, that whilst the group interviews he designed to retrieve soldiers' experiences might produce useful hypotheses about response, these had to be 'tested' by further 'experimental research'

(Merton 1987: 557). Qualitative methods could be included in inquiries, but only as junior and subordinate partners.

Ironically, while empiricists were looking at suitable ways of incorporating accounts of lived experience into their research, a number of those in the interpretive camp were embarking on a love affair with 'big science' in the form of structuralism. The discovery of a comprehensive grid of classifications and codes that seemingly ordered every aspect of social and symbolic life promised to give the human sciences a master key to chaos and contingency that could stand alongside the elegant helical structure of DNA. It was a delusion, a euphoric dream of scientificity. Structuralism was a 'yin–yang' system 'without a Book of Changes' (Sahlins 1987: xvi). Its pristine oppositions could not accommodate flux and contradiction. Reading structuralist accounts of contemporary culture was like walking into a bare white room furnished only with a Bauhaus chair. Its clean, angular lines were elegant, even beautiful, but you couldn't imagine dozing off in it, or making love in it, or sitting in front of the television eating diner from a tray. It resolutely banished any trace of the messiness of everyday life. There were no food stains, no animal hairs, no dust, no discarded newspapers. Though some researchers in cultural studies became caught up in the promise of structuralism, its working centre remained firmly anchored in the ebb and flow of social life and its heart lay with the small victories of refusal and remaking that arrested the onwards march of routine and conformity. It was a deeply Romantic sensibility.

' In searching for authenticity, researchers were drawn, like earlier writers, to groups who had slipped through the fine mesh of incorporation. Dick Hebdige's punks and rastas (1979) were the direct descendants of George Borrow's gypsies (1851) and Clarence Rook's London hooligans (1899). Cultural studies reported from beyond the boundaries of respectability, recuperating 'the experiences of otherwise un-voiced groups', and, by treating their cultures seriously, restored the capacity for rational action denied them by moral crusaders and headline writers (Atkinson and Coffey 1995: 48–9). This was as much a political intervention as an intellectual project. Because 'cultural studies has a . . . stake in social change, it requires a model that allows the marginal, the deviant, and the abnormal to be always granted significance and at times major significance' (Fiske 1994: 196). This focus on refusal and noncompliance left little room for an extended analysis of caution and conservatism. In cultural studies' hall of mirrors the centre became the margin. As a result it was unable to offer a convincing account of continuity and inertia. It was strong on disruption but weak on reproduction.

The Romantic sensibility underpinning interpretive work finds its fullest academic expression, however, in anthropology's trade in curiosities, bringing 'home' accounts of exotic and unsettling practices from unfamiliar places. It was, therefore, no accident that cultural anthropologists should be among the most vocal advocates of the interpretive turn in analysis or that the practice of ethnography should be presented as its methodological core. As Clifford Geertz argued in 1973, in one of the movement's key manifestos, 'Believing . . . that man is an animal suspended in webs of significance he himself has spun, I take culture to be those webs, and the analysis of it to be therefore not an experimental science in search of law but an interpretive one in search of meaning' (1973: 5). For him, 'Cultural analysis is guessing at meanings, assessing the guesses, and drawing explanatory conclusions from the better guesses' (1973: 20).

Cultural studies arrived in the academy just as this interpretive project was building up a head of steam and became inextricably bound up with it. It drew freely on diverse intellectual sources in anthropology, micro-sociology, textual analysis, social and cultural history, and psycho-analysis; and, through its own hybrid practices, generated new and distinctive syntheses that proved deeply attractive to a rising generation of students and young researchers. At the same time it also took over many of the methodological tensions and lacunae of the interpretive tradition. This considerably weakened its capacity to produce a compre-hensive account of contemporary culture and the forces shaping it.

Don't count on it

One conspicuous blind-spot concerns quantification. Most interpretive studies are centred on the qualitative analysis of texts, images, observa-tional notes or transcripts of everyday talk. The only numbers appear at the bottom of the pages of books or articles. Any form of counting or calculating is regarded as inadmissible, and the greater sensitivity of interpretive work is counterposed to empiricism's bone-dry presenta-tions. Where empiricism reduces texts, actions and beliefs to numbers, the interpretive approach insists on safeguarding their complexity and singularity. The resurgence of interpretation has reinforced this righteous disdain for statistics. During the 1970s 'the word got about that no good qualitative researcher would want to dirty his or her hands with any techniques of quantification' (Silverman 1993: 204). But, as with all lofty injunctions, this one is frequently breached in practice.

Reports of qualitative research often fall back on loose statements of how many people did or said something and how often. The recent exploration by Jane Roscoe and her colleagues (1995) of audience responses to a television drama-documentary on the IRA bombing of a pub in Birmingham is a case in point. The research is based on tran-scripts of twelve focus group discussions and uses verbatim quotations to illustrate the argument. But, at critical junctures, key points are underlined by statements of quantity. Two are particularly central to the case being made: 'There are *many occasions* in the group discussions where participants drew on their classified group membership to inform their reading' and 'There were *many instances* of participants moving outside the particular "interest" and "non-interest" classifications used in this study as they made sense of the issues' (Roscoe et al. 1995: 96, 98; emphasis added). These assertions appear contradictory, but we are not given the information that might allow for a resolution. We are not told how often each practice occurred, whether one was more common than the other, who was most likely to engage in them and in which contexts, or even whether they were different people or the same individuals at different points in the discussion. All of these features of the situation could be very simply expressed in numerical form. Far from reducing the complexity of the analysis, calculating these figures would deepen it by establishing the patterning of practice and by suggesting new dimensions of interpretation. As David Silverman argues, from his own experience of interpretive research, 'if you are trying to get some feel about your data as a whole or are actively pursuing deviant cases, it may sometimes be very useful to use certain quantitative measures' (1993: 204).

There is also a strong case for incorporating the results of large-scale surveys of cultural activities into the project of cultural studies. Given the distribution of funding for research, official statistics and commercially sponsored probes are the only sources of systematic national and international data on the social bases of cultural practice that we have. They have to be read and used with care and in the full knowledge of the way the materials have been obtained and put together. But, as Pierre Bourdieu demonstrates so forcefully in *Distinction* (1984), if the results are seen as posing puzzles and clues for further inquiry and interpretation, rather than as offering accomplished facts, they can play a vital role in extending the scope of cultural analysis. As he points out, a 'statistical relationship, however precisely it can be determined numerically, remains a pure datum, devoid of meaning' until it is interpreted (Bourdieu 1984: 18). Certainly, his own, very influential, model of the ties binding cultural practices to social locations consistently uses other people's often crude surveys as a jumping-off point for analysis.

It is useful to refer to available statistics alongside fieldwork materials since '[t]he more hints related to the mystery being solved, the more the researcher and the reader may trust in the solidity of the interpretation' (Alasuutari 1995: 18). Unfortunately, many students and researchers in cultural studies persist in seeing any move to incorporate what can usefully be counted as a concession to empiricism. This thins out the materials the analyst has to hand in constructing explanations and restricts the scope of inquiry. As David Silverman (1993: 203) points out, we might start 'to ask more interesting questions when we reject the polarities' erected by the rival camps. The importance of selected forms of quantification has been recognized by cultural anthropologists for some time. Roger Keesing argued in the early 1980s, as 'fieldwork in large-scale modern cultures, whether in the Third World or the West' has become more complicated with the increasing fragmentation and inter- play of different groups, so 'more concern with sampling, statistics, and methodological precision is needed' (1981: 6). Even so, thick description has remained at the heart of the ethnographic enterprise.

Thin and thick descriptions

Investigations in the human sciences pose four kinds of question: 'What is going on here?', 'Why is it happening as, when and where it is?', 'What does it mean to those involved?' and, measured against a declared set of ethical criteria, 'Is it, on balance, a good or a bad thing?' Runciman (1983: Chapter 1) usefully labels these: reportage, explanation, description and evaluation. Empiricists regard only two of these exercises – reportage and explanation – as legitimate. They see research as a matter of gathering basic data about an event, process or state of affairs and then offering an explanation of why it came to occur as it did. They resist any attempt to move from explanation to evaluation. They insist that their job stops with the analysis of 'facts' and that judgements are someone else's responsibility. Nor do they have any interest in developing descriptions. They accept that, unlike objects in the natural world, human beings have thoughts and feelings about their predicaments but argue that 'no methodological conclusion is to be drawn from' this except that, for better or worse, social researchers have an opportunity to 'submit the objects of their studies to verbal questionnaires' (Runciman 1983: 40). However, replies to these probes are taken as objective meas- ures of people's knowledge, beliefs and values which can be added to the stock of reported data to be explained. Empiricists refuse to accept that the distinctive problems of the human sciences are precisely prob- lems of description and that, in arriving at explanations, analysts have to account not only for what happened (as seen by an external observer) but for the ways in which it was perceived and acted on by those in the situation. One of the central tasks of non-empiricist research is, therefore, building 'thick descriptions' that capture the 'multiplicity of conceptual structures' operating on the ground, 'many of them superimposed upon or knotted into one another, which are at once strange, irregular, and inexplicit' (Geertz 1973: 10). Because it nominates the making and taking of meaning as its special focus, and lays claim to particular expertise and authority in this area, 'thick description' plays a central role in cultural analysis. This, in turn, privileges ethnography as a research practice.

Cultural studies has always supported a strong current of ethno- graphic work, from Paul Willis's work on the 'profane' culture of bike boys (1978) to recent studies of family television-viewing. It has also been shaped by powerful ties to literary criticism. Texts codify patterns of belief and structures of feeling. They bear the marks of the processes that produced them and extend invitations to interpretation. As Siegfried Kracauer argued in his ringing defence of qualitative analysis in the early 1950s, 'every word vibrates with the intentions in which they originate and simultaneously foreshadows the indefinite effects they may produce' (1952–3: 641). But interpreting texts cannot tell us how exactly they were made or how they are deployed in particular circumstances. To answer these questions we need ethnographies of cultural practice. As Geertz argues, although beliefs 'find articulation . . . in various forms of artefacts', these productions continually draw 'their meaning from the role they play . . . in ongoing patterns of life' (1973: 17). Anyone tempted to dismiss this as special pleading on the part of anthropologists should take note of Raymond Williams's staunch support. Although he held a chair in a department organized around textual analysis, he insisted that 'we have to break from the common procedure of isolating the object and then discovering its components' and concentrate instead on discovering 'the nature of a practice and then its conditions' (Williams 1980: 47).

Conducting ethnographies, however, is far from easy. Fieldwork uses up more time and commitment than most researchers are prepared to give. It is much more comfortable to take a short cut to compiling descriptions. One option is to view social action as a text and to deploy the armoury of literary analysis in teasing out its meanings and solving its riddles. Clifford Geertz expressly commends this approach to anthropologists in search of thick descriptions, arguing that 'doing ethnography is like trying to read (in the sense of "construct a reading of") a manuscript – foreign, faded, full of ellipses, incoherencies, suspicious emendations, and tendentious commentaries' (1973: 10). However, he is talking of interpretations built on sustained immersion in a situation and a full awareness of the diversity, fluidity and variability of people's accounts of their actions. This is not at all the same as an account based on brief encounters and spasmodic observations, as in Dick Hebdige's (1979) celebrated analysis of subcultural styles. What we are offered here is fine reportage but 'thin' description.

A second option is to stretch the definition of ethnography to cover almost any effort to collect extended accounts of people's beliefs, responses and experiences through, for instance, diaries and letters, individual depth interviews or focus group discussions. In this conveniently elastic usage, ethnography becomes synonymous with qualitative research. For academics hard pressed for research time, faced with dwindling resources for fieldwork and under mounting pressure to publish more often, this is an attractive proposition. And, as shown by Ien Ang's (1985) use of women's letters to explore their involvement in television soap operas, it can offer a solid basis for creative interpretation – but it cannot provide thick descriptions. What is missing is a rounded account of the ways that people's utterances, expressions and self-presentations are shaped and altered by the multiple social contexts they have to navigate in the course of their daily lives. However, as the current debate within contemporary anthropology demonstrates all too clearly, a return to ethnography is no simple matter.

Building sites

Empiricists are often cast in the role of unscrupulous property developers riding roughshod over customary rights and local sensibilities to realize their grand schemes. In contrast, anthropologists like to present themselves as working with the community, coaxing people to tell their stories and presenting their hopes, fears and beliefs to a wider audience. The aim of uncovering actors' conceptual worlds is not to provide information that might aid intervention and control, but, rather, to allow 'us' to 'converse with them' (Geertz 1973: 24); not as 'others' who are opaque and set apart, but as people like ourselves, facing the same basic dilemmas yet arriving at different solutions. This egalitarian promise is central to the very notion of 'fieldwork', with its strong connotations of labouring together to bring in a crop that everyone can share. The fields anthropologists enter, however, are never simply places. They are imaginative spaces in which identities, relations and histories intersect and collide (Auge 1995: 52). The analyst's first task is to unpack these ties and disconnections from the point of view of the actors in the situation. For interpretivists, being able to see the world through other people's eyes is an absolute precondition of understanding (Lindlof 1995: 30). This world is not already 'out there' to be simply located and mapped by technologies of inquiry. Unlike empiricism, interpretive work does not produce research 'findings', bringing to light cultural 'facts' which have lain buried like ancient iron objects awaiting a metal detector to pass over them. It constructs realities through the continual interchanges that take place between researchers and their subjects. The result 'is not the unmediated world of the "others", but the world between ourselves and the others' (Hastrup 1992: 117). Whereas a survey using a precoded questionnaire may smack of an interrogation, fieldwork is anchored in conversations 'in which the analyst is herself caught up and examined, much as the person she is submitting to investigation' (Bourdieu 1996: 21). Where empiricists strive to write themselves out of their accounts, claiming that an 'objective' presentation must be purged of any trace of subjectivity, contemporary ethnographers struggle to write themselves in. Empiricist research is based on distance and formal protocols. Interpretive work is rooted in intimate encounters. The slips, accidents and formative moments involved in constructing an account are as integral to the story being told as is the eventual product. As Laura Bohannan noted, after sharing a particularly difficult childbirth with one of her Tiv respondents in Nigeria, 'One can, perhaps, be cool when dealing with questionnaires or when interviewing strangers. But what is one to do

when one can collect one's data only by forming personal friendships?'
(Bowen 1954: 163). Interestingly, at the time she was writing, in the early
1950s, she felt she could only make this observation in a fictionalized
account of her work written under the pen name Smith Bowen. This is not
particularly surprising. In the classical anthropological tradition, ethnographers (most of whom were male) were expected to cultivate a certain
stiffness of the upper lip. Accounts of how the study was done were almost
always relegated to an appendix; though, as Raymond Firth grudgingly
acknowledged in introducing his pioneering work on the Tikopia (first
published in 1936), 'some account of the relations of the anthropologist to
his people is relevant to the nature of the results' (1965: 10).

The recent turn towards interpretation has moved these accounts to
the centre, producing texts in which 'the self of the ethnographer is
treated as being of equal interest to the actions of the observed' (Atkinson and Coffey 1995: 43). It has also prompted a much more sustained
engagement with the reflexive nature of fieldwork; the need to think
about the ways a researcher's actions may structure the responses
encountered and about how those reactions alter the researcher's own
perceptions. For some, like Pierre Bourdieu, fieldwork conversations 'can
be considered a sort of spiritual exercise', a baptism by total immersion
through which the researcher is 'born again', achieving 'through for-
getfulness of self, a true transformation of the view we take of others in
the ordinary circumstances of life' (1996: 24). Balancing autobiography
against history, confessional against realist accounts (Van Maanen 1988),
is by no means straightfoward. On the contrary, its difficulties are central
to anthropology's current crisis of method.

Cooking raw data

Despite its rejection of empiricist techniques of inquiry, classical ethnography's presentational forms relied heavily on the ideology of objectivity developed in two other major forms of social reportage that arose
alongside ethnography: investigative journalism and the classical film
documentary with its voice-of-God commentary directing the viewer's
gaze and reflections. All three offered accounts of other people's lives
from the vantage point of an 'impartial author whose point of view is the
dominant, even the sole one' (Atkinson and Coffey 1995: 51). 'Experience, both that of the enthnographer and that of the people, was erased
in favour of abstract analysis' (Callaway 1992: 38), producing a profound
paradox at the heart of the ethnographic endeavour. Whereas the ethos
of fieldwork was egalitarian, seeing 'observer and observed as inhabitants of a shared social and cultural field, their respective cultures
different but equal', the finished monograph presented respondents as
'others', 'rendered solely as the object of the ethnographer's gaze'
(Atkinson and Hammersley 1994: 256). Between writing up notes in the

field and writing them down for publication, subjects had become objectified. The intimacies of fieldwork were erased by the impositions of distance (Fabian 1983).

In an attempt to close this gap an increasing number of anthropologists have experimented with forms of writing that extend the range of voices in play within the text and give their spoken performances much more space. They have moved from authorship to orchestration, in much the same way as documentary film-makers have developed forms of video diary in which 'ordinary' people tell their stories in ways they have chosen. Other anthropologists have travelled in the opposite direction, towards more reflexive forms of authorship, experimenting with poetry, drama and fiction. Again, this parallels the recent shift towards a greater aestheticization of documentary forms within film and television (Corner 1996).

These movements may make anthropological work more enticing to read but, by presenting the central problem as one of exposition and representation, they paper over the enduring difficulties of doing fieldwork and constructing explanations. For all the rhetoric 'about dialogue, ethnographic practice implies intrusion and, possibly, pain' (Hastrup 1992: 123). It collects people's accounts with the intention of making a different kind of sense, mobilizing concepts and vocabularies they do not have access to. They know this. As one respondent told an ethnographer at their last meeting:

> You have all I can give you. Take it and do something with it. What it is I don't know. You have to take it in your own way. How you will do this with all your ignorance, I cannot think, but maybe something comes together and makes sense for you. We'll see. . . . Now, go home with all this package of stories. (Quoted in Hastrup 1992: 123)

In his recent book *La Misère du monde* (1993), which deals with the disappointments and small defeats of everyday life in contemporary France, Pierre Bourdieu wrestles with these problems in a particularly open way. His dilemmas are instructive since he is one of the major cultural theorists of our time, and one of the few to base his reflections on sustained empirical research using the full range of basic methodologies. In setting up the extended interviews for the study he broke with every conventional tenet of survey procedure. His sample was as far from random as it is possible to get. To encourage open, non-coercive, dialogue in the interviews investigators were free 'to choose their respondents from among or around people personally known to them' in the hope that familiarity would ensure trust and candour (Bourdieu 1996: 20). And to get around the problem that most university researchers move in somewhat restricted social circles, he recruited non-professional interviewers. The result was a dense and richly textured set of conversations. By offering their respondents 'an attentiveness and openness rarely met with in everyday life', Bourdieu claims that his team were able to go beyond 'ritualized talk of relatively common troubles' to tap the roots of popular miseries. At the same time, he recognizes very clearly that his procedures pose two major problems.

As with all interpretive studies, there is a strong residue of Romanticism, a desire to dig down, below surface conventions and elisions, to reach a solid bedrock of experience. As a result, the researcher runs a risk of being 'taken in by the "authenticity" of the respondent's testimony, because she believes she has access through it to a raw, dense, untarnished form of speech that others will not have known how to pick up or to provoke' (Bourdieu 1996: 27). The more confessional the interview the greater the researcher's claim to have produced 'an extra-ordinary discourse . . . which was already there, merely awaiting the conditions for its actualization' (1996: 24). This view conceals the extent to which all research outcomes are the product of particular social encounters, and colludes with empiricism's notion that 'findings' are, after all, 'out there' merely waiting to be discovered by skilled investigation. Interviews are never simply opportunities for vocalizing beliefs and experiences. They are always performances in which respondents assume identities and manage impressions. Much work in cultural studies conveniently forgets this and proceeds naively as though interview transcripts can be read as simple expressions of experience. Bourdieu is very well aware of this danger, but by encouraging interviews rooted in widely different degrees of social distance and familiarity he makes it impossible to address it in any consistent way.

Taking full account of the ways communication is organized by the immediate contexts of interaction is the first step towards a non-naive reading of transcripts of interviews, conversations or arguments. 'If attention is not paid . . . to the conditions of production of a text, to the reception and interpretation of it by the researcher', even the most 'subjective' sources of research material, such as personal narratives, are likely to produce a new kind of 'objectivism' (Melucci 1996: 387). The second step is to place the micro-settings of research and the competencies they call into play in the context of the wider formations that organize the distribution of key resources. As Bourdieu notes, respondents 'do not necessarily have access to the central causes of their discontent or their disquiet and the most spontaneous declarations can, without aiming to mislead, express quite the opposite of what they appear to say' (1996: 29). It is the analyst's task to illuminate these 'central causes' and to demonstrate how they work. This entails a move from description to explanation and from an analytical framework rooted in the interpretive tradition to one grounded in critical realism.

After interpretation

Interpretive research in search of thick descriptions sets out 'to take the capital letters off' the 'grand realities' that shape everyday life by anchoring them in the minutiae of situated action and the vagaries of biography (Geertz 1973: 21). It is social science with human faces. As Clifford Geertz rightly argues, 'There is a certain value, if you are going to run on about the exploitation of the masses in having seen a Javanese sharecropper turning earth in a tropical downpour or a Moroccan tailor embroidering kaftans by the light of a twenty-watt bulb.' He is equally correct to insist that 'the notion that this gives you the thing entire . . . is an idea which only someone too long in the bush could possibly entertain' (Geertz 1973: 22). As C. Wright Mills argued so eloquently, a comprehensive analysis needs to 'range from the most impersonal and remote transformations to the most intimate features of the human self . . . from examination of a single family to comparative assessment of the national budgets of the world . . . and to see the relations between the two' (1970: 14).

Teasing out the links between biography and history, the remote and the ready-to-hand, presents particular problems now, when the extension and deepening of globalization is incorporating local lives into an ever-denser network of transnational flows and power lines and reconstructing national formations in fundamental ways. The problem of portraying cultures 'shaped by an intense, continuous, comprehensive interplay between the indigenous and the imported' (Hannerz 1996: 5) is a key issue for contemporary cultural analysis. In a globalizing world, ethnography's traditional 'my people' values, which 'presumed the existence of bounded cultural entities – islands, literal or putative – into which the ethnographer might be incorporated, after a fashion . . . and learn to know, in a sense, from the inside', are no longer appropriate (Stocking Jr 1995: 955). Consequently, 'There is now a growing awareness among many anthropologists of the limitations of fieldwork and the need to pay greater attention to the heterogeneities within wider spaces and over longer time periods than personal observation allows' (Asad 1994: 76).

This difficulty is not confined to work with the 'peripheral' peoples who have been anthropology's stock-in-trade. It is central to the analysis of metropolitan life at the nodal points of contemporary capitalism. As the Brazilian anthropologist Ribeiro Durham has argued, 'The formation and life of the city escape us if we cannot show to what degree the narrow relationships we document in case studies are conditioned by . . . broader structures' (quoted in Garcia Canclini 1995: 743). Indeed, some of the central purposes of investigation 'are defeated when researchers get so close to "unique" lived experience that they have no generalizable wisdom to pass on . . . and can only see the complexities to be described and interpreted' (Berger 1995: 69–70). But integrating accounts of these structures into explanations that retain a proper emphasis on the fluid, reflexive, creative nature of everyday social practice has proved surprisingly difficult.

The separation between thick descriptions and concepts of structural determination has long been a major fault-line running through the social and human sciences. It has been reinforced within cultural studies by the flirtation with structuralism and, more recently, by celebrations of the seeming collapse of modernity's basic templates. Both perspectives have problems with history; structuralism freezes time; postmodernism accelerates it. Neither is adequate. Understanding change requires us to grasp inertia as well as dislocation, to recognize the resilience of basic structures over long loops of time as well as the breaks signalled by specific events. Projects for emancipation must grasp the brute force of 'necessity' as well as the contradictions and leaks that open the way for forward movement. They must continually test 'just how autonomous our choices are' and 'just how frequently we do or do not "give in" to the incentives, the intimidations, the temptations, the pressures that the social structure of our lives renders the flesh and spirit heir to' (Berger 1995: 7–8). This is the central aim of critical realism.

It begins by recognizing that there are social and cultural equivalents to the deep structuring processes of the natural world yet insists that these do not 'exist independently of the activities they govern' or of 'agents' conceptions of what they are doing in their activity' (Bhaskar 1979: 38). Social and cultural structures are always both constraining and enabling (Giddens 1984: 25). They 'determine' action by privileging certain possibilities while closing others off. At the same time, they are continually reproduced and altered by the ways that choices are understood and worked through on the ground. Research has to untangle these dialectical relations. To do this we need to develop working models of structures while retaining a commitment to thick description, to act as 'an interpretive humanist and a determinist' (Berger 1995: 70). Nestor Garcia Canclini makes this point particularly well in his reflections on conducting ethnographies in contemporary Mexico City:

> To ask ourselves about the meaning of the city is to explore the structure and the destructuring of demographic, socioeconomic, and cultural forms that have a certain objective 'reality'. But at the same time it calls for investigating the way in which the subjects represent those acts through which they inhabit these structures. . . . The meaning of the city is constituted by what the city gives and what it does not give, by what subjects can do with their lives in the middle of the factors that determine their habitat, and by what they imagine about themselves and about others. (1995: 751)

'Structure' is still an awkward term. It smacks too much of solidity and stasis. Because social and cultural structures differ from those in the natural world in having traceable histories and in being only 'relatively enduring' (Bhaskar 1979: 38), they are more usefully thought of as 'formations'. We can begin to explore their interplay with situated practice by looking at the ways they organize the distribution of key resources for action.

The making and taking of meaning in everyday life mobilizes three kinds of resource: material resources – command over money, 'free' time and usuable space; social resources – access to networks of support and affirmation; and cultural resources – competence in negotiating systems of discourse, performance and representation. Most research in cultural studies has paid a good deal of attention to the last two but very little to the first, assuming that any insistence on the central role of material assets involves accepting a strong form of economic determinism. This has produced a substantial hole at the heart of many accounts that is particularly disabling now, after fifteen years that have seen concerted moves towards the privatization of cultural facilities alongside widening income differentials and shifts in the structure of local economies and urban space that have major implications for the organization of cultural practice. Studies of emerging patterns of consumption and everyday creativity cannot be uncoupled from an analysis of the changing organization of production or the altering contours of inequality.

If cultural analysis is to provide thick descriptions of contemporary meaning-making and convincing accounts of the forces reshaping it, it must not only recover a suitably reflexive commitment to extended ethnography; it must also reconnect its concerns to critical analysis across the range of the social sciences, including areas that it has previously seen as marginal or irrelevant.

References

Alasuutari, P. (1995) *Researching Culture: Qualitative Method and Cultural Studies*, London: Sage Publications.

Ang, I. (1985) *Watching Dallas: Soap Opera and the Melodramatic Imagination*, London: Methuen.

Asad, T. (1994) 'Ethnographic Representation, Statistics and Modern Power', *Social Research*, 61(1) (Spring): 55–88.

Atkinson, P. and Coffey, A. (1995) 'Realism and its Discontents: On the Crisis of Cultural Representation in Ethnographic Texts' in B. Adam and S. Allan (eds), *Theorizing Culture: An Interdisciplinary Critique After Postmodernism*, London: UCL Press.

Atkinson, P. and Hammersley, M. (1994) 'Ethnography and Participant Observation', in N. Denzin and Y. Lincoln (eds), *Handbook of Qualitative Research*, Thousand Oaks, Calif.: Sage.

Auge, M. (1995) *Non-Places: Introduction to an Anthropology of Supermodernity*, London: Verso.

Berger, B. (1995) *An Essay on Culture: Symbolic Structure and Social Structure*, Berkeley: University of California Press.

Bhaskar, R. (1979) *The Possibility of Naturalism: A Philosophical Critique of the Contemporary Human Sciences*, Brighton: Harvester.

Borrow, G. (1851) *Lavengro: The Scholar, the Gypsy, the Priest*, London: John Murray.

Bourdieu, P. (1984) *Distinction: A Social Critique of the Judgement of Taste*, London: Routledge.

Bourdieu, P. (1993) *La Misère du Monde*, Paris: Seuil.

Bourdieu, P. (1996) 'Understanding', *Theory, Culture and Society*, 13(2): 17–36.

Bowen, E.S. (1954) *Return to Laughter*, London: Gollancz.

Callaway, H. (1992) 'Ethnography and Experience: Gender Implications in Fieldwork and Texts', in J. Okeley and H. Callaway (eds), *Anthropology and Autobiography*, London: Routledge.

Castells, M. (1996) 'The Net and the Self: Working Notes For a Critical Theory of the Information Society', *Critique of Anthropology* 16(1) (March): 9–38.

Corner, J. (1996) 'Documentary: The Re-socialization of a TV Aesthetic', in J. Gripsrud (ed.), *Media and Knowledge: The Role of Television*, University of Bergen: Department of Media Studies.

Fabian, J. (1983) *Time and the Other: How Anthropology Makes its Object*, New York: Columbia University Press.

Firth, R. (1965) *We The Tikopia*, Boston: Beacon Press.

Fiske, J. (1994) 'Audiencing: Cultural Practice and Cultural Studies', in N. Denzin and Y. Lincoln (eds), *Handbook of Qualitative Research*, Thousand Oaks, Calif.: Sage.

Garcia Canclini, N. (1995) 'Mexico: Cultural Globalization in a Disintegrating City', *American Ethnologist*, 22(4): 743–55.

Geertz, C. (1973) 'Thick Description: Toward an Interpretive Theory of Culture', in *The Interpretation of Cultures: Selected Essays*, New York: Basic Books.

Giddens, A. (1984) *The Constitution of Society: Outline of a Theory of Structuration*, Cambridge: Polity Press.

Hannerz, U. (1996) *Transnational Connections: Culture, People, Places*, London: Routledge.

Hastrup, K. (1992) 'Writing Ethnography: State of the Art', in J. Okeley and H. Callaway (eds), *Anthropology and Autobiography*, London: Routledge.

Hebdige, D. (1979) *Subculture: The Meaning of Style*, London: Methuen.

Keesing, R. (1981) *Cultural Anthropology: A Contemporary Perspective*, 2nd edn, New York: Holt, Rinehart and Winston.

Kracauer, S. (1952–3) 'The Challenge of Qualitative Content Analysis', *Public Opinion Quarterly*, 16(4): 631–42.

Lindlof, T. (1995) *Qualitative Communication Research Methods*, London: Sage.

Melucci, A. (1996) *Challenging Codes: Collective Action in the Information Age*, Cambridge: Cambridge University Press.

Merton, R. (1987) 'The Focused Interview and Focus Groups: Continuities and Discontinuities', *Public Opinion Quarterly*, 51: 550–66.

Mills, C.W. (1970) *The Sociological Imagination*, Harmondsworth: Penguin.

Rook, C. (1899) *The Hooligan Nights*, London: Grant Richards.

Roscoe, J., Marshall, H. and Gleeson, K. (1995) 'The Television Audience: A Reconsideration of the Taken-for Granted Terms "Active", "Social" and "Critical"', *European Journal of Communication*, 10(1) (March): 87–108.

Rosengren, K. (1996) 'Review Article: Klaus Bruhn Jensen: "The Social Semiotics of Mass Communication"', *European Journal of Communication*, 11(1) (March): 129–41.

Runciman, W. (1983) *A Treatise on Social Theory Volume 1: The Methodology of Social Theory*, Cambridge: Cambridge University Press.

Sahlins, M. (1987) *Islands of History*, Chicago: University of Chicago Press.

Silverman, D. (1993) *Interpreting Qualitative Data: Methods for Analysing Talk, Text and Interaction*, London: Sage.

Stocking Jr, G. (1995) 'Delimiting Anthropology: Historical Reflections on the Boundaries of a Boundless Discipline', *Social Research*, 62(4) (Winter): 933–66.

Van Maanen, J. (1988) *Tales of the Field: On Writing Ethnography*, Chicago: University of Chicago Press.

Williams, R. (1980) *Problems in Materialism and Culture*, London: Verso.

Willis, P. (1978) *Profane Culture*, London: Routledge.

10

Working Practices

Michael Green

In an editor's letter Jim McGuigan defined this book's main purpose as helping people 'cope with and find routes through the institutionalized academicism which they inevitably confront'. The distinctive purpose of this chapter, based on experiences in an English context of advising both postgraduate research students and undergraduate dissertation writers, was seen as 'bringing some of the issues of cultural studies down to ground in a very practical way'. What I have written is therefore intended as a kind of nuts and bolts or 'below stairs' contribution. It is concerned not with the implications for research processes of different theoretical/political paradigms but with the conditions of existence for research work in rapidly changing academic and social circumstances. It is a 'how to go about things' chapter.

As such it is primarily intended for imminent or existing postgraduate researchers, writing PhDs or engaged in funded research projects, but I hope some of it may also relate to the problems of dissertation writers in the final year of undergraduate programmes and on Master's degree programmes. The chapter draws on recent changes in British higher education but a dialogue about the rather different circumstances of cultural studies research in other countries' higher education systems would be illuminating. It may already be true in many countries that the position of the first degree is shifting so that research degrees become more of a usual, rather than exceptional, feature of educational experience.

The chapter has four sections. In the first I shall look at different models of ways of working, of the conditions and social relations within which research takes place. Second, I shall comment on the different stages which an extended piece of research would seem to have to go through – though other chapters in this book may impact upon these stages in particular ways. Third, I want to consider the distinctiveness, if any, of cultural studies research within the humanities and social sciences. This almost amounts to considering whether there is a specific academic subculture of cultural studies research. Last, I want to remark on the 'next phase' in cultural studies and on the features to be considered in constructing research conditions appropriate to the field 'thirty years on' and at the turn of the century.

Ways of working: four versions

Postgraduate research practices and the working relations, the social relations, of research continue to differ in startling ways between academic areas and between the education systems of various countries. It is possible, none the less, to see at least three prevailing models, and look towards an emerging, 'mixed economy', fourth.

1   *Research is individual*

Many traditional models of 'advanced research' have been intensely individual. The research student works alone, often in libraries, making contact intermittently with an advisory 'scholar' but accepting to a high degree that the onus of defining a topic, of producing research materials, and of analysing them, is a personal responsibility. Despite occasional research seminars and conversations with other people, the researcher works alone for long stretches and indeed is often rather lonely. S/he gets through this by high motivation, often with the aid of a sacrificial partner (cited in a footnote or dedication), and by inheriting a tradition, a liminal passage, in which the scholar is proved worthy through an initiation rite linked to near-poverty. It can also be argued, in favour of such practices, that much research of almost whatever type benefits from long stretches of uninterrupted concentration and dedication to the task in hand.

Such circumstances in many countries (though importantly not all) would have to be seen as going, going, gone. For one thing, funding rarely permits such time and space. For another, the model was often linked to a high rate of non-completion, or to completion only over very long periods of time which are particularly inimical to work in 'contemporary' cultural studies. Funding bodies and universities, now very attentive to completion rates (and for mainly positive reasons), will require attendance at research training courses and sessions, impose regular progress reviews and reports, and install pressures and sanctions towards successful completion within a defined and (over the last decade) ever-shortening length of time.

All this has brought into being a culture of research 'methodology' (to be resisted when it separates off 'theory' from 'how to do it' practice) and a self-consciousness about researching which was little developed in cultural studies (by comparison with political imperatives) twenty years ago. In addition a researcher now will be encouraged to network through a variety of dayschools, conferences and information sources and facilities and will in any case, full-time or part-time, be studying or teaching or earning money alongside the main piece of research. Indeed, time alone to think and write is becoming a scarce commodity and it may now be a question of securing and protecting this way of working as it almost passes out of existence. . .

2   *Research is collaboration between equals*

The former Centre for Contemporary (now Department of) Cultural Studies at the University of Birmingham was known for its postgraduate reading groups through which jointly written articles and books were developed. These research 'subgroups' arose both in protest against the damaging solitude of the 'loner' model, and more importantly because work in areas correctly described in letters to referees as 'new and uncharted' needed to gain from different disciplinary backgrounds and insights. There was a further shared, if loosely defined, socialist and then feminist belief in the value of mutual support, of working together, of joint authorship, of 'collective' production.

All these circumstances, combined with sustained encouragement in innovation from Claire L'Enfant at Hutchinson as publisher's editor, helped produce a distinctive series of books. These involved group authorship, a variety of contributors, but also co-written major pieces (the product of innumerable discussions and late nights) in which the resulting whole was far greater than the sum of individual contributors' inputs, for all the decisive 'leading role' taken by Stuart Hall (invariably) and by others (on occasion). The institutional visibility and consolidation of cultural studies, even despite Raymond Williams (eloquent at conferences and in debate, otherwise very much a 'lone' researcher), could not have happened except through the publications produced through these collaborative ways of working. It was not only a wide intellectual and political agenda, but also distinctive forms of intellectual organization which helped constitute the 'Birmingham School'.

These practices and circumstances must not be taken, for all their substantive and exemplary value, as constitutive of the difference of cultural studies. The conditions from which they arose would seem to have almost vanished, which is not to say that student-led reading groups, group work and joint authorship should be abandoned altogether.

It is rarely possible now for postgraduate students to spend long stretches of time working together. It has become important for people to finish a PhD to time, which may work against collaborative writing. Those who had a major intellectual role in such groups now have many other things to do at the same time. Institutions which understand co-authorship in the sciences seem strangely resistant in the humanities and social sciences. There is a demand to know who wrote what (as in the assessment exercise for research funding of British university departments). Perhaps also the 'launch phase' for cultural studies, in conjunction with other developments to be discussed, has allowed a more general confidence which makes intensive collective work less necessary, at least as the 'leading' model. These matters are worth debating, but few would think that conditions for such ways of working can still exist and (without romanticization, mourning or a failure to appreciate what was done) it has been necessary to move on, if possible retaining the collaborative social relations this model so valuably involved.

3   *Research is in team projects*

It seems, though, that what institutions and funding bodies might want to move towards is a 'natural science' model of the large-scale funded project. The pressure arises from intensified competition and associated rationalization into 'lead institutions', with benefits of scale and synergy, perhaps also (in the absence of a proper discussion towards which humanities and social science academics should be contributing) from various underlying, none too clear, assumptions about 'cutting edge' research.

In this third ideal type, successful research departments, units or teams (possibly working across departmental, institutional or national boundaries) attract major funded projects led by senior researchers or investigators around whom are constituted a series of research groups. A group's project is made up of a number of linked pieces of research which contribute to a shared goal and are variously carried out by academic staff, by research fellows (usually post-doctoral) and in PhD topics linked to the main concerns. This mode of research is said to generate a distinctive synergy, sometimes linked with particular library resources, or with the needs of particular user groups, while it encourages a concentration of research expenditure in a smaller number of larger units. There are also implicit or explicit labour-saving and cost-cutting elements, creating a pressured environment of serial contract researchers. There are clear signs in Britain that this model is being pursued in social science funding bodies, and even in the humanities, linked with a more firmly steered national definition of priorities in research – priorities which, though open to many readings, both allow and yet do not specifically encourage cultural studies research as such.

A small number of teams who might attract such support from foundations, charities or research councils already exist. If cultural studies research is to be supported, this way of working will need to be seriously grasped, including welcome participation in large-scale projects and in equally welcome (but not straightforward) collaboration with existing subject areas and disciplines. There have been the first signs of such developments in Britain in the competition (in 1995) for media research monies through the Economic and Social Research Council.

Cultural studies – in and against English/sociology/media studies, whatever, or standing alone – cannot and should not ignore these changes. The 'best side' here could include collaboration between different departments and between groups in different countries. Finding time to think big about major research projects is obviously desirable, and could conceivably fund both doctoral and post-doctoral research with a defined and useful public outcome. This would be to ask that 'useful knowledge' in cultural studies should have policy implications and be useful in areas outside higher education. Requirements of clarity, public accountability and potential usefulness to a wider community of 'beneficiaries' are in many ways welcome, though to be debated and sometimes struggled over.

At the same time the problems of trying to go down this route are very striking. There is the question of who defines priorities and how, and of the apparent marginalization of 'theoretical', 'disinterested' or so called 'blue skies' research, even more of research in areas of cultural studies which look to be fruitfully quirky or unorthodox. There is the danger of constant disappointment and of disillusion since, even in wealthier countries and institutions, funding is unlikely to be realized in any regular or sufficient way. Even should a few such projects be generated it is likely that most institutions and groups would fail to gain any part in them, potentially incurring instead heavier teaching loads with less space for research and less room for this new kind of 'research culture' with PhDs and shorter-term funding contracts at its centre.

4   *Research is not quite any of these: enterprise and pragmatics*

For many people now starting postgraduate research the current picture is more mixed and less clear than in the previous three types. This is partly because the departments and institutions in which they will be working are feeling their way very tentatively in the new circumstances, perhaps lurching towards other models which are not substantially realized at the moment. Nor have those working in cultural studies spent much time debating these issues, which is why I make some tentative suggestions at the end of this chapter. Currently, making the best use of opportunities and of circumstances is an important skill in itself.

It is the current view of funding bodies in Britain that a taught Master's degree should precede thesis research. A very limited number of grants for Master's work are available[1] using course work and the dissertation to 'set up' and focus more clearly potential PhD topics. It is also possible to take a Master's by thesis, probably taking in addition research training elements of the taught course. In practice the system is rather more open and it is still occasionally possible to go straight into a PhD route. Whatever the circumstances, elements of research training courses (typically ranging from ethnographic to quantitative method) are becoming steadily more important and will normally be found useful. By January of the final undergraduate year, say, it will be necessary to consider possibilities for PhD work, including finding an appropriate institution and adviser. Only some graduates are going to get money for research, from a funding body, charity, research project, studentship or just possibly outside agency or sponsor.[2] This means being willing to have a go at a number of research applications in quick succession. They must stress the main aim of the research, its point and what it will yield, what it will involve in what stages and against what timescales, its connection with previous work and its possible outcomes in terms of other research later. A cumulative set of concerns, through coursework and dissertation into the proposal, perhaps stressing distinctive knowledges or connections or experiences, will be helpful. Alternatively there is a skill in applying for a studentship linked to a stated theme in an ongoing project. Either way, applications should be clear and readable, not only to those within the particular area, and it needs to be possible to produce them to short order in response to advertisements.

For many people, probably the majority, research is not going to be funded at all but undertaken part-time alongside other activity. Its motivation should be interest and a determination not to accept a three-year degree as the final limit of experience in higher education. Many first degrees leave an appetite for more developed further work. Many European countries produce graduates after five or seven years, not three, as in England and Wales. Many who have graduated are able to consider PhD work, work-related or not, alongside full-time or part-time employment. Many are concerned to research an area properly, irrespective of its outcomes. This is no longer a period in which higher degrees normally lead on to employment in higher education, but evidence of research abilities may be useful in contract research and in other areas of employment, particularly where the topic area was policy-related.

In current circumstances a full-time or part-time research student should have various 'reasonable expectations' about day-by-day conditions, which need to be worked on and secured. The institution and department should offer appropriate library resources, including access to networks, archives and data banks; working space and access to word processing and computing facilities; research training and work in progress seminars (an important feature of developing a PhD's argument, and for gaining feedback); and some help with attendance at appropriate conferences and dayschools, including a chance to present a paper. There may be opportunities for some undergraduate teaching, including training in such teaching (a useful text here is Allan 1996). It should be possible to have informal reading and support groups with other research students, to make contact with people in other departments, to make sure of meeting with people working in related areas, sometimes at other places. There may be chances for short-term pieces of funded research. There should be a committee or forum in which research students' concerns and needs are discussed with responses from the department.

The contrast with first degree work is marked. Instead of proceeding through with the same large cohort, the research student is placed in a more amorphous constituency, whose members may be taking from two up to six years on their work, meeting less regularly and with less routinized support. Yet it is still possible and desirable to create a working research culture, and to liaise through Web pages and the Internet with other groups in other departments and countries (for the Birmingham site, see http://www.birmingham.ac.uk/CulturalStudies/).

The other important contrast and new feature is the relationship with a PhD adviser or sometimes advisers, working together or alternately for different aspects. This relationship is full of promise for both partners (it is a privilege to work with a highly motivated research student), but has to be negotiated carefully and worked at from both ends. Cultural studies is unlike, say, specialist areas of physics in that the adviser may sometimes know less than the researcher about a topic which is opening up new issues and material, in a field where publishers' catalogues reveal an exploding universe, and where the social and cultural world constantly generate new questions. This relationship is likely to be centred not only on detailed specialist knowledge (there will usually be books and articles to be found out about) but on enthusiasm for the topic, consistent support and determination in holding a PhD to two things: to being like a PhD (and not a polemic, encyclopaedia or set of related essays); and to an achievable schedule. This implies regular meetings, regular drafts and, at the far end, discussion about issues which might arise in a viva.

This picture would suggest a model of PhD work which is fundamentally crowded and where time needs to be protected for progressing the writing of a long piece of work. Not a loner, not in a tight collective, not a paid member of a hierarchical research team, the cultural studies research student will be earning money and/or teaching while networking in various ways, attending a variety of courses and seminars, meeting an adviser regularly, looking for appropriate material and keeping up with new publications, thinking of the future, living a social life and doing other things. The PhD in many Western countries is becoming more like a major task undertaken out of interest in complex and fast-changing circumstances. It is no longer a 'life's work' and, above all else, it needs to be completed.

Producing a longer piece of research

In this section I want to consider issues which, for all the differences of approach characterized in other chapters of this book, are often involved in producing a doctoral thesis or indeed a shorter dissertation.

Comments of this kind are quite hard to get right/make appropriate, and are open to parody. Advice can miss the target in a number of ways, coming across as a set of maxims, proverbs or handy hints. There is a strong danger of banality ('keep references on 5.28 inch file cards') or of excessive generality ('formulate a research hypothesis'). As with car manuals, washing machine guides and other such documents, the discourse of the helpful pointer may be unreadable until the moment it's wanted – and then insufficiently precise. Perhaps such comments have to be made orally in a working relationship, not on the page. Maybe things have to be said (and said several times) at particular stages in a process, not all at once. There are issues of temperament about how much comment of this kind is wanted. There is also a generalized resistance in cultural studies to an academic-bureaucratic codification which lines us up with 'fellow researchers' in the hierarchies of academic labour.

And yet. Hoping that something can still be usefully taken from experiences of the research process, I want to comment on typical issues/ problems as I've encountered them through and with different people. I notice, though, that problems of 'finding a topic', sometimes discussed in the literature on research, have not at all been part of my experience. Which topic, yes, and how to pursue it, but not a blankness about 'finding' one at all, nor a danger of 'duplicating' other work. With a deep breath then, a series of points:

1 *This piece of work is finite.* No research, not even a doctorate, is the last or most comprehensive account of a topic, and in looking at contemporary culture timeliness is important. Two earlier models of PhD research are now disadvantaged. One, the enormously ambitious and theoretically exploratory PhD, often over-length, which felt the pressure to grasp every relevant issue over a wide field. The other, the 'serial doctorate', written and researched in episodes between other work, twice a year or at weekends. Though part-time working is still the likeliest basis for many PhDs, there is a price to be paid in changes impacting upon the object of study; in maintaining concentration and coherent writing; in new work being published. The dissertation or PhD thesis is an important but particular piece of work, to be done to time, and which forms the basis for later work and for publication. It is not a lifetime labour but a stage. Do it, move on from it!

2 *Plans are important and will change.* There are people who work to a very tight schedule and structural plan (in one case, a PhD writer used a daily working plan for a year ahead which was successfully adhered to), others prefer to write long chunks and cut/revise later. Either way it can be predicted that there will be a series of shifts and movements in what is being done. It is impossible starting out to be certain what the most productive aspect of a topic will be, or the best way of handling it. A lot may depend upon available resources, on lucky or unlucky accidents, on what you can get access to, on who will talk productively, on the clearer realization of what's not been looked at properly before. There is often an implicit or even quite explicit logic to these changes of direction and it is often possible to put them to use in reflections upon the research process towards its conclusion.

3 *Research may use different approaches and resources.* The aim is to use a research strategy which most appropriately and productively illuminates the chosen topic. It is better not to fetishize either 'theory'/'paradigms'/'models' or alternatively empirical/'concrete' work/case studies. Other writers' 'theoretical' work should come to life and find its place in dialogue with this particular research or not at all. Equally, empirical material does not exist straightforwardly but is produced, prioritized and made sense of through particular choices. It must always prompt reflection upon the personal, intellectual, political alignments which gave it a place in the research. If empiricism has denied or repressed issues about the ways in which (as Althusser observed) knowledge constructs its object, then conversely there has sometimes been a reification of theory, presented as though separated off from or merely enlivened and made plausible by various kinds of evidence. There are many contemporary cultural research areas where existing work, 'theoretical' or otherwise, is not immediately obviously to hand, where research strategies will need to be innovative, where more general observations will be produced through the work as it goes along. The dissertation, thesis (and, where appropriate, the viva) will want to show why the work was done as it was and not otherwise.

4 *Research happens through a process of writing.* Research is constituted through a long piece of writing; it is not 'done' and then 'written up'! A researcher should write often, whatever the circumstances, as a matter of routine. This working pattern, the advice of novelists, is even more apposite when word processing allows (sometimes excessively) material to be rewritten, used elsewhere, shifted around, rescrambled, taken to bits and put to work in other places. To be negative, the experience of accumulating material, deferring writing, finding more material, deferring writing again, and then later trying to write about it all, is likely to be difficult, if not disastrous, because it is overwhelming. To be positive, many things happen during writing (connections, insights, metaphors) which are discovered and only happen in and through the writing process. If there was one thing academic about which I would like to have been told at twenty, this is it!

5 *'The river flows underground.'* Despite this plea for regular writing, there are obviously times when the going gets hard and work becomes difficult. Paul Willis, once asked during a job interview(!) to comment on problems in research work, surprised his interviewers by replying unhesitatingly and with characteristic fluency that in his view three things could cause problems: first, the realization that the initial approaches or paradigms were not helping with the work at hand; second, personal unhappiness getting in the way of working; third, and most memorably, 'at times the water flows underground in the dry river valley, bubbling up later'. To these I would add the

severe discouragement that can result from a recurrent failure to get to people, institutions or sources thought to be essential, and sometimes a sense of having too many directions, themes and purposes. It would be unusual and very good fortune if none of these occurred during research. Most of them can be worked through, while the river metaphor is apposite and illuminating.

6 *Research has to be balanced against other activities.* There's a difficult and shifting balance between research and other activities. Even those with full-time money will probably be doing some teaching and other work, concentrated if possible on certain days of the week. Seminars, networking, emailing, conferences, trying out work-in-progress are all valuable but take time. Some (enviably, unlike this writer) can fit research and writing into odd hours of the day or night; others will need protected spaces given to this work alone. Even with 'fieldwork' involved, research is not often a gregarious activity but needs concentration, and almost uninterrupted ownership of the process and of the writing itself. Getting right this combination of sharing ideas, other activities and working alone is almost harder, in current conditions, than anything in the research itself.

7 *An adviser should be made use of.* A research student will have at least one adviser and the relationship with the adviser is an important one (to each partner). The adviser will be interested but it is the researcher who is doing the new work. An adviser should be able to offer intellectual and personal support, through thick and thin; to keep a clear eye on progress, schedules, lengths of writing, what needs doing by when; to give the response line by line of a careful reader who may want things clarified or expanded; to suggest changes in the order, ask for the structure to be changed; to have some ideas about other relevant resources; to help with the last stages and with putting the research to use when finished. From an adviser's point of view it's important to be kept in touch with reading, ideas and progress and be shown drafts of writing (sometimes as a precondition for meeting) on a regular basis, and not to have to 'chase up' after periods of silence . . .

8 *There is*, or so I believe, *a typical shape to a dissertation or thesis*, however much this may be modified in particular cases.

- Towards the beginning the exploration of relevant current writing shows a grasp of the literature, situates the work in contemporary debates, is an opportunity for a proper, measured critique of other writers' work, and most of all sets up what this research will do which has not been done in this way before and redresses absences in other accounts.

- There is a need to 'set the stage' by way of contextualizing and clarifying what's being discussed, what resources are being brought to bear upon it, what strategies have been adopted and what stages the thesis will go through.

- There will be a detailed exploration of aspects of the topic in a thorough, even exhaustive, certainly if possible a cumulative way.
- The research will get nearer to a distinctive issue, feature, problem or argument, arising from the wider scene-setting. Many outstanding books would not have made research theses because they are wide-ranging and perhaps a series of 'horizontal' linked essays. A research thesis gets deeper into one area progressively.
- The significance of what's been done will be reflected upon and opened up in various ways. These are very important substantive features, not summaries or a brief late afterthought or recapitulation. There should be reflections upon what was done and problems and issues arising, including what could not or did not happen and why, presented in the most positive light and not defensively.[3] Equally, implications for future work might be discussed. This section allows the fullest possible yield from what was done and also permits, entirely reasonably, an account of what was not intended or could not have happened in this particular piece of work.
- Finally, and written last, there will be a clear introduction to where the work was coming from, its intentions, its shape and logic – as a reader's guide or preferred version of what follows for someone who does not know the thesis, as by now you do, inside out. A title and subtitle should also focus what is, and isn't, relevant.
- Time should be planned in for a rewrite, based on comments by adviser and friends, since the rewriting process is likely to enhance the overall clarity very significantly indeed.

Other matters concern not the general progression and shape but details of effective writing. The reader should be told, almost to the point of pedantry, chapter by chapter, what the thesis will be doing, is doing and has done – what the chapter has provided and why the next chapter is now necessary. Each chapter, as much as the overall thesis, should have a specific contribution to make, and a distinctive argument. Sources, footnotes and bibliography need to be checked with extreme care and accuracy. Last, it's possible to put into appendices or really substantive footnotes (normally escaping the word limit) issues and material for which there was no space or obvious place in the text; all of these are useful, particularly for documents which may not be available elsewhere, and can be drawn on by others.

9 *Give time to prepare for the oral examination* by an internal and external examiner, which, in addition to written reports, is part of the British

PhD process. The viva happens, usually, once in a lifetime and is often fraught, while also being a disturbingly under-discussed part of higher degrees. Except in fortunate cases where a successful pass is indicated in the opening moments, a viva should be seen as a chance to put across a view of exactly what the thesis was trying to do and not trying to do, and a chance also to have an engaged discussion with two informed readers who have given the thesis a considerable amount of attention. As I have known them, and all such experiences differ, vivas may reveal considerable misunder-standings which need patient and meticulous clarification (despite the tensions and power relations of the occasion). To a writer who has long lived with a project its purpose may seem obvious. A reader coming straight to the work in a hurry, from other starting points, may have questions or perspectives which may puzzle, 'throw' or even considerably anger the writer. The writer needs to keep calm and talk this through, particularly to avoid being asked to rewrite sections or chapters. This task is a common viva outcome and often an opportunity for huge improvements, while passing straight through without even correction of spellings and so forth may now be quite rare – there are no available figures. As in other interviews, it's useful to have things to want to talk about and bring in, whatever the shape of the questioning, but, above all, it's important to state a purpose and chosen method, defend both, acknowledge other interesting approaches and dimensions which were not however the concern of this project, and to be able to defend the aims and achievement of the thesis while showing a close knowledge of areas discussed – and indeed, if necessary, of what was written in the second paragraph of page 267, which may suddenly be turned to for clarification. Is the viva (or elsewhere the committee or public dialogue) the appropriate way of approving research in cultural studies? This has been very little discussed to date.

10 *Finishing a piece successfully is most definitely not the end of it.* Rather, the writing becomes an important platform (and indeed some of this should ideally have happened already) for: articles both about the research and about the processes of research; a book; further work arising from these beginnings; applications for funded research projects; postdoctoral work; the construction of profiles for different job applications; becoming known in research networks. For those staying in higher education, this may be the longest space for writing ever achieved! For those leaving education, the successful management of the process and of such a length of writing, prob-ably also connections and contacts made during the work, are assets to be drawn upon. Increasingly, too, with any research, the clear writing up in summary form of its outcome and the promotion of the research through networks, conferences, media, reviews and the

Internet is not only satisfying but likely to be required by funders. As with other forms of publication, there should be energetic work to secure reactions, readers and rejoinders, not just the 'lodging of a deposit copy in the university library'.

But is it cultural studies?

Much of what has been said so far could apply to many other departments, fields and disciplines. There may be a feeling that these recommendations (in a field where many well-known names either never began, or never finished, a PhD of their own) amount to excessive conformity to an institutional model of research.

In part I would argue that there is no longer a choice about this, or about the need for achieved outcomes within shorter periods of time. Nor, in truth, were there great advantages in 'impossibilist' PhD topics, or in endlessly deferred (and sometimes non-completed) theses whose contemporary concerns began to be repositioned or overtaken by events. Other chapters in this book are concerned with paradigms and ways of working appropriate to different kinds of cultural studies work, while this chapter has a more how-to-complete concern. Even so, it may be worth asking whether a new phase in which longer pieces of research are certified by universities (as PhDs) or funded externally (as projects bearing useful knowledge) – a phase which is well under way and which this book both signals and contributes to – constitutes, to excess, cultural studies 'going straight'. Perhaps the space for difference and resistance was always rather romantically savoured, but much more was at stake. Some of the best-known texts of the field were and are quirky, eclectic, surprising, exploratory and bold. The argument about the problem of existing disciplines was important:

> At a minimum, cultural studies must pursue an anti-disciplinary practice. . . . I do not see any possibility of elaborating a 'line', a unified theory, or even a political center to orient the whole of the enormous and diverse project. . . . [The] student-scholar of cultural studies should work . . . with . . . a sense of the political effects of her theoretical and practical choices, beginning with the choice of cultural studies itself. (Rooney, 1996: 214)

Should Ellen Rooney's remarks and many similar arguments give us pause about the attempt to produce successful PhD theses? I do not think so.

For one thing, many of the relevant 'disciplines' are now much more open, more self-conscious and less fixed than was the case earlier, more interested in the 'cultural turn' and themselves (as in cultural geography) more experimental. For another, whether cultural studies activity be regarded as interdisciplinary, cross-disciplinary, post-disciplinary or 'undisciplined', it normally (at its best) has no taken for granted 'core' domains such as the past, space, the text. It will bear the marks of a mix of sources, disciplines and approaches.

There are several other distinguishing features (which do not need, however, to become codified as necessities). Topics are often very much contemporary and arise from new social and cultural forms for which there may be few obvious existing guides: they are importantly and almost inevitably innovative in their concerns, which 'matter' outside as well as inside the academy. They also represent choices about which the writer is encouraged to write openly, indicating personal, intellectual and political starting points, where the project is coming from, why it matters to this author at this time. There should be encouragement for openness and more self-consciousness about the intellectual labour-process, about forms of writing, forms of argument, indeed what con-stitutes a distinctive cultural studies argument and how it could be made use of or evaluated. Since also the research may be written up, presented, made available in other media, for other audiences and purposes, it is hard to see that 'the PhD form' or even 'the funded project form' are of themselves inimical to the heterogeneity and contemporaneity of the best cultural studies work.

More bothersome to me is Rooney's reminder, quoting Margaret Ferguson, that 'in an old women's studies adage' it was said that 'changes in the *content* of the curriculum' should be correlated with 'changes in the *forms* of instruction' (Rooney 1996: 217). This area gives me more unease (and I know of no published commentaries on the PhD labour process by those who went through it). The individual student; the individual adviser; the 'external and internal examiners'; the very troubling ritual of the viva – together they would seem to reproduce an age-old form of working at the heart of the institutions and of their apprenticeship and accreditation procedures. All of this is not much thought about, little reconstructed, little problematized. Joint advisers, 'mentors', more continuously active advisory panels, may emerge quite quickly. All of it could be discussed within the structures of 'professional associations' which those working in cultural studies have so far had difficulties in constructing. Alternatively, it may be in places where graduate students and researchers are working together (almost but not quite those 'graduate schools' which universities seek to standardize) that different ways of working will be found. As yet all of this is very under-discussed in the 'secret garden' of research, where people are groping with difficulty towards finding the 'best side' of new condi-tions.

To what is research a 'contribution'?

Since cultural studies cannot straightforwardly answer 'work worthy of publication by a learned society' I want to end by looking at extended research within the larger situation of cultural studies work at the end of the century, at the end also (in part) of a long period of New Right dominance and (again in part) of Western supremacy and Western-centred knowledge. This is by way of tentative contribution towards another unheld discussion about the 'direction' of cultural studies research and about 'priorities' in research for the next few years.

Direction? Priorities? Perhaps again the words fit badly with the unpredictability of cultural studies work, its responsiveness to new paradigms, new politics, new circumstances. Yet these may be necessary words and questions. Time is at a premium for research, as against either teaching or metareflection (theorization, recombination, political questioning of other work): suggestive articles abound, fully researched books do not. At the same moment, many of us are being required, as never before, to set our research 'strategies' out to funders, or to work to imperatives set by them, as a condition of funding.

Cultural studies in many places is through its 'launch phase' and subsequent 'legitimation phase' (though a flurry of attacks on media and cultural studies in the British press in 1996 remind us that gains can be reversed rapidly in a period of cuts). Now there are starting to be intelligent commentaries on what has happened, and not happened, in work to date,[4] and by implication on where work needs to be done.

All this has been accompanied by very drastic political and more general ('global') changes which position cultural studies work in very new contexts. Within academic knowledge forms it is perhaps now not so much cultural studies 'in and against the disciplines' as convergences of interest in particular areas and questions between cultural studies work and work on literature, cultural geography, critical linguistics, anthropology, and so forth.

All of this suggests, ineluctably from where I write, that the larger point of particular research activities will need to be more consciously promoted within the ambiguous demands and categories of funding bodies. Under stress there will have to be research priorities. PhDs and other research projects will increasingly take a visible and designated place within a research culture with declared emphases, needs and indeed 'goals'. This will require negotiation within new languages (for example, the current Economic and Social Research Council priority theme of 'inclusion and exclusion'), but however coded a negotiation, it cannot be a cynical one. Researchers will be required to say what matters and why, including why it should matter to a wide variety of off-campus research 'users', some of whom will be on project steering committees. This is also the context in which proposals to do research will be made and judged.

This new phase will begin to impact in various ways, some far from clear, on cultural studies work. The absence, particularly given Web sites and the Internet, of an adequate exchange of information about work in cultural studies world-wide is regrettable and surely cannot persist. Departments and researchers will have to think less on their own about what they do and be aware of their activity in a wider context and also, very importantly and to be welcomed, in collaboration with other groups, other institutions, and with users of research. It is possible too, far less attractively for many of us, that groups in particular places will begin to specialize in offering and clarifying what they can do well in research, and that this may be narrower than before. Built into the funding model is competition between institutions in research, assessments and in gaining funding, which subverts (to me) any known previous version of what cultural studies was about.

This also inhibits willingness to suggest, explicitly, what kinds of research could be valuable in the next few years, as does the further question of what constitutes valuable research in our area, by what criteria, and to whom. Perhaps that question was always there but only evaded to date, though there will be a heterogeneity of definitions of value, straining the canons of 'professional judgement' in the 'institutionalized academicism' to be confronted.

For all this, the moment is one for optimism on balance, despite many other circumstances. Research, meaning extended research rather than essays and commentaries, will be of higher significance. Cultural studies work is, despite everything, accepted as an important site of ideas, and, while without clear institutional space, is not necessarily going to meet with resistance or exclusion from research projects, particularly if it argues its worth in a positive and comprehensible way. There will be a lot of encouragement for PhD projects, for research teams, for co-funded ventures and for research with a variety of user groups and institutions and services. In the setting out of interests and priorities and purposes in research, and especially given our common position in the same intellectual and social moment, 'students' of various kinds, researchers and paid academics will be, for all the serious dangers of competition between institutions (offset by official encouragement for collaboration between them!), working together.

As for the graduation ceremonies, vivas and thirty-page application forms in triplicate, perhaps for the interest of what we do we can live with them.

Notes

1. At the time of writing, taught Master's courses in England and Wales receive either British Academy (humanities) or Economic and Social Research council (social science) recognition. The institutions applied to will offer advice, and it is possible to go through both routes at different places. There may also be 'quota' awards offered by the department concerned, or an opportunity to enter a highly competitive national 'pool' of awards. Deadlines and procedures, involving referees and confirmation of first degree results, are complex and quite rigid; they need some time. Advice should be available from the first degree or intended higher degree institution.

2. As with the taught courses, it is possible to submit versions of a proposal, respectively stressing the humanities or social science dimensions, to different funding bodies through different institutions whose departments will advise. There is an increasing stress on a

good 'match' between what a potential supervisor has done and the prospective student. We are in this together!

3. One good example from Willis would be his discussion of puzzling or frustrating encounters in ethnographic work:

> Why has the subject behaved in this way? Why do certain areas remain obscure to the researcher? What differences in orientation lie behind the failure to communicate? . . . in terms of the generation of 'new' knowledge, we know what it is precisely *not* because we have shared it – the usual notion of empathy – but because we have *not* shared it . . . . (1980: 92).

He adds that he is 'not necessarily arguing that the final account should show the several stages of this often tortuous process' (1980: 93), whereas I would argue that reflection upon and clarification of the stages, precisely asking what made them tortuous or difficult, can be a strongly beneficial feature of a PhD.

4. Welcome examples include Sparks (1996a, 1996b), McGuigan (1992), McRobbie (1992) and the exemplary Corner (1995).

References

Allan, D. (ed.) (1996) *In at the Deep End: First Experiences of University Teaching*, Lancaster, Unit for Innovation in Higher Education.

Corner, J. (1995) 'Media Studies and the Knowledge Problem', *Screen*, 36(2): 147–55.

McGuigan, J. (1992) *Cultural Populism*, London: Routledge.

McRobbie, A. (1992) 'Post-Marxism and Cultural Studies', in *Post-Modernism and Popular Culture*, London: Routledge.

Rooney, E. (1996) 'Discipline and Vanish: Feminism, the Resistance to Theory, and the Politics of Cultural Studies', in J. Storey (ed.) (1996) *What is Cultural Studies?*, London: Edward Arnold.

Sparks, C. (1996a) 'The Evolution of Cultural Studies . . .' in J. Storey (ed.), *What is Cultural Studies?*, London: Edward Arnold.

Sparks, C. (1996b) 'Stuart Hall, Cultural Studies and Marxism', in K.-H. Chen and D. Morley, (eds), *Stuart Hall: Critical Dialogues in Cultural Studies*, London: Routledge.

Willis, P. (1980) 'Notes on Method', in S. Hall, D. Hobson, A. Lowe and P. Willis (eds), *Culture, Media, Language*, London: Hutchinson.

Index